OBJECTIVITY, RATIONALITY AND THE THIRD REALM:
JUSTIFICATION AND THE GROUNDS OF PSYCHOLOGISM

NIJHOFF INTERNATIONAL PHILOSOPHY SERIES

VOLUME 16

General Editor: JAN T.J. SRZEDNICKI (Contributions to Philosophy)
Editor: LYNNE M. BROUGHTON (Applying Philosophy)

Editorial Advisory Board:

For a list of other volumes in this series see final page of the volume.

Mark Amadeus Notturno

Objectivity, Rationality and the Third Realm: Justification and the Grounds of Psychologism

A Study of Frege and Popper

1985 **MARTINUS NIJHOFF PUBLISHERS**
a member of the KLUWER ACADEMIC PUBLISHERS GROUP
DORDRECHT / BOSTON / LANCASTER

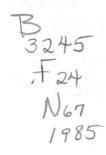

This is a volume in the subseries 'Logic and Applying Logic'.

Distributors

for the United States and Canada: Kluwer Academic Publishers, 190 Old Derby Street, Hingham, MA 02043, USA
for the UK and Ireland: Kluwer Academic Publishers, MTP Press Limited, Falcon House, Queen Square, Lancaster LA1 1RN, UK
for all other countries: Kluwer Academic Publishers Group, Distribution Center, P.O. Box 322, 3300 AH Dordrecht, The Netherlands

Library of Congress Cataloging in Publication Data

```
Notturno, M. A.
   Objectivity, rationality, and the third realm.

   (Nijhoff international philosophy series ; v. 16)
   Revised version of the author's doctoral dissertation.
   Includes bibliographical references and indexes.
   1. Frege, Gottlob, 1848-1925. 2. Popper, Karl Raimund,
Sir, 1902-    . I. Title. II. Series.
B3245.F24N67 1984    121'.092'2    84-3971
ISBN 90-247-2956-4
```

ISBN 90-247-2956-4 (this volume)
ISBN 90-247-2331-0 (series)

PRINTED IN THE NETHERLANDS

Giving grounds, however, justifying the evidence, comes to an end; − but the end is not certain propositions' striking us immediately as true, i.e. it is not a kind of *seeing* on our part; it is our acting, which lies at the bottom of the language-game.

If the true is what is grounded, then the ground is not *true*, nor yet false.

Ludwig Wittgenstein

Thus in the end truth is reduced to individuals' taking something to be true. All I have to say to this is: being true is different from being taken to be true, whether by one or many or everybody, and in no case is to be reduced to it.

Gottlob Frege

But this method of fixing belief, which may be called the method of tenacity, will be unable to hold its ground in practice. The social impulse is against it. The man who adopts it will find that other men think differently from him, and it will be apt to occur to him in some saner moment that their opinions are quite as good as his own, and this will shake his confidence in his belief. This conception, that another man's thought or sentiment may be equivalent to one's own, is a distinctly new step, and a highly important one. It arises from an impulse too strong in man to be suppressed, without danger of destroying the human species.

Charles S. Peirce

For Henry Miller,
and the IRT Broadway Local

CONTENTS

PREFACE

It is somewhat ironic that the preface to a literary work is usually the last part to be written. Mine is no exception. Insofar as this is concerned, I feel the strong temptation to present an overview: a summary of the major points argued and a comment on the limitations of results. I will avoid this temptation — primarily because someone else might then feel the temptation to read the preface, but not the book. Instead, I want simply to tell a few anecdotes which I hope will, in one way or another, reveal my motivations for writing.

It would be too simple to say that this work originated as a doctoral dissertation. In reality, its roots run far deeper and most probably can be traced to my early elementary education. Having been raised as a strict Roman Catholic in parochial schools, I soon came to feel an uneasiness with the realization that in order to accept this religious faith I would be obliged to ignore many of the alternative claims made by other religions and philosophies. Perhaps more important, I also soon came to despise the fear, suspicion, and hatred that was all too often directed against those who took these alternative claims seriously. When my natural impulse to sin tempted me to undertake an investigation into the nature and grounds of these alternative claims, my parish priest advised me to pray to God. But praying to God did not produce the desired result. For I soon came to feel that in praying to God I was simply talking to myself. By the end of my adolescence I had reached the decision that, eternal damnation or not, I could not live the rest of my life in fear. And with that decision, I embarked upon the study of philosophy.

My introduction to philosophy was as personal as it was narrow. It was personal in that my philosophical problems were never academic, but motivated by very real and deeply felt anxieties concerning the existence of God and the cognitive authority for moral laws. It was narrow in that my first philosophy professors viewed philosophy, and the world in general, from the perspective of Logical Positivism. As I now see it, Logical Positivism, like Roman Catholicism, was a truly comforting ideology. Whereas Catholicism had reduced any question of substance to dogmatic faith, Logical Positivism offered a methodology of inquiry according to which any question could be recognized as empirically or analytically decidable, or simply nonsensical and hence not problematic at all. It would be difficult to exaggerate the impression that my first positivist teacher made upon me. Appearing as old and as wise as Socrates, he would lecture twice a week on *Existentialism*. Losing himself completely in these lectures, he would periodically raise his head to pronounce in a tone of profound seriousness, "But all this, of course, is rubbish!" Owing perhaps to my early religious training, I at first accepted these pronouncements as if spoken *ex cathedra*. But in time, old anxieties resurfaced. The verifiability criterion of meaning and an overdeveloped sense of the analytic had given me the intellectual confidence to dismiss traditional philosophical problems as nonsensical. But what provided me with the confidence for Positivism? My break with Positivism was a minor trauma. As my teacher persistently tried to avoid commitment, I as persistently pressed the question. Finally, with no place left to move, the answer came, "No, God does not exist." It was then that I fully realized what I had somehow known all along. Neither he nor anyone else could answer that question for me.

As my philosophical education progressed, my concern about the existence of God naturally translated into a concern for the possibility of objective certainty. And here, I became obsessed with the question, "What, if anything, can be known *a priori*?" It seemed to me that philosophical disputes ultimately reduced to the question of foundational principles. But unless there was some way to adjudicate between competing claims concerning such principles, all hope for objective certainty was just that — hope. Here I was struck by the realization that philosophical systems, in their efforts to be presuppositionless, all too often proceed by begging the very questions at issue. And part and parcel of this realization was the recognition that philosophers were, all too often, simply talking past each other. With time, I despaired of the hope for *a priori* certainty. And strange to say, the sky did not fall and the earth did not crumble. Nevertheless, this despair raised very deep problems concerning the possibility of real philosophical criticism and justification, i.e., criticism and justification that addresses foundational problems, but is not simply preaching to the converted. Since few philosophers seemed to share my concerns, I naturally gravitated to those who did. But even here I felt frustration. For I soon found that even those philosophers who explicitly denied the possibility of *a priori* certainty, nonetheless appealed to such principles in practice. More important, such philosophers seemed to be generally unaware of the consequences of this denial. When one such philosopher (call him "R") denounced the possibility of *a priori* certainty, I asked him, "But then how is philosophical criticism and justification possible?" He replied, "We do it all the time." That much I knew. But my question concerned the philosophical grounds for those activities. When he began to expand on his answer by saying, "Well, it's analytic to the concept of justification...", I felt the rub. Where did he get "analytic"?

For a number of years these problems weighed heavily on my mind, all the more because I was, in the process of completing my graduate work, actively engaged in the very sort of criticism and justification I no longer considered meaningful. In the midst of all this, I one day ran into Ernest Nagel outside the subway station at Broadway and 116th Street in New York. At the time, I was busy writing a paper on the Carnap/Popper dispute. Nagel and I chatted for a while about their divergent views, and then, as we were parting, he said, "Have fun". These rather innocent words were spoken not sarcastically, but seriously. They stuck in my mind, and have haunted me ever since. I've now come to realize that in my quest for certainty (permanence, truth, God, or what have you), I was missing a very real part of what philosophy is and should be all about. In many ways, this book is the product of that realization.

As I've already indicated, this book, or a version of it, was first written as my doctoral dissertation. Originally, I had intended to include in that dissertation several chapters on Wittgenstein that would, I had hoped, serve to mediate the transition from Frege to Popper. But some of the members of my committee strongly advised against this. So when the dissertation was completed and the members of my committee urged that I seek publication, I resolved not to do so until I had added the chapters on Wittgenstein. Nevertheless, Martinus Nijhoff had learned of my work from a request for permission to quote, requested to see the manuscript, and then offered to publish it without revision. Since Nijhoff wanted to publish the book in 1984, and I was suffering under the teaching load of four courses per semester without chance for released time, I soon realized that I would not even have the time to adequately revise what I had written, much less produce the chapters on Wittgenstein. While I am not altogether happy about this situation, I am nonetheless resigned to it. What we cannot speak about we must pass over in silence.

December, 1983   M.A. Notturno

ACKNOWLEDGMENTS

The thoughts expressed in this book have evolved through the course of arguments spanning many years, and my intellectual debts are heavy. It would be impossible to mention all of the philosophers, professional and otherwise, who have contributed to these arguments and, in one way or another, influenced my views. But I owe a special gratitude to faculty and students connected with Columbia University. Among these, I am deeply indebted to Arthur Danto, Robert Merton, Jonas Soltis, and Herbert Terrace for the time and care they took to read and criticize a version of this work in its guise as a doctoral dissertation. Also, I must thank James Higginbotham, Isaac Levi, Ernest Nagel, David Palmer, Gregory Silverman, and Ted Talbot for the many long hours that they willingly devoted to the discussion and criticism of my views. Finally, I cannot exaggerate the deep intellectual and moral debt I owe to Charles D. Parsons. His singular example of philosophical integrity has provided me with a regulative ideal which I can only hope to approximate. Having suffered through his many criticisms, I am tempted to say that whatever errors still exist in this work must surely be his. But I know better.

I am, of course, also indebted to people not connected with Columbia. My gratitude is owed to Bill Bartley, Bill Larkin, John McEvoy, Audrey McKinney, Peter Munz, Anthony O'Hear, and Karl Popper — each of whom read this work, or parts of it, and offered valuable criticism and encouragement. Chapter eleven was originally commissioned by and presented before the Department of Psychiatry and Behavioral Sciences at The Johns Hopkins Medical Institutions in Baltimore, Maryland. I am thankful to Dr. Paul McHugh and Dr. Godfrey Pearlson for making that invitation possible, and to the members of that department for their hospitality, generosity, and interest. I wish also to thank Alexander Schimmelpenninck van der Oye and Elisabeth Erdman-Visser of Martinus Nijhoff for their invaluable help in publishing this book. Finally, I am grateful to Susan Petri, Lynda Simon, and Connie Tekulve for their assistance in the typing (and retyping) of the manuscript, and to David Trunnell and David Weinberg — for being there.

I am also indebted to a number of institutions. Research for this work was, in part, funded by a Chamberlain Fellowship from Columbia University and an Eliza Buffington Research Fellowship from Vassar College. The assistance of Columbia and Vassar is gratefully acknowledged. Also, a number of these chapters have already found their way into print as slightly altered journal articles. Chapter five first appeared as "Frege and the Psychological Reality Thesis" in *Journal for the Theory of Social Behaviour*. Chapter six has been published as

"Frege's Justificationism: Truth and the Recognition of Authority" in *Metaphilosophy*. And chapter eleven has appeared in *Psychological Medicine* as "The Popper/Kuhn Debate: Truth and Two Faces of Relativism". I wish to thank these journals for their permission to use this material here. Finally, I wish to thank the various publishers and copyright holders who have granted permission for quotation. My thanks, therefore, to: Basil Blackwell, publisher of *Translations from the Philosophical Writings of Gottlob Frege*, edited and translated by Peter Geach and Max Black, and copyright holder of Gottlob Frege's *The Foundations of Arithmetic*, translated by J.L. Austin, and "The Thought: A Logical Inquiry", translated by A.M. and Marcelle Quinton; Cambridge University Press, publisher of *Criticism and the Growth of Knowledge*, edited by Imre Lakatos and Alan Musgrave, Susan Haack's *Deviant Logic* and *Philosophy of Logics*, and Hilary Putnam's *Mathematics, Matter and Method*; Columbia University Press, publisher of Ernest Nagel's *Teleology Revisited*; Dover Publications, copyright holder of Kant's *Logic*, translated by Robert Hartman and Wolfgang Schwarz; Harper & Row, publisher, and Gerald Duckworth & Co., Ltd, British Commonwealth and Canadian copyright holder of Michael Dummett's *Frege: Philosophy of Language*; Harvard University Press, first publisher, and the President and Fellows of Harvard University, copyright holders of W.V.O. Quine's *From a Logical Point of View*; Humanities Press, publisher, and Routledge & Kegan Paul, world copyright holders of Edmund Husserl's *Logical Investigations*, translated by J.N. Findlay, and Franz Brentano's *Psychology from an Empirical Standpoint*, edited by Linda L. McAlister, and translated by Antos C. Rancurello, D.B. Terrell, and Linda L. McAlister; Oxford University Press, publisher of John Locke's *An Essay concerning Human Understanding*, edited by P.H. Nidditch; Karl Popper, author and copyright holder of *Conjectures and Refutations: The Growth of Scientific Knowledge, Objective Knowlege: An Evolutionary Approach, The Logic of Scientific Discovery*, and *Unended Quest: An Intellectual Autobiography*; St. Martin's Press, publisher, and Macmillan & Co., Ltd, copyright holder of Immanuel Kant's *Critique of Pure Reason*, translated by Norman Kemp Smith; The Putnam Publishing Group, copyright holders of John Dewey's *The Quest for Certainty*; University of California Press, publisher of Gottlob Frege's *The Basic Laws of Arithmetic*, translated by Montgomery Furth; University of Chicago Press, publisher of Thomas S. Kuhn's *The Structure of Scientific Revolutions*; and University of Toronto Press, publisher, and Routledge & Kegan Paul, British Commonwealth copyright holder of John Stuart Mill's *A System of Logic* and *An Examination of Sir William Hamilton's Philosophy*, both edited by J.M. Robson.

The writing of this book has involved many long and sleepless nights. It was my great fortune that many of these nights were spent in the company of Fyodor Dostoevsky, Søren Kierkegaard, Henry Miller, and Ludwig Wittgenstein who provided inspiration, moral support, and criticism when no one else was available. Finally, I cannot say enough to express the debt I owe to my wife Andrea who read every page of this work as it came off the typewriter and provided much desired (and undesired) stylistic criticism. More important, without her love, patience, understanding, and encouragement, I would not have had the courage to see those nights through.

M.A. Notturno

1. EPISTEMOLOGICAL PARADIGM SHIFTS: A GAME OF CHESS

Wittgenstein used to liken language to the game of chess. Words are like chess pieces which speakers, like chess players, use to make moves. The rules of syntax and semantics were similarly likened to the rules of chess: they restrict the moves possible in the game. This analogy gave birth to Wittgenstein's seminal notion of language games. And that notion, in turn, gave birth to a radically new concept of language and of the relationship between language and the world, a concept which ultimately helped to reshape twentieth century philosophy's perspective concerning the nature and cognitive authority of human knowledge. It is interesting that Wittgenstein also regarded linguistic analysis as the first *and last* move to be made in philosophy. For in another sense, the whole of philosophy can be likened to the game of chess. If we conceive of the separate squares of the chessboard as distinct philosophical positions, the analogy becomes clear. Here, the rules of chess find their philosophical counterparts in the logical and epistemological rules for criticism and justification. Good philosophical *Weltanschauungen*, like good chess games, are tight. And good philosophers, like good chess players, usually hold one position in order to protect another. As in chess, first moves are logically arbitrary. They are justified not with reference to prior moves, but with what is to follow. So the analysis of a philosophical thesis is never idiosyncratic. As in chess, the examination of an isolated move can never yield an evaluation of its worth or of its significance in the game. For that, we need to survey the entire board.

It is in the spirit of this analogy that I conduct the following discussion. For an investigation of the psychologism/anti-psychologism debate is without point unless it considers the implications that psychologism holds for our concept of objective knowledge. And an examination of our concept of objective knowledge is inadequate unless it considers our concomitant presuppositions concerning justification, rationality, and the third realm. These five concepts are held together in a logical tension that constitutes one of the major strategic blocks on the chessboard of philosophy, a strategic block the purpose of which is to respectively defend and attack opposing claims concerning the nature and ground of cognitive authority. Failure to appreciate this tension is a failure to appreciate the significance of the psychologism/anti-psychologism debate. But this extension of Wittgenstein's analogy is likely to cause intellectual despair in some. For it will readily be seen that a complete analysis of any one philosophical position requires an analysis of all philosophical positions. And that is impossible. And that is the way it must be. So my analysis of the psychologism/ anti-psychologism debate suffers. It is necessarily incomplete. Nevertheless, this necessary incompleteness need not cause intellectual despair. For as in good chess games, the joy of philosophy comes not in the winning, but in the playing.

Much of the following discussion will be devoted, at least ostensibly, to a critical and comparative examination of the anti-psychologisms of Gottlob Frege and Karl Popper, and to the implications of this examination for twentieth century analytic philosophy. But one of the major underlying themes of this discussion can be readily expressed in terms of our analogy. It is that much of the confusion in twentieth century analytic philosophy results from the fact that philosophers have unwittingly been playing their game according to different rules. It is as if one player has, in a way undetected by his opponent, been moving his castle diagonally across the board. Explicitly: it is my belief that the twentieth century has witnessed an epistemological paradigm shift that has left the intuitions of many contemporary analytic philosophers straddling two distinct and incompatible concepts of objective knowledge. In the course of this epistemological paradigm shift, labels of positions and concepts instrumental in the framework of the old paradigm have been used to name *different* positions and concepts instrumental in the new without sufficient recognition and explication of the differences in their use. Hence, while Fregean and Popperian anti-psychologisms are nominally identical, they in fact point in diametrically opposed epistemological directions and appeal to radically different concepts of objective knowledge, rationality, and the third realm. In this period of conceptual change, confusion results from a failure to recognize and draw taut the conceptual slack between these two epistemological paradigms. And this confusion is illustrated in the tendency to evaluate the theories and positions of the one paradigm according to the standards and goals of the other. Hence, many contemporary philosophers have adopted the new epistemological paradigm in principle without suitable modification of the cognitive goals, methodological rules, and regulative ideals that govern their own critical practice. And this all too often results in the twin tendencies: (1) to criticize theories in a way which presupposes a sort of justification that is much stronger than what the new paradigm considers possible; and (2) to claim a sort of cognitive authority for their theories that is much stronger than what the new paradigm considers appropriate. While the resulting situation is not quite that of a private language, it is one in which philosophers are simply talking past each other. Now a detailed account of the shift from the old epistemological paradigm (henceforth "EP$_1$") to the new (henceforth "EP$_2$") would provide an interesting and important chapter in the history of modern philosophy. But such a history is well beyond the scope of the present discussion. For our purposes it will suffice to give a brief statement of the conceptual essentials of these two paradigms.

According to EP$_1$, scientific and philosophical inquiry was considered a quest for objective and absolute certainty. Here, knowledge was considered to be a sort of justified true belief, viz. knowledge was construed to be just that sort of belief whose justification was sufficient to eliminate any doubt of its truth. The objectivity of such certainty was thought to be guaranteed by the identification of justification with logical proof. The justification of a statement was thus thought sufficient to eliminate any doubt of the truth of that statement because the justification of a statement demonstrated that statement as a deductive consequence of other statements whose truth was already considered self-evident and beyond doubt. Here, rationality emerged as a function of logical justification. Simply put, a belief was considered rational only to the extent to which it was considered self-evident, or validly deducible from other statements which were themselves considered self-evident. Here, what was considered to be rationally self-evident was, like objective knowledge itself, regarded as eternally and immutably so. And in order to maintain these concepts of objective knowledge, justification, and rationality without falling into scepticism, EP_1 philosophers generally found it necessary to separate the *objects* of objective knowledge from the natural world. This, because the objects of the natural world are in no sense absolute, but decidedly temporal and changing. Hence, EP_1 philosophers appealed, either explicitly or implicitly, to a supernatural third realm of eternal and immutable concepts and truths, and to a cognitive source whose function it was to apprehend these concepts and truths. But regardless of whether these third realm entities were called "Forms", or "essences", or "God", and regardless of whether this cognitive source was called "the Reason", or "the Intellect", their epistemological function was the same: they provided the ultimate ground for cognitive authority. Hence, Popper, in tracing the scientific roots of philosophical problems, writes:

> The earliest version of Plato's famous theory of 'Forms' or 'Ideas' may indeed be described, somewhat roughly, as the doctrine that the 'Good' side of the Table of Opposites constitutes an (invisible) Universe, a Universe of Higher Reality, of the Unchanging and Determinate 'Forms' of all things; and that True and Certain Knowledge (*episteme= scientia=science*) can be of this Unchanging and Real Universe only, while the visible world of change and flux in which we live and die, the world of generation and destruction, the world of experience, is only a kind of appearance of which no True and Certain Knowledge can be obtained. All that can be obtained in the place of Knowledge (*episteme*) are the plausible but uncertain and prejudiced opinions (*doxa*) of fallible mortals.[1]

From the perspective of EP_1, any justification which rests upon the changing phenomena of the natural world must itself be temporal and uncertain, and, hence, subjective and irrational. For objective and rational knowledge is knowledge that is not in a state of flux, that is not subject to revision over the course of time. Hence, objective knowledge cannot be justified by desiderata from the natural world. From the EP_1 perspective, objectivity and certainty were considered *criteria* of knowledge (as opposed to regulative ideals), scientists and philosophers were obliged to direct their inquiries into the realm of timeless truths (into the Absolute), and any attempt to justify theories with sense perceptions of natural phenomena was considered to be the first step down the slippery slope toward scepticism.

Now philosophy and science assume an entirely different character within the framework of EP_2. According to EP_2, philosophy and science may *aim* at objectivity and certainty, but these are no longer considered to be criteria of knowledge. This is because EP_2 *begins* with the assumption that objective certainty is, strictly speaking, unattainable. Rather, fallibilism is accepted as a simple epistemological truth, part and parcel of a more naturalistic conception of human cognition. Here, philosophy and science are considered to be human investigations into natural phenomena. Hence, whatever objective knowledge is obtained is thought to be both temporal and uncertain, by its very nature evolutionary and subject to revision. To the extent to which the justified true belief theory of knowledge is retained, justification is no longer construed as entailing the truth of the statements justified. At best, it is thought of as entailing the *probability* of the truth of the statements justified. Hence, the evidence considered necessary to justify a statement or a belief need no longer eliminate *all* possibility of doubt. Insofar as this is concerned, rationality is no longer associated solely with knowledge justified by logical proof, and there is generally no longer thought to be any need to introduce either a third realm of eternal and immutable truths or a special cognitive source to apprehend them. Rather, such third realm entities are considered fairly irrelevant to science and philosophy. Insofar as this is concerned, Dewey, in characterizing the differences between these two views, writes:

> In the traditional theory, which still is the prevailing one, there were alleged to exist inherent defects in perception and observation as means of knowledge, in reference to the subject-matter they furnish. This material, in the older notion, is inherently so particular, so contingent and variable, that by no possible means can it contribute to *knowledge*; it can result only in opinion, mere belief...
>
> In the older theory, sense and experience were barriers to true science because they were implicated in natural change. Their appropriate and inevitable subject-matter was variable and changing things. Knowledge in its full and valid sense is possible only of the immutable, the fixed; that alone answers the quest for certainty. With regard to changing things, only surmise and opinion are possible, just as practically these are the source of peril. To a scientific man, in terms of what he does in inquiry, the notion of a natural science which should turn its back upon the changes of things, upon events, is simply incomprehensible. What he is interested in knowing, in understanding, are precisely the changes that go on...[2]

From the EP_2 perspective, the ancient quest for certainty enjoys the same status as attempts to square the circle or corral a unicorn. But here, it is not so much thought that philosophers have *failed* to achieve the EP_1 epistemological goal as that they have come to recognize that goal as unrealistic to begin with.

The epistemological paradigm shift from EP_1 to EP_2 might thus be most simply understood as the abandonment of the quest for certainty in favour of fallibilism. That such an historical shift has occurred is, in my view, uncontroversial. And, as the passages cited from Popper and Dewey indicate, it has already been recognized and documented. So it is not my intention to, in any way, claim novelty for the recognition of this shift. Insofar as this is concerned, my use of the phrases "epistemological paradigm" and "epistemological paradigm shift" are, of course, conscious allusions to Thomas Kuhn's "scientific paradigm" and "scientific paradigm shift". If there is anything in philosophy that qualifies as a paradigm in the Kuhnian sense, it is the conception of knowledge as entailing objective certainty. And if there is anything in philosophy that resembles a paradigm shift, it is the recognition of knowledge as fallible. But thus said, let me hasten to add that my allusion to Kuhn is intended primarily as a heuristic. While I do believe that Kuhn has contributed an important conceptual framework for the interpretation of the history of ideas, I here commit myself to none of the normative or historical *details* of the Kuhnian picture as it relates to science. Nevertheless, I do feel that my use of the phrase "epistemological paradigm shift" is appropriate. For it underscores the fact that the rejection of the quest for certainty in favour of fallibilism involved not simply a change in the concept of knowledge, but changes in many other key epistemological concepts and problems as well. Hence, it is important to recognize that from the perspective of EP_1, the very adoption of EP_2 and the theories proposed within it is viewed as a concession to scepticism. For what, EP_1 philosophers might ask, is fallibilism, but scepticism made humble? From the perspective of EP_1, what I have called an "epistemological paradigm shift" is nothing more nor less than the admission that objective and rational knowledge is impossible after all. And it is, at least initially, important to recognize the justice of this view. If knowledge is equated with or understood as entailing objective certainty, then to deny the possibility of objective certainty *is* to deny the possibility of knowledge. Hence, to say that we have or can have objective knowledge, albeit fallible, *is* to contradict oneself. But thus acknowledged, it is equally important to recognize the sterility of this view. Regardless of how we characterize it or what we call it, it would simply be silly to deny the existence of the wide and logically interrelated network of theory and fact that is commonly called "scientific knowledge". And to the extent to which scientific knowledge differs from and makes a stronger claim to our rational assent than other non-scientific systems, it is incumbent upon philosophy to explain the basis for that claim. Hence, from the perspective of EP_2, this accusation of scepticism is viewed as callow and immature, as the product of a primitive epistemology. That primitive epistemology was forced to regard as sceptical any theory which denies the possibility of objective certainty. Contrary to this, EP_2 philosophers regard the EP_1 *concept* of knowledge as itself the first step toward scepticism. For having set their goals unrealistically high, EP_1 philosophers were bound to fall short of them. From the EP_2 perspective, the denial of the possibility of objective certainty is regarded not as a concession to scepticism, but as a first and necessary step toward a more seasoned epistemology. So for those who object to my use of the phrases "epistemological paradigm" and "epistemological paradigm shift", it will suffice if they allow simply: (1) that many contemporary philosophers have rejected the traditional quest for certainty and have, at least in principle, embraced fallibilism; and (2) that those philosophers' understanding of some of the traditional epistemological concepts and problems has, as a result, undergone revision.

The gradual but persistent shift away from EP_1 toward EP_2 was only in part due to the success of philosophical arguments. What was, perhaps, more important were the repeated failures of philosophers and scientists to provide objective and certain (or at least convincing and enduring) justification for their theories, coupled with the success of the specific sciences in applying the so-called "inductive" or "experimental" method to natural philosophy. It is important to appreciate just how gradual a shift this was. While the discussion of inductive inference can be traced at least to Aristotle, Dewey, as late as 1930, regarded what we have called "EP_1" as the then prevailing view. And even an understanding of the mechanics of the inductive method was not a matter of course. Insofar as this is concerned, Kneale writes:

> ... the deliberate pursuit of knowledge by this method is a comparatively recent enter-prise of mankind: at the beginning of the 17th century, when Bacon wrote his *Novum Organum*, it was a novelty not very well understood; and a thinker as great as Descartes could maintain that there was no essential difference between physics and geometry. A hundred years later, after the founding of the Royal Society and the great triumphs of Newton, the method was still something that could arouse debate among intelligent men, as may be seen from the curious remarks of Newton in the *General Scholium* that he added at the end of his *Principia*. In 1730 Hume, who thought Newton "the greatest and rarest genius that ever rose for the ornament and instruction of the species," found him-self driven nevertheless to the conclusion that induction could be nothing but customary association of ideas (which Locke had called "a sort of madness") because it was clearly not to be justified as a form of deduction. If the method or policy now seems obviously wise, that is because we understand our situation better than our predecessors did and are therefore no longer inclined to think that we can get what we want in any other way.[3]

Now it is, perhaps, obvious that the shift from EP_1 to EP_2 is closely related to the decline of classical rationalism and the emergence of empiricism. Still, I do not wish to suggest that EP_1 and EP_2 should be *identified* with classical rational-ism and empiricism. Many EP_1 philosophers who embraced empiricist principles were naturally led as a consequence to scepticism – just because induction can-not guarantee objective and rational certainty. And still other EP_1 philosophers were inspired to develop theories that attempted to show that and how inductive inference can yield objective and rational certainty. Even Newton, who knew full well that the argument to "general conclusions from the consent of phenom-ena" could not be demonstrated *a priori*[4] and could be regarded as accurately or very nearly true "till such time as other phenomena occur, by which they may either be made more accurate, or liable to exceptions",[5] nonetheless considered his rules of reasoning in philosophy as the only method "possible to determine settled agreement in any science".[6] Explicitly: the shift from EP_1 to EP_2 con-cerned not so much the *means* considered requisite to acquire objective and rational knowledge, but the *nature* of objective and rational knowledge itself.

I have emphasized this gradual character of the shift from EP_1 to EP_2 pri-marily for two reasons. (1) In saying that the twentieth century has *witnessed* this epistemological paradigm shift, I do not wish to be misinterpreted as suggest-ing that the view that knowledge is fallible is in any way idiosyncratic to the twentieth century, or that it is now common among *all* twentieth century philosophers. As has already been shown, its roots can be traced at least to the 17th century. And, strange as it may seem, there still exist today Platonists, Thomists, Cartesians, and Kantians (among others), all of whom maintain theories that fall well within the conceptual framework of EP_1. What is new in the twentieth century is not EP_2 itself, or even its universality, but simply its widespread acceptance on the part of many philosophers dealing with contemporary problems. Nevertheless, this widespread acceptance is itself significant. For it indicates that many contemporary philosophers no longer regard fallibilism as a form of scepticism, but as a positive theory of knowledge. Simply put, fallibilism is now in ascendance. (2) In giving these brief statements of the conceptual essentials of EP_1 and EP_2, I do not wish to be misunderstood as suggesting that these two epistemological paradigms have always been separate and monolithic, or that philosophers have always worked exclusively in one or the other. Rather, the shift from EP_1 to EP_2 involved a long and piecemeal process of conceptual evolution, the course of which gave birth to many theoretical mutants regarding the nature of objective knowledge, justification, rationality, and the third realm. Moreover, as explicitly stated earlier, it is my perception that many contemporary analytic philosophers have been caught straddling these two epistemological paradigms, and thereby wedding incompatible concepts and methodologies.

Now I have yet to offer definitions or explications of "psychologism" and "anti-psychologism", nor will I attempt to do so here. For we will embark upon a discussion of the psychologism/anti-psychologism debate, in both its epistemological and metaphysical versions, in the immediately succeeding chapter. Nevertheless, having offered these brief statements of the conceptual essentials of EP_1 and EP_2, the question that should immediately arise is, "How is this epistemological paradigm shift pertinent to the psychologism/anti-psychologism debate, and to our proposed critical comparison of the anti-psychologisms of Frege and Popper?" Now the answer to the first part of this question may seem controversial. But in my view, it is really quite simple. And in chapters three through six I will argue that Fregean anti-psychologism, and EP_1 anti-psychologism in general, was maintained in order to oppose fallibilism — in Frege's case, fallibilism with regard to logic and mathematics, but more generally, fallibilism in whatever domain of knowledge for which EP_1 anti-psychologism is held. The answer to the second part of this question, however, is somewhat more intricate, though no less controversial. For if the purpose of EP_1 anti-psychologism is to oppose fallibilism, then it might seem as if anti-psychologism and fallibilism are incompatible theses. Nevertheless, Karl Popper has presented an epistemology that weds fallibilism with anti-psychologism in an explicit attempt to combat scepticism. While most commentators regard this wedding as indicative of a deep inconsistency in Popper's thought, I will argue, in chapters seven through eleven, that the inconsistency is merely apparent and can be resolved through an appreciation of Popper's rejection of justification as a criterion of knowledge. And in so doing, I will attempt to draw taut some of the conceptual slack between EP_1 and EP_2.

8

NOTES AND REFERENCES

1.   Popper, Karl R.; "The Nature of Philosophical Problems and Their Roots in Science";
in *Conjectures and Refutations: The Growth of Scientific Knowledge* by Karl R. Popper;
Harper & Row (New York, 1963) pp. 78-79. Popper, incidentally, traces the problem of
knowledge to the problem of change, and both of these problems to Heraclitus:
> Here I wish to stress that Heraclitus' philosophy, by appealing to thought, to the word,
> to argument, to reason, and by pointing out that we are living in a world of things whose
> changes escape our senses, though we *know* that they do change, created two new prob-
> lems — *the problem of change* and *the problem of knowledge*.
("Back to the Presocratics"; in Conjectures and Refutations; p. 133).

2.   Dewey, John; *The Quest for Certainty*; George Allen & Unwin (London, 1930) pp. 80-
82.

3.   Kneale, William Calvert; "Scientific Method"; in *Encyclopedia Britannica*; William
Benton (Chicago, 1964) Volume 20, p. 128.

4.   See, e.g., Newton's draft of his letter to Cotes (28 March 1713) in: Hall, A. Rupert and
Laura Trilling, eds.; *The Correspondence of Isaac Newton*, Volume V; At the University
Press (Cambridge, 1975) pp. 398-399.

5.   See: Isaac Newton; *Mathematical Principles of Natural Philosophy*; trans. by Andrew
Motte; University of California Press (Berkeley, 1974) Volume II; p. 400.

6.   See Newton's letter to Oldenburg for Pardies (10 June 1672) in: Turnbull, H.W., ed.;
The Correspondence of Isaac Newton, Volume I; At the University Press (Cambridge, 1959)
p. 164.

2. WHAT IS PSYCHOLOGISM?

Our discussion of the psychologism/anti-psychologism debate is intended to function simultaneously on four different levels. (1) It is intended to clarify the senses of "psychologism" and "anti-psychologism" as they are used in the literature of twentieth century analytic philosophy. (2) It is intended as a critical examination of the anti-psychologisms of Gottlob Frege and Karl Popper — anti-psychologisms which, while nominally identical, in fact point in epistemologically opposed directions. (3) It is intended, through this critical examination of Fregean and Popperian anti-psychologisms, to illustrate the terminological confusions engendered by the epistemological paradigm shift mentioned in chapter one. (4) It is intended to sketch and defend the function of critical philosophical inquiry within an epistemological framework which denies the necessity for and possibility of the justification of rational knowledge. An answer to the question raised in the title of this chapter is, in many ways, dependent upon the completion of each of these tasks. And since these tasks are interrelated, such an answer will emerge only toward the end of our discussion. Still, it is best to raise this question early on and to use this chapter as a propaedeutic to our discussion of Frege and Popper, if only to direct our attention to the philosophical space and the terminological pitfalls that surround the psychologism/anti-psychologism debate.

For the past one hundred and fifty years, "psychologism" has been used as an umbrella term to cover a multitude of philosophical sins, both metaphysical and epistemological. As a result, the meaning of the term has remained systematically obscure, and even today there is little clarity as to exactly what is being charged when an author labels a theory "psychologistic". There is, of course, little doubt that "psychologism" is intended to connote, and to denigrate, the use of psychological methods in philosophical and scientific investigations. But far from clarifying matters, this simply contributes to the elusiveness of the charge. For the various methodological perspectives adopted by the different schools of psychology are so diverse that any reference to psychological methods itself suffers from the same obscurity as "psychologism". And this is significant. For it might be thought that a critical examination and differentiation of these diverse methodological perspectives would be an essential prerequisite for any discussion of psychologism. At least, it has been suggested[1] that one way to acknowledge the primacy of psychological methods and at the same time avoid the anti-psychologistic critique is to adopt a suitable methodology of psychological inquiry. Nevertheless, it is a central thesis of this discussion, and one to be argued in the body of its text, that these charges of psychologism can generally be traced to a common ground, and to one which, ironically, has less to do with psychological methods than with epistemological theses concerning the ultimate justification of and cognitive authority for philosophical and scientific theories.

The initial difficulty that confronts any attempt to define "psychologism" is that few philosophers have ever willingly characterized their own theories as "psychologistic", or themselves as proponents of psychologism. This, of course, is not to say either that few philosophers have ever willingly held positions that were characterized by others as "psychologistic", or that such descriptions were never accurate, or, as is often maintained, that the psychologistic elements of such theories were always the result of conceptual confusions which, once revealed, would be willingly resolved through the adoption of an anti-psychologistic methodology. Rather, it is simply to note that "psychologism", as used in the philosophical literature, is a term of ill-repute. As Franz Brentano wrote, "psychologism" is a word which "when it is spoken many a pious philosopher — like many an orthodox Catholic when he hears the term Modernism — crosses himself as though the devil himself were in it".[2] Simply put, psychologism is, most often, something of which philosophers are *accused*, and something of which they then try to prove themselves innocent.

The pejorative connotations of "psychologism", like the ameliorative connotations of "objectivity" and "rationality", are as real today as they were in the nineteenth century. And, in my view, a sensitivity to such connotations will prove essential for an understanding of the central thesis of this discussion. While I am most sympathetic to the view that the relationship between a word and the object which it denotes is logically arbitrary, I nonetheless feel that it would be too naive to think that the persuasive force of philosophical argumentation functions on the level of logic alone. While the rigour of logical analysis is surely a regulative ideal to which most philosophers aspire, it is also one of which they often fall short. And in their efforts to secure a ready and sympathetic audience, philosophers, like most everyone else, describe the doctrines they support and characterize the positions they oppose, respectively, with terms already possessing generally acknowledged positive and negative evaluative contents. While an explanation of the mechanics of a philosophical term's acquisition of an evaluative content would provide an interesting chapter in the sociology of philosophy, this much, at least, seems clear: once such a term has acquired a *negative* evaluative content, it is almost impossible to cleanse it. The result is that the term ceases to function on a purely descriptive level (if, in fact, it ever did), and philosophers generally avoid its use to characterize positions for which they desire to muster support. But while this practice may prove most effective as a rhetorical device, it does so only at the price of casting a conceptual fog across the philosophical dialectic. For whatever agreement is predicated solely on such linguistic tact is oftentimes merely nominal, and at best serves to camouflage the deep differences in attitude that are characteristic of most philosophical disputes.

In its least pernicious form, sensitivity to the evaluative contents of philosophical terms leads philosophers to replace terms possessing pejorative contents with descriptively identical terms possessing neutral or preferably ameliorative evaluative contents. The fact that descriptively identical terms may differ in evaluative content is, perhaps, ironic. But it is a fact nonetheless. And if one might find an audience more sympathetic to a description of Metaphysics as "unverifiable", as opposed to "nonsensical", then it would seem less than prudent to deliberately opt for the pejorative term. This form of linguistic tact is evident on all linguistic levels. And it might even be regarded as benign since it seldom results in ambiguity. Nevertheless, to the extent to which it masks significant philosophical issues, e.g., ones *attitude* concerning the unverifiable, it can only serve to hinder communication.

Somewhat more pernicious is the tendency to use terms which originally designated one philosophical position in order to refer to one or more of its near contraries. This tendency usually increases with the passage of time, and usually when the untenable character of the original position has done little to tarnish the ameliorative character of the term that labelled it. A contemporary illustration of this tendency may be found in the works of certain epistemologists who label as "realist" positions which might have more accurately been described as "conventionalist", had that term not acquired a pejorative content. I have often argued that in this particular case the principle of charity must be liberally applied. What these epistemologists really want to say is, "Let's be *realistic*, human knowledge is, at base, a matter of decision!" Be this as it may, most everyone likes to think of knowledge, and themselves for that matter, as in some way rational and objective. For these, of course, are ameliorative terms. But just because most everyone likes to think of knowledge as rational and objective, these terms have also acquired different and contradictory senses. They have become systematically ambiguous. And because they have become systematically ambiguous, their descriptive contents should be regarded as suspicious at best.

But what is, to my mind, most pernicious is the tendency to *oppose* a position in *name* while at the same time cleaving to its substantial content. And in my view, this tendency is amply illustrated by much of the contemporary opposition to psychologism. Many contemporary philosophers, well aware of the stigma associated with "psychologism", continue to denounce theories as psychologistic despite their acceptance of the epistemological and metaphysical planks traditionally thought essential to and definitive of the psychologistic platform.[3] It would, perhaps, be more apt to say that what these philosophers oppose is not psychologism, but "psychologism". In any event, this situation poses a threat to any understanding of the philosophical dialectic concerning psychologism, and of the epistemological paradigm shift that has characterized twentieth century analytic philosophy.

Here I do not wish to be misunderstood. These comments have not been motivated by a priggish attitude concerning the sanctity of language, nor by a desire to replace natural language with an artificial calculus. Rather, my concern is with understanding. In my view, natural language is and should be in a continual state of evolution. For any attempt to halt the evolutionary process of natural language can only result in the stifling of creativity. But just because language is in a continual process of evolution, understanding demands that we take care in interpreting the words of others. Now, since few philosophers have characterized themselves as proponents of psychologism, it will be necessary to turn to the anti-psychologists for a characterization of the position. And here, a sensitivity to the pejorative nature of "psychologism" is important. For it will not, perhaps, be too surprising to find that the theories called "psychologistic" by philosophers of an opposing camp are characterized with more ameliorative terms by the philosophers who propose them.

Nicola Abbagnano has traced the use of "psychologism" to German writings in the first half of the nineteenth century. According to Abbagnano, the term was first used to characterize a philosophical movement, contrary to the then dominant Hegelianism, that was defended by Jakob Friedrich Fries and Friedrich Eduard Beneke. These philosophers, in their defense of the "rights of experience", held that "the only instrument philosophical inquiry has at its disposal is self-observation (or introspection) and that there is no way to establish any truth other than by reducing it to the subjective elements of self-observation".[4] From this perspective, psychology is the fundamental philosophical and scientific discipline, and introspection is the proper method of psychology. All other philosophical and scientific inquiries thus receive their theoretical data and ultimate justification from the results of self-observation. To that extent, Fries and Beneke can be characterized as holding that such scientific and philosophical disciplines are, in the more contemporary sense, *reducible* to introspectionist psychology. Abbagnano also notes that Fries and Beneke regarded Kant as their intellectual predecessor in that he too was a spokesman for the "rights of experience". But here it is interesting that these philosophers were nonetheless critical of Kant's efforts to derive the categories of reason from *a priori* intuition – a form of intuition which Kant thought was not dependent upon sensuous experience, but prerequisite for the very possibility of such experience. Contrary to Kant, Fries claimed that the critique of reason, like any other science, must itself be based upon introspection. And this is significant, for it suggests that, whatever else "*a priori* intuition" might mean, it was not considered by Fries to be a synonym for "introspection". Hence, *a priori* intuition was *not* regarded as a *psychological* source of knowledge.

As Abbagnano's etymology indicates, the historical relationship between psychologism and introspectionism is strong. In my view, it is too strong to be denied. Nevertheless, I will argue that anti-psychologism, at least in its Fregean and Popperian varieties, was not targeted against introspectionist psychology alone. Hence, Abbagnano's characterization of psychologism will need refinement if we are to understand Frege's and Popper's opposition to the thesis.

When Franz Brentano's theory of knowledge was accused of psychologism, Brentano sought an explication of the term. Edmund Husserl and others told him that "it means a theory which contests the general validity of knowledge, a theory according to which beings other than men could have insights which are precisely the opposite of our own".[5] More recently, John Wild has elaborated on this view by locating the essence of psychologism in its characterization of reason as in some way dependent upon something non-rational in character.[6] As such, psychologism should be understood not as a particular thesis, but as a tendency which motivates a wide range of theses, e.g., relativism, scepticism, idealism, and subjectivism. Gregory Currie has lent some credence to this view. According to Currie, psychologism is "the view according to which we are to give a subjective, mental explanation of the nature of these concepts" viz. truth, validity, and knowledge.[7] In Currie's view, Frege's anti-psychologism was thus designed to avoid relativism and scepticism.[8] Finally, Leszek Kolakowski writes that "Husserl was sure that psychologism ended in scepticism and relativism, that it made science impossible, and that it devastated the entire intellectual legacy of mankind".[9] Now the characterization of psychologism in terms of relativism, scepticism, idealism and subjectivism demands further clarification. For the systematic ambiguity of these terms renders them, without qualification, too fragile to bear the weight of philosophical explication. But what is, in my view, interesting about these characterizations of psychologism is that they contain no reference at all to either psychology in general or introspectionism in particular. Rather, they focus on: (1) psychologism's denial of the rational foundation of reason and the general validity of knowledge; and (2) the epistemological consequences of this denial. And what this, perhaps, suggests is that the focus on psychology and introspectionism is, ironically, only incidental to the anti-psychologistic critique.

Husserl himself tells us that his struggle against psychologism was neither a struggle against the psychological grounding of Logic as methodology, nor against the descriptive-psychological elucidation of logical concepts. Rather, it was a struggle against an *epistemological position*.[10] According to Husserl, "The basic error of Psychologism consists ... in its obliteration of this fundamental distinction between pure and empirical laws of psychology".[11] Here, the "epistemological position" Husserl opposed is that which holds that the laws of logic and mathematics are knowable only *a posteriori*, and hence contingent upon the "givenness of a fact and a factual world". Such a position, Husserl maintained, cannot do justice to the strict universality and necessity, the "unconditioned generality", usually associated with logical and mathematical laws. Contrary to the view that the laws of logic and mathematics are knowable only *a posteriori*, Husserl held that:

> "Prior" to the givenness of a fact and a factual world, we could be *a priori* unconditionally certain of the fact that, what we state as logicians or as arithmeticians must be applicable to everything that may be encountered as the corresponding factual reality.[12]

But the failure of such unconditioned certainty, Husserl thought, was more the result of a strictly empirical approach to psychology than of a psychological approach to epistemology. With this in mind, Husserl followed Brentano in distinguishing between (what we would call) purely descriptive or empirical psychology and *a priori* (eidetic-intuitive) psychology. Both philosophers argued that it is only the latter form of psychology that can provide a foundation for epistemology, logic, and mathematics.

Here, it is important to note that the above distinction — between purely descriptive or empirical psychology and *a priori* (eidetic-intuitive) psychology — is framed in contemporary terminology and bears an ironic relationship to Brentano's own characterization of the distinction. In the contemporary idiom of analytic philosophy, a descriptive statement is contrasted with a normative statement,[13] and a descriptive science is generally regarded as descriptive of empirical facts. But for Brentano, descriptive psychology, or *psychognosy*, was more than a purely empirical science. Rather, Brentano opposed descriptive psychology to genetic psychology. While the latter was conceived as purely empirical, the former was based upon *a priori* insight and carefully distanced from both introspectionist and behaviourist methodologies. Insofar as this is concerned, Oskar Kraus writes:

> Like nearly all the great logicians before him Brentano clearly bases logic, as the theory of how correct judgements are made, on psychology. But in his opinion there is both a descriptive and a genetic psychology; and so there are correspondingly, two kinds of logical rule. One kind comprises those which utilize the factual truths of genetic psychology and are concerned with empirical regularities. ... The other kind of rule is based on *descriptive* psychology, and hence both on the factual truths of inner perception, of secondary consciousness, and on those *a priori* truths which we spoke of earlier. Such truths as these tell us, for example, that two persons making contradictory judgements having the same temporal mode, the same modality, etc., cannot possibly both be judging correctly at one time. We have, then an immediate *a priori* insight into the correctness of judgements, into their validity or justification; and with this we have a criterion for deciding whether or not a given judgement can be a correct judgement, that is a judgement as it should be.[14]

It is not my purpose here to adjudicate between these competing claims for the title "descriptive psychology". Nor is it my purpose to evaluate the success of Brentano's and Husserl's attempts to eradicate all traces of empirical intuition from eidetic psychology. Still, this distinction between *a priori* and empirical psychology is of interest to our discussion — if only because it provides an illustration of the linguistic tact mentioned earlier. We have already seen that Fries did not regard Kant's *a priori* intuition as a psychological source of knowledge. Still, it might be argued that Brentano and Husserl did and, hence, the thesis that the laws of logic and mathematics are based upon eidetic psychology is an instance of psychologism. I do not wish to dispute this. But here, the point to be made is that if this reduction of logic and mathematics to *a priori* intuition is a form of psychologism, then it is not the form of psychologism which Husserl (and Frege) opposed. Insofar as this is concerned, Kraus writes that "We can ...

find in Brentano an anti-psychologistic attitude, insofar as this means simply the acknowledgement of a logical ought, of thinking that is justified in and of it-self".[15]

More recently, Dallas Willard has characterized logical psychologism as "the view that the non-normative statements made by logicians in their business are about, and draw their evidence from the examination of, the particular conceivings, assertings, and inferrings of particular persons — a range of facts commonly thought to belong ultimately to the science of psychology alone".[16] According to Willard:

> If Psychologism were correct, then when a logician is speaking in general and non-normative terms, about propositions, statements, proofs, arguments or inferences, his claims could have only that degree of probability provided by actual *observation* of instances from the classes of psychical or linguistic facts to which he refers.[17]

But what is curious about Willard's account is his restriction of logical psychologism to the view that the *non-normative* statements made by logicians are based upon empirical observations. For here, logical psychologism would be fully compatible with that "anti-psychologistic attitude" characterized by Kraus. Willard not withstanding, I will argue that logical psychologism is characterized, in part, by the view that logical *norms* are either based upon empirical observations or are entirely without foundation.

Here, the suggestion I wish to make, and for which I will argue in succeeding chapters, is that the ground of psychologism is neither a commitment to introspectionism nor, ironically, even a commitment to the primacy of psychological methods of inquiry. Rather, it is a commitment to the epistemology of empiricist justificationism. At least, it was the consequences of this epistemological position, and not the reduction of scientific and philosophical inquiry to psychology *per se*, that provoked the charge of and attack on psychologism. More explicitly, albeit aphoristically, Kolakowski writes that "the controversy between the psychological and Husserlian interpretations of logic is the controversy between empiricism and the belief in transcendental Reason".[18] And to the same effect, but more succinctly, Hans Sluga writes that "Psychologism, as it was understood in the nineteenth century, and also by Frege, implies the denial of *a priori* truth".[19] Again, I do not wish to be misunderstood. It may well turn out that a fully consistent rendering of the empiricist justificationist programme would require that psychology be regarded as the ultimate base for knowledge. And it might even turn out that such a psychology must, at its own base, be introspectionist in nature. While this is certainly not the direction in which most contemporary renderings of empiricist justificationism proceed, it might, nonetheless, be the one to which they are ultimately committed. Still, it is not obvious that the denial of *a priori* truth entails a commitment to introspectionism. And, in any event, the thesis for which I will argue is that the anti-psychologistic arguments of Frege and Popper are directed not against the reduction of knowledge to introspectionist psychology *per se*, but against the epistemological consequences of this move. And here, the point to be made is that these epistemological consequences are not idiosyncratic to the reduction of knowledge either to introspectionist psychology in particular or to empirical psychology in general. Rather, they are the epistemological consequences entailed by any programme that regards the ultimate justification of knowledge as empirical in nature. If this is correct, then its upshot is that the empiricist moves to (a) replace introspectionism with another more "objectivist" methodology of empirical psychology, or (b) replace psychology with a different empirical science as the foundation of knowledge will not, in themselves, suffice to meet the Fregean and Popperian critiques.

Thus far we have focussed upon the epistemological significance of the psychologism/anti-psychologism debate. But "psychologism" has also been used to designate a metaphysical or ontological thesis. And insofar as this is concerned, the battle between psychologism and anti-psychologism has often been fought, at least explicitly, on metaphysical rather than epistemological grounds. Nicola Abbagnano, for example, notes that during the same period in which Fries and Beneke were pressing the "rights of experience", Vincenzo Gioberti branded as "psychologism" all of modern philosophy from Descartes on. According to Abbagnano, what Gioberti meant by "psychologism" is "the philosophical procedure that claimed to go from man (that is, from experience) to God".[20] Gioberti thus contrasted psychologism with ontologism, which is the philosophical procedure which moves from God to man. At first glance, this characterization of psychologism might also appear epistemological in nature. For Descartes claimed to *justify* or *demonstrate* the existence of God on the basis of the fact that he possessed an idea of infinite substance, an idea of which Descartes argued he could not have been the cause. Nevertheless, Gioberti's ontologism has also been characterized as the thesis that being is present to the intellect as thought, i.e., "the being which is present to the mind is not merely the being of the mind but being itself".[21] And in this characterization, the dispute between psychologism and ontologism is the dispute whether the being apprehended in thought is (a) essentially mental and exists only as a mode of the human mind, or (b) essentially non-mental and exists completely independent of the human mind. Now it is obvious that psychologism and ontologism, thus construed, have significant implications for the Cartesian attempt to demonstrate the existence of God on the basis of introspection. For that attempt relied heavily on Descartes' questionable assumption that the cause of an idea must have at least as much formal reality as the idea has objective reality.[22] And it is interesting that most Platonist versions of ontologism ascribe to third realm entities many of the same properties traditionally associated with God, i.e., both are described as eternal, immutable, immaterial, and objective. At least, this characterization of third realm entities raises the question whether and to what extent Fregean thoughts might be functionally regarded as a semantic substitute for the God-in-the-(epistemological?) machine. Still, it should not be thought, not at least without further argument,[23] that the meta-physical dispute between psychologism and anti-psychologism is essentially theological in nature. Regardless of whether or not what is apprehended in thought must or should be regarded as eternal, immutable, and immaterial, the thesis that it must be *objective*, i.e., ontologically independent of the human mind, is a recurring theme in the anti-psychologistic literature.[24]

When, for example, Franz Brentano replied to his anti-psychologistic critics that he had always firmly rejected and opposed subjectivism and therefore should not be regarded as a proponent of a psychologistic epistemology, he was informed that his epistemology was psychologistic nonetheless because it did not admit of something outside the human mind that corresponds to the true judg-ment.[25] And Edmund Husserl, despite his later and extensive criticism of and opposition to both metaphysical and epistemological psychologism, was sharply criticized by Frege for the failure of his *Philosophy of Arithmetic* to clearly distinguish between the presentation of an object and the object itself:

> The present attempt belongs to those which undertake this cleansing in the psychological washtub. This offers the advantage that in it, things acquire a most peculiar suppleness, no longer have as hard a spatial impact on each other and lose many bothersome par-ticularities and differences. The mixture of psychology and logic that is now so popular provides good suds for this purpose. First of all, everything becomes presentation. The references of words are presentations. In the case of the word "number", for example, the aim is to exhibit the appropriate presentation and to describe its genesis and com-position. Objects are presentations. Thus J. St. Mill, with the approval of the author, lets objects (whether physical or mental) enter into a state of consciousness and become constituents of this state... But might not the moon, for example, be somewhat hard to digest for a state of consciousness? Since everything is now presentation, we can easily change the objects by now paying attention, now not. The latter is especially effective.[26]

According to Frege, failure to distinguish sharply between the presentation of an object and the object itself leads readily to a blurring of the distinction between the objective and the subjective. "Everything is shunted off into the subjective. But it is precisely because the boundary between the subjective and the objective is blurred, that conversely the subjective also acquires the appearance of the ob-jective."[27]

Frege's critique of Husserl's *Philosophy of Arithmetic* is a watershed in the history of the psychologism/anti-psychologism debate. Nevertheless, whether and to what extent Frege's critique was either justified or influential in the de-velopment of Husserl's own anti-psychologism are controversial questions that bask in obscurity.[28] But here, it is not my intention to adjudicate between the conflicting views that have been expressed concerning these questions. On the one hand, questions concerning the history of influences are notoriously difficult to resolve. On the other hand, the highly satirical (and at times sarcastic) style of Frege's critique makes it difficult to determine whether Frege's attack was targeted against Husserl's position, or against Husserl's *expression* of his position, or against the consequences of taking Husserl's expression of his position too literally.[29] In any event, the specific points of Frege's anti-psychologism are not idiosyncratic to his critique of Husserl and will later be examined as they are expressed in a number of Frege's less controversial works. Whatever the case may be, Husserl's *Logical Investigations* launched a devastating attack on psychologism which can, in part, be understood as a retraction of the views expressed in his earlier work. And here, it is important to recognize that the dispute between psychologism and anti-psychologism, in its metaphysical version, is not *simply* the dispute whether or not there exist objects independent of the human mind. For one might well admit that such objects exist, both spatio-temporal and transcendent, while at the same time denying that any such are identical with mathematical objects, senses, or thoughts. Insofar as this is concerned, Husserl, in speaking of the significance of his *Logical Investigations*, writes:

> ... first: as against logical psychologism it [the *Logical Investigations*] defended the already mentioned irreality, the ideal objective and identical being of such objects as concepts, propositions, inferences, truths, true proofs, etc... This included the thesis that these objects are unities of meaning of such a kind that in the content of the meanings themselves there is nothing of the psychic acts and other subjective experiences which constitute the changing consciousness of the objects concerned, that they are in no way tied to the real men or other subjects. Psychic acts, like their subjects, belong to the real world. Secondly, and in close connection with the above: correlative to the ideal objectivities, there are also pure, ideal truths which say nothing about the world or about anything real. Pure logic, in the theory of the syllogism, speaks about pure concepts and pure propositions, just as pure arithmetic states truths and theories about pure numbers or the number series, in whose meaning not the least is said about the spatio-temporal, factual world. Irrespective of whether there is a world or not, the truth that $2 + 2 = 4$ subsists in itself as a pure truth. It does not contain in its sense the least information about real facts. The same holds good of the law of non-contradiction and other such laws. Pure ideal truths are "*a priori*", and are seen to be true in the unconditioned necessity of their generality.[30]

More recently, Michael Dummett has characterized psychologism as "the intrusion or appeal to mental processes in the analysis of sense".[31] Insofar as this is concerned, Frege's anti-psychologism was predicated upon an ontology that sharply distinguished between the sense of an expression and the mental idea or ideas associated with that expression. As we shall see shortly, this distinction involved the hypothesis of third realm objects that were construed as ontologically independent of the human mind. Such third realm objects were characterized as immaterial in that they are not spatio-temporal entities, but objective in that they exist independently of any knowing subject. And since third realm entities are immaterial, they cannot be perceived through the senses. Rather, Frege held that they are grasped or apprehended by the Reason (presumably a sort of intellectual sense organ) without compromise to their objectivity. Now many contemporary analytic philosophers, impressed with Frege's defense of objective truth but wary of objects not accessible through sense perception, have minimized the importance of Frege's third realm. Nevertheless, I will argue that Frege regarded the third realm as a necessary ontological component of anti-psychologism since it is only the characterization of truth as a third realm entity that can account for its objectivity. Insofar as this is concerned, the psychologism/anti-psychologism debate, in its metaphysical version, might well be understood as the dispute concerning whether or not third realm entities exist. At least, Popper, despite his disagreement with Frege concerning the properties of third realm entities, has characterized psychologism as resulting from "the neglect or even denial of the third world".[32]

Now the purpose of this chapter, and the definitions and passages cited herein, has been to orient our ideas — to direct our attention toward the philosophical space surrounding the arguments concerning psychologism. As such, my attempt has been to sketch the epistemological and metaphysical grounds of the debate. In distinguishing between these grounds, I do not wish to suggest that these epistemological and metaphysical theses are logically independent or held in isolation. Rather, I will argue that the metaphysical hypothesis of the third realm was held primarily to provide the ontological prerequisites for objective knowledge. Still, the connections between these theses remain vague and inexact. And it will be the burden of much of what follows to make these connections explicit. But in order to attain a more exact view, we must turn to the *arguments* of the anti-psychologists for a statement of the specific theses condemned as "psychologistic" and the reasons for those condemnations. For it is, I think, only when we see what is being defended that we will understand what is being attacked. But as a first approximation toward such an understanding, we will denote by "psychologism" a family of views, all tending to deprecate or deny distinctions between epistemology and metaphysics on the one hand and psychology on the other. Accordingly, by "anti-psychologism" we will initially understand any tendency or inclination to keep such alleged distinctions sharply in focus. Unmodified, these terms denote not theses, but families of theses. In the following chapter, we will identify some of the more salient members of these families.

NOTES AND REFERENCES

1.   See: e.g., Sober, Elliott; "Psychologism"; *Journal for the Theory of Social Behaviour* Volume 8, No. 2; July 1978.

2.   Brentano, Franz; *Psychologie vom empirischen Standpunkt*; Duncker & Humblot (Leipzig, 1874) ed. by Linda L. McAlister; trans. by Antos C. Rancurello, D.B. Terrell, and Linda L. McAlister; *Psychology from an Empirical Standpoint*; Humanities Press (New York, 1973) p. 306.

3.   It is *not* my claim that either Frege or Popper are guilty of this tendency.

4.   Abbagnano, Nicola; "Psychologism", trans. by Nino Langiulli in *The Encyclopedia of*

20

Philosophy; ed. by Paul Edwards; Macmillan Publishing Co., Inc. & The Free Press (New York, 1967) Volume 6, p. 520.

5.   *Op. cit.*; Brentano; p. 306.

6.   Wild, John; "Husserl's Critique of Psychologism: Its Historic Roots and Contemporary Relevance", in *Philosophical Essays in Memory of Edmund Husserl*; ed. by Marvin Farber; Greenwood Press (New York, 1968) p. 20.

7.   Currie, Gregory; *Frege: An Introduction to His Philosophy*; Harvester Press (Sussex, 1982) p. 13.

8.   Currie, Gregory; "Frege on Thoughts"; *Mind*, Volume LXXXIX, No. 354; p. 245.

9.   Kolakowski, Leszek; *Husserl and the Search for Certitude*; Yale University Press (New Haven, 1975) p. 17.

10.   Husserl, Edmund; "A Reply to a Critic of my Refutation of Logical Psychologism"; *Zeitschrift für Psychologie und Physiologie Sinnesorganie*, Volume 31, 1903; p. 287-294; trans. by Dallas Willard; in *Readings on Edmund Husserl's Logical Investigations*; ed. by J.N. Mohanty; Martinus Nijhoff (The Hague, 1977) p. 35.

11.   *Ibid.*; p. 39.

12.   Husserl, Edmund; "Phanomenologische Psychologie"; *Husserliana* Volume 9; trans. by J.N. Mohanty as "The Task and the Significance of the *Logical Investigations*"; in *Op. cit.*; *Readings on Edmund Husserl's Logical Investigations*; p. 198.

13.   This characterization is independent of positivist worries concerning whether or not sentences that express norms are or should be considered *statements*, i.e., sentences that possess truth values. Nor do I wish to suggest that a *sharp* distinction between normative and descriptive statements is tenable. The idea that there is a *sharp* distinction between statements of fact and statements of value has recently been attacked from two fronts. On the one hand, empiricists argue that normative statements can only be justified naturalistically, i.e., by facts concerning the values that people actually hold. On the other hand, rationalists argue that all observation is theory-laden, and that all theory is value-laden. Nevertheless, we can continue to speak intuitively of a distinction between normative and descriptive statements. But in my view, neither normative nor descriptive statements are ultimately justifiable. And while all observation may be both theory-and-value-laden, no theory or value is *a priori* valid.

14.   See: "Introduction to the 1924 Edition by Oskar Kraus"; in *Op. cit.*; Brentano; pp. 390-391.

15.   *Ibid.*; p. 391.

16.   Willard, Dallas; "The Paradox of Logical Psychologism: Husserl's Way Out"; in *Op. cit.*; *Readings on Edmund Husserl's Logical Investigations*; p. 43.

17.   *Ibid.*; pp. 45-46.

18.   *Op. cit.*; Kolakowski; p. 28.

19. Sluga, Hans; "Frege's Alleged Realism"; *Inquiry*, 20, p. 229. It is interesting that this passage occurs in a context critical of Dummett's characterization of Fregean anti-psychologism as directed against post-Kantian idealism. There, Sluga quotes from Frege's *Nachgelassene Schriften* to demonstrate that what Frege opposed was "the sensualism of Locke and the idealism of Berkeley".

20. *Op. cit.*; Abbagnano; p. 520.

21. Caponigri, A. Robert; "Vincenzo Gioberti", in *Op. cit.*; *The Encyclopedia of Philosophy*, Volume 3, p. 324.

22. Descartes seems to use "objective reality" to refer to an object as it is represented in an idea, and "formal reality" to refer to an object as it exists independent of such representation. While Descartes distinguished between the power of imagination and the power of understanding, associating the former with the senses and the latter with the intellect, the objects of both imagination and understanding were characterized as mental entities. This is, in a way, interesting. For Descartes' "objective reality" and Frege's "objective reality" seem to be antonyms.

23. I cannot develop such an argument in detail here. Later, I will argue that the epistemological function of Frege's third realm was to provide the possibility of objectively certain knowledge. But if this is correct, then it is, at least, interesting that God fulfilled the same epistemological function for Descartes. And since Frege's third realm entities, like Descartes' God, are described as eternal, immutable, immaterial, and objective, my speculative suggestion is that God has here not been removed from the system, but simply renamed.

24. Popper also introduces a third realm to account for the objectivity of knowledge. But contrary to Frege, Popper characterizes the objects of the third world as *products* of the human mind. Hence, for Popper, third realm objects are neither eternal nor immutable. Their objectivity consists solely in the fact that they are not mental entities. And this is interesting since, for Popper, the epistemological function of the third realm is *not* to provide the cognitive authority for objectively certain knowledge.

25. *Op. cit.*; Brentano; p. 306.

26. Frege, Gottlob; Review of E. Husserl; *Philosophie der Arithmetik; Zeitschrift für Philosophie und Philosophische Kritik*, 103, pp. 313-332. Trans. by E. Kluge as "Review of Dr. E. Husserl's *Philosophy of Arithmetic*"; in *Mind*, 81, pp. 323-324.

27. *Ibid.*; pp. 324-325.

28. In my view, much of this obscurity results from the unfortunate sociological fact that Frege and Husserl are regarded as founding fathers of philosophical schools that have, in the twentieth century, been regarded as competing methodological alternatives for philosophical investigation. Regardless of whether or not this is the most fruitful way to view the relationship between logical analysis and phenomenology (and in my view it certainly is not), their characterization as competing methodological alternatives has proved unfortunate for the history of philosophy. For historians of each tradition seem to regard the demonstration of the anti-psychologistic priority of its founder as something of a vested interest. It is as if the philosophical fortunes of logical analysis and phenomenology rise or fall with the determination of Frege's influence on Husserl. So on the one hand, we find the portrait of Frege as the clear-minded and dispassionate surgeon who cut through the impenetrable fog of Husserl's rhetoric to locate the cancer of psychologism lurking in the very bowels of phe-

nomenology. But phenomenologists, on the other hand, tend to dismiss this view, insisting instead that Frege repeatedly misses the mark in his criticism of Husserl, that Husserl's *Philosophy of Arithmetic*, while psychologistic, is so on grounds different than those mentioned by Frege, and that Husserl had, in any event, already correctly diagnosed this psychologism and had taken the anti-psychologistic cure prior to Frege's critique and on his own accord.

29. This last possibility is, perhaps, suggested by Frege himself: "But isn't it really a very harmless pleasantry to call, for example, the moon a presentation? It is – as long as one does not imagine that one can change it as one likes, or produce it by psychological means. But this is all too easily the result". (*Op. cit.*; Frege; "Review of Dr. E. Husserl's *Philosophy of Arithmetic*"; p. 325.)

30. *Op. cit.*; Husserl; "The Task and the Significance of the *Logical Investigations*"; pp. 198-199.

31. Dummett, Michael; *Frege: Philosophy of Language*; Harper & Row (New York, 1973) p. 659.

32. Popper, Karl; *Objective Knowledge*; Oxford University Press (New York, 1972) p. 162.

3. PSYCHOLOGISM: A FREGEAN PERSPECTIVE

Perhaps the most constant and influential opponent of psychologism in the late nineteenth and early twentieth centuries was the German mathematician and philosopher of logic, Gottlob Frege. Edmund Husserl, Rudolf Carnap, and Karl Popper have also been influential opponents of psychologism. Popper's anti-psychologism will be the focus of our attention later in this discussion. But Carnap's glossary definition of "psychologism" as the "wrong interpretation of logical problems in psychological terms"[1] is the most terse, if not the most dogmatic, statement of the thesis. And the first volume of Husserl's *Logical Investigations* contains the most developed polemic against psychologism in the literature. But each of these philosophers has acknowledged his anti-psychologistic debt to Frege.

In this chapter we will take Frege's anti-psychologistic arguments as illustrative of the position, and we will attempt to characterize psychologism in terms of them. In at least one respect it would have been easier to take Husserl as the central figure in this chapter. The epistemological considerations which motivate the anti-psychologistic critique are stated with greater clarity and in more detail in Husserl's writings than in Frege's. But while Frege and Husserl are both great and seminal anti-psychologistic thinkers, it would be too naive to ignore the fact that they are figures in, if not founders of, different philosophical movements. It is sometimes said that the analytical and phenomenological movements address the same problems but in different idioms. Still, the fact remains that the idioms *are* different. Since our discussion will eventually focus on the differences between Popperian anti-psychologism and the more traditional thesis, Frege seems the more appropriate figure to begin with. But this, of course, entails a sacrifice of perspicuity for continuity.

Frege was clearly opposed to the subjectivist tendencies associated with the introspectionist psychology of his day. But Frege's anti-psychologism was not limited to an attack on introspectionism alone. Rather, Frege's arguments attempt to undermine the suggestion that *any empirical psychology* (introspectionist or otherwise) can provide the foundations for logic. This lends credence to Wild's view. In speaking of Husserl, Wild writes:

> Ever since the time of Hume, "empiricist" philosophers had dreamed of psychology, or the "science of human nature", as the basic science to which all other sciences are relative. Hence Husserl adopted the name psychologism for the tendency to relativize reason, or to make it dependent upon something not itself.[2]

According to psychologism, reason is dependent upon the data of empirical psychology. This link between psychologism and empiricism is important, and we will carry it one step further. Far from being limited to an opposition to introspectionism, Frege's refusal to countenance empirical *psychology* as the foundation for logic was itself incidental. An examination of Frege's anti-psychologistic arguments reveals that he would have been opposed to the suggestion that *any empirical science* can provide foundations for logic. That Frege focused on psychologism was due to the fact that the reduction of logic to psychology was the then dominant empiricist move. But were Frege alive today, he might have well have initiated an attack on 'biologism'.

There are at least four specific anti-psychologistic theses to be gleaned from Frege's philosophical writings: (1) logic is a normative and not a descriptive or natural science; (2) meanings, or senses,[3] are third realm entities and neither mental entities nor objects of the real world (i.e., spatio-temporal entities); (3) mathematical objects, e.g., numbers, are third realm entities and neither mental entities nor material objects nor properties of material objects; and (4) questions of justification are distinct from questions of discovery, and statements concerning the psychological genesis of a belief are irrelevant for the justification of that belief. These four theses are like spokes connected to a more general and catalytic hub. To that extent, the spokes of this wheel exist for the sake of its hub. The hub of Frege's anti-psychologistic thought is that (5) truth and knowledge are, in some rather literal sense, objective. What is assumed is that the truth value of a thought is objective (i.e., that truth is independent of the judging subject, or that being true is distinct from being thought to be true), and that thoughts can be known without compromise to the objectivity of their truth values. (1) through (4) are then introduced as what must be the case if (5).

In the remainder of this chapter I will offer brief sketches of (1) through (4). In so doing, I will be concerned both with what distinguishes them as separate theses, and with what characterizes them in common as anti-psychologistic. In addition to reciting Frege's reasons for holding (1) through (4), I will cite historical examples of contrasting psychologistic theses. My narrative will here be expository rather than critical. The examples cited are intended only as illustrations. And the positions sketched are definitely not the only versions or instances of psychologism and anti-psychologism to be found in the literature. Nevertheless, it is hoped that by focusing on these examples we will be able to fix the locus of the debate, i.e., we will determine why some philosophers have consciously advocated psychologistic theories while others have been so intent upon opposing them. Finally, I will make no attempt to adjudicate between (1) through (4) and their psychologistic counterparts. I am here not so much interested in determining whether psychologism is true or false as I am in identifying a certain movement in contemporary analytic philosophy as psychologistic and in clarifying the implications of that movement for the philosophical activities of justification and criticism. Moreover, I really do not know what would count as a demonstration that psychologism is true or that it is false. Such a demonstration would, of course, involve an argument. But as will become evident in a later chapter, unless that argument unveils a contradiction internal to the psychologistic position (as opposed to a contradiction between the psychologistic theory and some statement or statements thought to be true by anti-psychologists but denied by psychologism), it will only succeed in begging the question against psychologism. Indeed, insofar as psychologism is thought to result in logical relativity, it is not even clear that the demonstration of a contradiction would count as a refutation to radical supporters of the position. If the only way to "prove" a thesis is by appealing to "facts" which the opponents of that thesis deny, then we should really question the point of giving a proof in the first place. Such "proofs" may foster solidarity among the supporters of a position, but they will only provide comic relief for its opponents.

Logical Psychologism

(1) concerns the task and scope of logic. It is thesis about what constitutes the subject matter of logic. And it is, in effect, a directive about what logicians should be doing. We can contrast (1) with what might be called "logical psychologism".[4] According to logical psychologism, logic is a natural science descriptive of the human acts of asserting, thinking, judging, and inferring. Logical laws are thus characterized as inductive generalizations discoverable only through empirical investigation. What is usually meant by "empirical investigation" in this context is, no doubt, self-observation. But the data for such inductive generalizations need not be derived from introspection alone. Observation reports concerning the linguistic behaviour of a community of language users could also provide psychologistic evidence for the laws of logic. Exactly what one's psychology is may vary. But what distinguishes logical psychologism from anti-psychologism and from other versions of empiricism and naturalism is that it conceives of our knowledge of the laws of logic as based upon the evidence of empirical psychology.

It is important to emphasize that what anti-psychologistic writers understand by "psychology" is *empirical* psychology. Husserl, for example, writes:

> ...psychology is concerned with "empirical consciousness", with consciousness from the empirical point of view, as an empirical being in the ensemble of nature, whereas phenomenology is concerned with "pure" consciousness...any psychologistic theory of knowledge must owe its existence to the fact that, missing the proper sense of the epistemological problematic, it is a victim of a presumably facile confusion between pure and empirical consciousness. To put the same in another way: it "naturalizes" pure consciousness.[5]

Pure consciousness is, presumably, distinguished from empirical consciousness in that it is unadulterated by elements gleaned from sensuous experience. That "introspection" was construed by anti-psychologistic writers as introspection of *empirical* consciousness is due to the fact that the radically empiricist psychologies they opposed had denied the existence of a consciousness unadulterated by elements gleaned from sensuous experience. According to such radically empiricist psychologies, the mind prior to sensuous experience is a blank slate, and whatever exists in the mind and can be introspected can be traced ultimately to sense perceptions.

According to logical psychologism, our belief that, e.g., any and every meaningful sentence of the form -(P & -P) is true is, at least in part, a result of the fact that we live in a world in which the law of non-contradiction "holds". It is, moreover, a psychological result of that fact. Whether the law of non-contradiction "holds" in this world due to the linguistic conventions of its inhabitants or to the physical composition of its stuff is, for the psychologistic logician, irrelevant. In either case, our belief in the truth of the law of non-contradiction is explained by the psychologistic logician as a result of our past and continuing sensuous experience of that world. What is essential to logical psychologism is that our knowledge that the laws of logic "hold" in our world cannot be *a priori*. It follows from this that the laws of logic cannot be known to be either necessary or strictly universal. And it follows from this that they cannot be known with anything greater than empirical certainty. Had our sensuous experience been different, then our logical laws might have been other than what they in fact are. And should we have sensuous experience which cannot be explained without appeal to logical laws which differ from our own or can be explained with much greater simplicity by appealing to logical laws which differ from our own, then beliefs concerning the truth of our laws of logic may well undergo revision.

It is often thought that psychologistic logicians appeal to induction for justification of the logical laws. It is, no doubt, true that such logicians often give inductive accounts of logic. But if such accounts are taken as attempts at justification, then the question reiterates. For what justifies induction? To this extent, logical psychologism denies that there is, ultimately, any question of justifying a logical law over and above that of whether or not it is actually used in practice. Justification is thought to be either unnecessary, or given in survey. But more often than not, the appeal to induction is made to account for how we come to know the laws of logic. It is not so much that questions of genesis are confused with questions of justification as that questions of justification are simply ignored. In any event, what is essential to logical psychologism is that justification by appeal to *a priori* truths is ruled impossible.

Logical psychologism is also associated with the denial of an objective and unique criterion for rationality. Philosophers, especially those influenced by the development of logic, have long been prone to equate rationality with logicality, i.e., strict adherence to the laws of logic. But if this equation is to yield a unique criterion of rationality, then it must assume that the laws of logic are themselves unique. Indeed, EP_1 philosophers consider adherence to the laws of logic suitable as an objective criterion of rationality precisely because they regard the laws of logic as objective, unique, and incorrigible, i.e., not subject to revision. Toulmin, for example, in discussing the problem of rationality and the resolution of conceptual diversity and philosophical disagreement, writes:

From early on, however, all the philosophical theories proposed as solutions to this problem began to develop in a single direction. The need for an impartial forum and procedures was understood as calling for a single, unchanging, and uniquely authoritative system of ideas and beliefs. The prime exemplar of such a universal and authoritative system was found in the new, abstract networks of logic and geometry. In this way, 'objectivity', in the sense of impartiality, became equated with the 'objectivity' of timeless truths; the rational merits of an intellectual position were identified with its logical coherence; and the philosopher's measure of a man's rationality became his ability to recognize, without further argument, the validity of the axioms, formal entailments, and logical necessities on which the claims of the authoritative system depended. Yet this particular direction of development – which equated *rationality* with *logicality* – was never compulsory. On the contrary ... accepting this equation made an eventual clash with history and anthropology inevitable.[6]

Be this as it may, when confronted with beings who reason according to different and incompatible logical laws, the psychologistic logician can only describe the facts. It is not that he *cannot* judge which, or whether any of these beings are rational. But from the EP_1 perspective, the *objectivity* of his judgments is suspect since they are, at best, based on consensus and subject to revision in the light of further experience.

Logical psychologism thus denies: (a) that the laws of logic are knowable *a priori*; (b) that the laws of logic can or need to be justified *a priori*; and (c) that the laws of logic can function as an objective and unique criterion of rationality. Positively, logical psychologism attempts to give a naturalistic account of our logical knowledge that does not appeal to *a priori* valid statements and does not presuppose sources of knowledge over and above the ordinary sense perception of empiricist psychology.

The best illustration, if not the strongest statement, of logical psychologism can be found in the philosophy of John Stuart Mill. While Mill was vehemently opposed to the nominalist view that the laws of logic express merely verbal conventions (a view which he thought distorts their significance), he was equally opposed to the view that they are knowable *a priori*. Rather, he considered the logical laws to be well-entrenched but corrigible inductive generalizations which could be known through introspection of our psychological states of belief and disbelief. In discussing the law of non-contradiction, Mill writes:

I consider it to be, like other axioms, one of our first and most familiar generalizations from experience. The original foundation of it I take to be, that Belief and Disbelief are two different mental states, excluding one another. This we know by the simplest observation of our own minds. And if we carry our observation outwards, we also find that light and darkness, sound and silence, motion and quiescence, equality and inequality, preceding and following, succession and simultaneousness, any positive phenomenon whatever and its negation, are distinct phenomena, pointedly contrasted, and the one always absent where the other is present. I consider the maxim in question to be a generalization from all these facts.[7]

It should not, moreover, be thought that Mill's reference to the psychological states of belief and disbelief is an unconscious oversight. On the contrary, Mill elsewhere criticizes Sir William Hamilton for his refusal to recognize belief as any element in the scientific analysis of a proposition.[8]

Now Mill sometimes writes as if the laws of logic express psychological necessities. But this does not mean that Mill thought it psychologically impossible for a person to believe contradictory propositions. A person can for example, believe contradictory propositions through forgetfulness, believing the affirmative at one time and its negation at another. And a person might "yield a passive assent to two forms of words, which, had he been fully conscious of their meaning, he would have known to be, either wholly or in part, an affirmation and a denial of the same fact."[9] But Mill thought it "totally impossible" for a person to believe a proposition *once he is made to see that it involves a contradiction.*[10] Nevertheless, Mill remains agnostic regarding both the scope of the universality of the laws of logic and the question whether or not they reflect the native structure of the mind:

> I readily admit that these three general propositions (the laws of identity, non-contradiction, and the excluded middle) are universally true of all phenomena. I also admit that if there are any inherent necessities of thought, these are such. I express myself in this qualified manner, because whoever is aware how artificial, modifiable, the creatures of circumstances, and alterable by circumstances, most of the supposed necessities of thought are (though real necessities to a given person at a given time), will hesitate to affirm of any such necessities that they are an original part of our mental constitution. Whether the three so-called Fundamental Laws are laws of our thoughts by the native structure of the mind, or merely because we perceive them to be universally true of observed phenomena, I will not positively decide: but they are laws of our thoughts now, and invincibly so. They may or may not be capable of alteration by experience, but the conditions of our existence deny to us the experience which would be required to alter them. Any assertion, therefore, which conflicts with one of these laws − any proposition, for instance, which asserts a contradiction, though it were on a subject wholly removed from the sphere of our experience, is to us unbelievable. The belief in such a proposition is, in the present constitution of nature, impossible as a mental fact.[11]

In saying that *if* there are any inherent necessities of thought, then the laws of logic are such and that it is "totally impossible" for a person to believe a proposition once he sees that it involves a contradiction, I take it that Mill is asserting that the laws of logic are at least as well-entrenched as any other of our beliefs. In other words, it is totally impossible for a person to believe a proposition once he sees that it involves a contradiction *given the present state of our experience.* So the extent to which such laws are thought universal is the extent to which we have yet to encounter phenomena that contradict them.

It might seem that we are here involved in a vicious circle, i.e., an appeal to phenomena that contradict the law of non-contradiction in order to revise the law of non-contradiction. The situation seems somewhat analogous to the paradox of fallibilism. When the fallibilist asserts that all of his beliefs are fallible, he is inevitably confronted with the quip, "Including that one?" But Mill seems to have been generally unimpressed with such arguments. In reply to Hamilton's assertion that "those who would assert the possibility of contradictions being at once true, in fact annihilate the possibility of truth itself, and the whole significance of thought", Mill writes:

Assuming it to be true that "to deny the universal application of the three laws" as laws of existence "is to subvert the reality of thought:" is anything added to the force of this consideration by saying that "this subversion is itself an act of thought?" If the reality of thought *can* be subverted, is there any peculiar enormity in doing it by means of thought itself? In what other way can we imagine it to be done? And if it were true that thought is an invalid process, what better proof of this could be given than that we would, by thinking, arrive at the conclusion that our thoughts are not to be trusted? Sir W. Hamilton always seems to suppose that the imaginary sceptic, who doubts the validity of thought altogether, is obliged to claim a greater validity for his subversive thoughts than he allows to the thoughts they subvert. But it is enough for him to claim the same validity, so that all opinions are thrown into equal uncertainty.[12]

The laws of logic may be the laws of our thoughts *now*, and "invincibly so", but Mill is always prepared to allow that future experience may lead to their revision. Such a circumstance may well, at any present moment, be inconceivable. But Mill is also generally sceptical concerning what, if anything, the inconceivability of a proposition shows:

This, therefore, is the principle asserted: that propositions, the negation of which is inconceivable, or in other words, which we cannot figure to ourselves as being false, must rest on evidence of a higher and more cogent description than any which experience can afford.

Now I cannot but wonder that so much stress should be laid on the circumstance of inconceivableness, when there is such ample experience to show that our capacity or incapacity of conceiving a thing has very little to do with the possibility of the thing itself; but is in truth very much an affair of accident, and depends on the past history and habits of our own minds. There is no more generally acknowledged fact in human nature, than the extreme difficulty at first felt in conceiving anything as possible, which is in contradiction to long established and familiar experience; or even to old familiar habits of thought. And this difficulty is a necessary result of the fundamental laws of the human mind. When we have often seen and thought of things together, and have never in any one instance either seen or thought of them separately, there is by the primary law of association an increasing difficulty, which in the end may become insuperable, of conceiving the two things apart.[13]

This passage is interesting for two reasons: (1) insofar as Mill's radical empiricism denies the possibility of *a priori* knowledge, it *a fortiori* denies the existence of analytic truths. In this passage Mill denies the validity of what is, for all intents and purposes, the test of analyticity; (2) despite his psychologistic tendencies, Mill clearly does not equate being true with being thought to be true, not even when the negation of what is thought to be true is thought inconceivable.

Experience, according to Mill, shows that our beliefs concerning what is conceivable and what is inconceivable are themselves results of experience. Hence, whatever necessity, psychological or otherwise, the laws of logic may have, the most that Mill thinks can be justifiably affirmed is that our belief that such laws are necessary is based upon habits formed through association. Such necessity may be psychologically real in the sense that it is, at a given time, really impossible for a person to, e.g., simultaneously and consciously believe a proposition and its negation. But whether or not it will always be impossible is another question, and one which cannot be answered in the same breath. So while Mill is prepared to grant the laws of logic the strictest universality, necessity, and certainty that experience will allow, this is, nonetheless, the strictest universality, necessity, and certainty that *experience* will allow.

Frege opposed logical psychologism with the doctrine that logic is a normative and not a natural science:

> It will be granted by all at the outset that the laws of logic ought to be guiding principles for thought in the attainment of truth, yet this is only too easily forgotten, and here what is fatal is the double meaning of the word "law". In one sense a law asserts what is; in the other it prescribes what ought to be. Only in the latter sense can the laws of logic be called 'laws of thought': so far as they stipulate the way in which one ought to think. Any law asserting what is, can be conceived as prescribing that one ought to think in conformity with it, and is thus in that sense a law of thought.[14]

But stated thus simply, the question whether logic is a normative or a descriptive science might appear to be a red herring. On the one hand, anti-psychologists also conceive of the logical laws as describing what is the case. Indeed, it is only to the extent that the laws of logic truly describe what is that they can justifiably prescribe what ought to be. But Frege argued that what the logical laws describe is not (necessarily) what is the case concerning how human beings in fact reason. On the other hand, there is nothing contradictory in the use of inductive generalizations which describe how humans in fact reason as norms, or guiding principles, for how they should reason. To that extent, the psychologistic logician might find little fault in the doctrine that the task of logic is to state how human beings should reason, i.e., in the doctrine that logic is a normative science. But the psychologistic logician would insist that these norms must be based on facts concerning how human beings generally reason or on human decisions concerning the methods of reasoning which are pragmatically most efficacious. Hence, the psychologistic logician could maintain that logic is (in part) a normative science, but that the normative laws of logic are relative to human beings, or to some subset thereof, and may be subject to revision in the light of further empirical evidence or a change in our practical goals.

But this masks the deeper issue. The deeper issue concerns the scope of the logical laws qua normative laws of thought and, ultimately, the possibility of their revision. What the psychologistic logician's adherence to empiricist methodology commits him to doubt is the "unconditional and eternal validity" of the laws of logic.[15] If logical psychologism is correct, then the descriptive and normative value of such laws would be relative to our thought as it is now, or as it was during a certain period of time and for a certain community of language users. Thus, Frege wrote:

...the expression "law of thought" seduces us into supposing that these laws govern thinking in the same way as laws of nature govern events in the external world. In that case they can be nothing but laws of psychology: for thinking is a mental process. And if logic were concerned with these psychological laws it would be a part of psychology; it is in fact viewed in just this way. These laws of thought can in that case be regarded as guiding principles in the sense that they give an average, like statements about 'how it is that good digestion occurs in man', or 'how one speaks grammatically', or 'how one dresses fashionably'. Then one can only say: men's taking something to be true conforms on the average to these laws, at present and relative to our knowledge of men; thus if one wishes to correspond with the average one will conform to these. But just as what is fashionable in dress at the moment will shortly be fashionable no longer and among the Chinese is not fashionable now, so these psychological laws of thought can be laid down only with restrictions on their authority. Of course — if logic has to do with something's being taken to be true, rather than with its being true![16]

But for Frege, the laws of thought are not psychological laws, but "boundary stones set in an eternal foundation, which our thought can overflow, but never displace."[17] For Frege, the normative value of the laws of logic is not relative to time, place, or community of language users. Rather, it ranges universally over all rational beings, at all times, and in all places. Linguistic expression may, of course, vary, but the reference of the logical laws is fixed. "Anyone who has once acknowledged a law of truth has by the same token acknowledged a law that prescribes the way in which one ought to judge, no matter where, or when, or by whom the judgment is made."[18]

Husserl, in opposing the thesis that logic is a natural science, seems to echo Frege's concern:

No natural laws can be known a priori, nor established by sheer insight. The only way in which a natural law can be established and justified, is by induction from the singular facts of experience. Induction does not establish the holding of the law, only the greater or less probability of its holding; the probability, and not the law, is justified by insight. Logical laws must, accordingly, without exception, rank as mere probabilities. Nothing, however, seems plainer than that the laws of 'pure logic' all have a priori validity. They are established and justified, not by induction, but by apodeictic inner evidence. Insight justifies no mere probabilities of their holding, but their holding or truth itself.[19]

What Husserl thinks is guaranteed by the a priori validity of a proposition is the strict universality, necessity, and, hence, incorrigibility of that proposition. Truths which are a priori valid thus truly are boundary stones set in an eternal foundation. This issue of incorrigibility is significant for our later discussion. For it is the possibility of revision which the fallibilist maintains, and it is the denial of a priori valid statements which usually leads to fallibilism. Husserl, on the other hand, considered the possibility of the revision of the laws of logic an "open absurdity":

We know that, in view of ineliminable observational imprecision, it would be foolish to look for a uniquely true law. Such is the situation in the exact factual sciences, but by no means in logic. The justified possibility of the former becomes the open absurdity of the latter. We have insight into, not merely the probability, but the truth of the logical laws.[20]

Now Frege does not deny that rational beings can "break" the logical laws, that their thought can "overflow" these logical boundary stones. Indeed, the utility of the laws of logic as normative laws of thought would be naught were it not possible for humans to violate them. Insofar as norms are concerned, the sense of a law presupposes an ability to break it. Nor does Frege deny that certain rational beings might recognize these logical laws only empirically:

> ...the possibility remains of men or other beings being discovered who were capable of bringing off judgments contradicting our laws of logic. If this were to happen? Herr Erdmann would say: here we see that these principles do not hold generally. Certainly! – if these are psychological laws, their verbal expression must single out the family of beings whose thought is empirically governed by them. I should say: thus there exist beings that recognize certain truths not as we do, immediately, but perhaps by some lengthier route of induction.[21]

But what the logical laws, thus understood, provide for Frege is a standard by which to measure the rationality of *any* creature. It is this objective and eternal standard that the psychological logician lacks:

> ...what if beings were even found whose laws of thought flatly contradicted ours and therefore frequently led to contrary results even in practice? The psychological logician could only acknowledge the fact and say simply: those laws hold for them, these laws hold for us. I should say: we have here a hitherto unknown type of madness. Anyone who understands laws of logic to be laws that prescribe the way in which one ought to think – to be laws of truth, and not natural laws of human beings' taking a thing to be true – will ask, who is right? Whose laws of taking-to-be-true are in accord with the laws of truth? The psychological logician cannot ask this question; if he did he would be recognizing laws of truth that were not laws of psychology.[22]

The justified true belief theory of knowledge coupled with the EP_1 characterization of justification as logical demonstration points to the epistemological need for an objective criterion of rationality. Here, adherence to the laws of logic as an objective criterion of rationality provides a standard for the evaluation of the rationality of any proposed justification. But unless such a criterion were *a priori* valid, it would itself stand in need of rational justification, and hence could not provide the standard for such evaluations. Husserl, in linking psychologism to empiricism, developed this line of thought and argued that radical empiricism renders rational justification impossible:

> Extreme empiricism is as absurd a theory of knowledge as extreme scepticism. *It destroys the possibility of the rational justification of mediate knowledge*, and so destroys *its own possibility* as a scientifically proven theory. It admits that there is mediate knowledge, the product of various validating connections, and it does not reject principles of validation. It not only admits that there is a logic, but itself helps to construct

it. If, however, all proof rests on principles governing its procedure, then we should either be involved in a *circle* or in an infinite *regress* if the principles of proof themselves required further proof, in a circle if the principles of proof used to justify the principles of proof were the same as the latter, in a regress if both sets of principles were repeatedly different. Plainly, therefore, the demand for a fundamental justification of all mediate knowledge can only have a sense if we can both see and know certain ultimate principles on which all proof in the last instance rests. All principles which justify possible proofs must therefore be deductively inferrible from certain last, immediately evident principles, so that even the principles of the deduction in question all themselves occur among such principles.[23]

We will need to return to this argument in greater detail in our discussion of Popper's anti-psychologism. For now, suffice it to say that this argument is devastating to the psychologistic position only to the extent to which it equates rationality with logical justification.

Frege's opposition to logical psychologism was meant neither to demean psychology as an empirical science nor to cast doubt upon the significance of empirical facts concerning how human beings reason. Frege clearly acknowledged such empirical facts as the legitimate concern for certain fields of inquiry, e.g., empirical psychology. But insofar as logic is concerned, Frege thought them to be of interest only as curiosity. So, far from being a red herring, the thesis that logic is a normative science, as understood by Frege, is of primary importance. It is true that logic is both a descriptive and a normative science. But the anti-psychologist and the psychologistic logician differ with regard to the facts that logic describes. The anti-psychologist believes that as a descriptive science logic describes what is the case, i.e., the laws of logic as opposed to the facts concerning how humans reason (the laws of thought as opposed to the laws of thinking). And this descriptive account is thought to engender logic's normative role by providing the unconditional and eternal guiding principles of how humans should reason. Finally, what hangs on the existence of such unconditional and eternal guiding principles is, from the EP_1 anti-psychologistic perspective, the very possibility of critical science.

Linguistic Psychologism

(2) is a thesis in the theory of meaning and concerns the ontological character of senses and thoughts, or what have commonly been called "meanings". Such concerns should be sharply distinguished from what might be called "the logic of meaning", i.e., issues concerning whether and to what extent we need to distinguish between sense and reference, between connotation and denotation. Nor does (2) concern the issue whether or not meanings exist. Granted that meanings exist, (2) is a statement concerning what sorts of things meanings are. We can contrast (2) with what might be called "linguistic psychologism". According to linguistic psychologism, the meanings of words and sentences do not exist independently, but bear some ontological relation to the human mind, i.e., meanings

are in some way dependent upon the human mind for their existence. They are entities created by, or existing within, or describable only with reference to the human mind. (2), on the other hand, denies that meanings are mental entities (objects of the second world) or have any "essential"[25] relation to the human mind. But (2) also denies that meanings are material or spatio-temporal entities (objects of the first world). In so doing, (2) posits the existence of a so-called "third realm", i.e., a world consisting of objects which are timeless and immaterial, but objective in that they can be apprehended in common by different individuals.

But why are questions concerning the ontological status of meanings significant? Specifically, why should anyone care whether meanings are spatio-temporal objects, ideas in the mind, or third realm entities? An answer to this question presupposes an appreciation of the connections that have been traditionally thought to obtain between epistemology and the philosophy of language. Such connections will be investigated in later chapters. For now, suffice it to say that truth is a semantic notion, i.e., what is called "true" or "false" are the meanings of indicative sentences. Hence, since human knowledge consists of true propositions,[26] one of the primary motivations for the philosophical investigation of language is the hope that it will shed light on the nature and extent of human knowledge. Here, the intuition is that if propositions and their constituents are ultimately the products of sense perception, then human knowledge must itself be limited to that which can be perceived through the senses, and the certainty of such knowledge can be no greater than that which is afforded by sense perception. If, on the other hand, propositions and their constituents are not ultimately the products of sense perception, but are objects which can be apprehended by some faculty other than the senses (e.g., the Intellect, or the Reason), then it is at least possible that human knowledge transcends that which can be perceived by the senses, and it is possible that humans achieve something greater than "mere" empirical certainty.

These seem to be some of the intuitions which motivate philosophical investigation into the ontological character of meanings. But it would be too naive to think that such investigations can proceed independently of general epistemological maxims. This, of course, is because an investigation of the ontological character of meanings itself seeks knowledge. So, we should not be surprised if an investigation which limits itself to the tools of sensation and reflection fails to discover entities which cannot be discovered by sensation and reflection alone. But nor should we be surprised if an investigation which does not restrict itself to sensation and reflection does discover entities which cannot be discovered by sensation and reflection alone. Such considerations may suggest that the epistemological motivations for an investigation into the ontological character of meanings are ill-founded. Nevertheless, these seem to have been the traditional motivations.

The most radical version of linguistic psychologism can, perhaps, be found in the

philosophy of John Locke. In *An Essay concerning Human Understanding*
Locke sharply criticized the view that man is privy to innate ideas. All of the
mind's ideas (i.e., the *"Phantasm, Notion, Species*, or whatever it is, which the
Mind can be employ'd about in thinking"[27]), according to Locke, are the products of experience. Specifically, ideas have their sole sources in either sensation
or reflection, the latter being the perception of the operations of our own
minds.[28] Since Locke held that man is conscious of nothing other than the ideas
in his own mind,[29] it is no great surprise that he maintained that *"Words in their
primary or immediate Signification, stand for nothing, but the* Ideas *in the Mind
of him that uses them* ... Nor can any one apply them, as Marks, immediately to
any thing else, but the Ideas, that he himself hath"[30] :

> Man, though he have great variety of Thoughts, and such, from which others, as well as
> himself, might receive Profit and Delight; yet they are all within his own Breast, invisible,
> and hidden from others, nor can of themselves be made appear. The Comfort, and
> Advantage of Society, not being to be had without Communication of Thoughts, it was
> necessary, that Man should find out some external sensible Signs, whereby those invisible
> *Ideas*, which his thoughts are made up of, might be made known to others. For this pur-
> pose, nothing was so fit, either for Plenty or Quickness, as those articulate Sounds,
> which with so much Ease and Variety, he found himself able to make. Thus we may con-
> ceive how *Words*, which were by Nature so well adapted to that purpose, come to be
> made use of by Men, as *the Signs of* their *Ideas*; not by any natural connexion, that there
> is between particular articulate Sounds and certain *Ideas*, for then there would be but
> one Language amongst all Men; but by a voluntary Imposition, whereby such a Word is
> made arbitrarily the Marks of such an *Idea*. The use then of Words, is to be sensible Marks of
> *Ideas*; and the *Ideas* they stand for, are their proper and immediate Signification.[31]

To that extent, Locke considered truth to be "nothing but" the joining or
separating of Signs, as the Things signified by them, do agree or disagree one
with another,[32] and knowledge as "nothing but" the perception of the con-
nexion and agreement, or disagreement and repugnancy of any of our Ideas.[33]

This "nothing but" is, if nothing else, indicative of the deep repugnancy
Locke felt for the sort of cognitive authoritarianism usually associated with the
doctrine of innate ideas. Locke's naturalization of human knowledge, which
results from his denial of innate ideas and his restriction of cognitive sources to
sensation and reflection, is, in effect, a movement from cognitive authoritarianism toward fallibilism. While the possibility of certainty is not wholly denied,
what certainty there is does not much transcend the perception of the agreement
or disagreement of ideas.

Now Locke is not wholly consistent concerning the possibility and degrees
for certainty of real knowledge. With regard to degrees of certainty, Locke
writes:

> ...a Man cannot conceive himself capable of a greater Certainty, than to know that any
> *Idea* in his Mind is such, as he perceives it to be; and that two *Ideas*, wherein he perceives
> a difference, are different, and not precisely the same. He that demands a greater Cer-
> tainty than this, demands he knows not what, and shews only that he has a Mind to be a
> Sceptick...[34]

And concerning the extent of our knowledge, Locke writes that it falls short even of the extent of our own ideas, let alone the reality of things.[35] Insofar as Locke considers "real knowledge" to be the knowledge of things, i.e., the extent to which the agreement of our ideas conforms to the reality of things,[36] he would seem here to deny the existence of real knowledge. At least, he seems to deny that man can ever be certain of real knowledge. Now Locke anticipated criticism on this point. But while he hoped to show that certainty transcends bare imagination, he nonetheless restricted it to the knowledge of our own ideas:

> If it be true, that all Knowledge lies only in the perception of the agreement or disagreement of our own *Ideas*, the Visions of an Enthusiast, and the Reasonings of a sober Man, will be equally certain. 'Tis no matter how Things are: so a Man observe but the agreement of his own Imaginations, and talk comfortably, it is all Truth, all Certainty...
>
> To which I answer, That if our Knowledge of our *Ideas* terminate in them, and reach no farther, where there is something farther intended, our most serious Thoughts will be of little more use, than the Reveries of a crazy Brain; and the Truths built thereon of no more weight, than the Discourses of a Man, who sees Things clearly in a Dream, and with great assurance utters them. But, I hope, before I have done, to make it evident, that this way of certainty, by the Knowledge of our own *Ideas*, goes a little farther than bare Imagination: and, I believe it will appear, that all the certainty of general Truths a Man has, lies in nothing else.[37]

Be this as it may, Locke nonetheless affirms the possibility of having "perfect certainty" of "instructive *real Knowledge*":

> We can know then the Truth of two sorts of Propositions, with perfect *certainty*; the one is, of those trifling Propositions, which have a certainty in them, but 'tis but a *verbal Certainty*, but not instructive. And, secondly, we can know the Truth, and so may be *certain* in Propositions, which affirm something of another, which is a necessary consequence of its precise complex *Idea*, but not contained in it. As that *the external Angle of all Triangles, is bigger than either of the opposite internal Angles*; which relation of the outward Angle, to either of the opposite internal Angles, making no part of the complex Idea, signified by the name Triangle, this is a real Truth, and conveys with it instructive *real Knowledge*.[38]

But why geometry should provide any greater certainty of the conformity of our ideas to the reality of things is a mystery. Perhaps what is inconsistent here is Locke's use of "real Knowledge". In any event, these passages suggest that for Locke certainty of real knowledge, i.e., certainty that the agreement or disagreement of ideas conforms to the reality of things, is, at best, tenuous.

Locke, of course, was not the only proponent of linguistic psychologism. On the contrary, the view was doctrinaire among the British Empiricists, despite disagreements concerning the logic of meaning. Mill, for example, criticized Locke by distinguishing between two aspects of meaning, the connotation and the denotation of names.[39] Names, according to Mill, denote things, not ideas.[40] Nevertheless, Mill held that common names and definite descriptions connote attributes of the things which they denote. Such attributes, however, Mill

thought to be grounded on states of consciousness, i.e., on the sensations which
we receive from material bodies.[41] Hence, "The object of belief in a proposition,
when it asserts anything more than the meanings of words, is generally ... either
the co-existence or the sequence of two phenomena"[42]:

> The proposition which asserts that one attribute always accompanies another attribute,
> really asserts thereby no other thing than this, that one phenomenon always accom-
> panies another phenomenon; insomuch that where we find the latter, we have assurance
> of the existence of the former. Thus, in the proposition, All men are mortal, the word
> man connotes the attributes which we ascribe to a certain kind of living creatures, on the
> ground of certain phenomena which they exhibit, and which are partly physical phenom-
> ena, namely the impressions made on our senses by their bodily form and structure, and
> partly mental phenomena, namely the sentient and intellectual life which they have of
> their own. All this is understood when we utter the word man, by any one to whom the
> meaning of the word is known. Now, when we say, Man is mortal, we mean that wherever
> these various physical and mental phenomena are all found, there we have assurance that
> the other physical and mental phenomenon, called death, will not fail to take place.[43]

What Mill and Locke agree upon is their denial that meanings exit independently of the human mind and their affirmation that meanings originate in sensuous
intuition. To that extent, both philosophers deny that meanings are third realm
entities.

Frege opposed linguistic psychologism with the doctrine that senses, and hence
thoughts,[44] are third realm entities. But one could oppose linguistic psychologism
without thereby being committed to the existence of a third realm. If, for example, one were a naive realist one could practice both anti-psychologism and
ontological birth control by maintaining that meanings are spatio-temporal entities. One might, for example, maintain that the meaning of a term is the sign itself. More plausibly, one might maintain that the meaning of a term is the object
which the sign denotes. Both of these theories are anti-psychologistic in that
they construe meanings as ontologically independent of the human mind. And it
is interesting to note that Frege considered and rejected each in turn before he
distinguished between the sense and reference of proper names. That Frege rejected the thesis that meanings are spatio-temporal entities is not surprising.
Both versions of this theory are anti-psychologistic. But each engenders special
difficulties of its own.

   One well known difficulty arising from the construal of meanings as spatio-
temporal entities concerns the explication of the identity relation. In his *Begriffsschrift*[45] Frege assumed that the signs flanking the identity sign refer to
themselves, i.e., that identity is a relation not between objects but between the
names of objects. Here Frege reasoned that a theory which contrues identity as a
relation between objects would be unable to account for the difference in cognitive status between statements of the form "a=a" and those of the form
"a=b":

> ...a=a and a=b are obviously statements of differing cognitive value; a=a holds *a priori*

and, according to Kant, is to be labelled analytic, while statements of the form a=b often contain very valuable extensions of our knowledge and cannot always be established *a priori*. The discovery that the rising sun is not new every morning, but always the same, was one of the most fertile astronomical discoveries. Even today the identification of a small planet or a comet is not always a matter of course. Now if we were to regard equality as a relation between that which the names 'a' and 'b' designate, it would seem that a=b would not differ from a=a (i.e., provided that a=b is true.)[46]

But in "On Sense and Reference" Frege criticized his *Begriffsschrift* position as inadequate. While taking identity to be a relation between objects would seem to imply that all true identity statements are tautologous, taking identity to be a relation between the names of objects seems to imply that whatever knowledge is expressed by true identity statements is merely verbal. If identity is a relation between the signs of objects, then:

> ...the sentence a=b would no longer refer to the subject matter, but only to its mode of designation; we would express no proper knowledge by its means. But in many cases this is just what we want to do. If the sign 'a' is distinguished from the sign 'b' only as object (here, by means of its shape), not as sign (i.e. not by the manner in which it designates something), the cognitive value of a=a becomes essentially equal to that of a=b, provided a=b is true.[47]

Criticism of both horns of this dilemma led Frege to his famous distinction between the sense (*Sinn*) and reference (*Bedeutung*) of proper names. But if we ignore ontological considerations, Frege's distinction between sense and reference, considered as a theory of the logic of meaning, bears a striking resemblance to Mill's distinction between the connotation and denotation of names. From a logical perspective, what distinguishes the two theories is that Mill denied that personal names, e.g., "John", "Robert", "Mary", etc., have connotation. From an ontological perspective, the differences are more acute. Whereas Mill's theory was psychologistic in that it identified the connotations of names with ideas associated with those names, Frege sought to avoid this psychologism by distinguishing between the idea (*Vorstellung*) associated with a sign and the sense of that sign:

> The reference and sense of a sign are to be distinguished from the associated ideas. If the reference of a sign is an object perceivable by the senses, my idea of it is an internal image, arising from memories of sense impressions which I have had and acts, both internal and external, which I have performed. Such an idea is often saturated with feeling; the clarity of its separate parts varies and oscillates. The same sense is not always connected, even in the same man, with the same idea. The idea is subjective: one man's idea is not that of another. There result, as a matter of course, a variety of differences in the ideas associated with the same sense.[48]

But Frege's argument is not simply that taking ideas to be the meanings of names would make communication *difficult*. Rather, Frege thought it rendered communication impossible. Different men may associate different *senses* with the same name. And the same man may, at different times, connect different senses to a given sign. So the problem with taking ideas to be the meanings of names is not simply that ideas are *variable* among men. Rather, the problem is that they are essentially private to the individual consciousness that bears them.[49] Senses may vary from individual to individual. The same sense, however, may be apprehended by different men. But the same idea cannot even in principle exist in the minds of different men. Hence, if communication involves the apprehension of the same thought, i.e., one and the same object, by different individuals, then meanings cannot be mental entities.[50]

Frege seemed to think that any theory which identifies meanings with mental entities inevitably results in a private language. But the distinction between sense and idea was not motivated by concern for the possibility of communication alone. In his *Philosophical Investigations*[51] Wittgenstein fought the spectre of a private language with the doctrine that meaning is use. But Frege would have found this doctrine equally objectionable. A second and equally important motivating factor for Frege's distinction between sense and idea was a concern for the absolute character of truth.[52] We have said that the hub of Frege's anti-psychologistic thought is that truth is objective and independent of the judging subject. Now thoughts are the meanings (senses) of indicative sentences. And thoughts, according to Frege, are also the bearers of truth value. Thoughts are just those things which are true or false. Hence, thoughts are the objects of knowledge. Frege opposed the doctrine that meanings are mental entities not only because it results in a private language, but because it also relativizes truth to individuals. If thoughts were ideas, "no contradiction between two sciences would then be possible and it would really be idle to dispute about truth"[53]:

If someone takes thoughts to be ideas, what he then recognizes to be true is, on his own view, the content of his consciousness and does not properly concern other people at all.[54]

According to Frege, the doctrine that thoughts are mental entities challenges the very possibility of critical science. Wittgenstein's doctrine that meaning is use may escape the trap of a private language. But it also relativizes truth — if not to individuals, then to the language games that individuals and groups play. If the meaning of a sentence is its use, then meaning is dependent on the existence of language users. And if truth value attaches to the meaning of sentences, then truth itself is also relativized to language users.

Frege thought linguistic psychologism objectionable for two reasons: (1) it inevitably results in a private language thereby making communication and objective knowledge impossible; (2) it relativizes truth to the language user thereby making objective critical science impossible. Frege, of course, could not have been aware of Wittgenstein's *Philosophical Investigations*. Insofar as (2) follows from (1), he may have thought it sufficient to argue against the private language thesis. In any event, Frege's concern for the absolute character of truth is explicit. As Wittgenstein has shown, truth can be, in some sense, objective without its thereby being absolute. Frege, however, does not seem to have separated the notion of relativity from that of objectivity. Rather, he seems to have accepted the traditional notion that the dichotomy between what is absolute and what is relative coincides with that between what is objective and what is subjective. Being reluctant, for the reasons mentioned above, to identify meanings with spatio-temporal objects, Frege was led to the introduction of the third realm. Thoughts are neither things of the spatio-temporal world nor ideas[55]:

> A third realm must be recognized. What belongs to this corresponds with ideas, in that it cannot be perceived by the senses, but with things, in that it needs no bearer to the contents of whose consciousness to belong. Thus the thought, for example, which we expressed in the Pythagorean theorem is timelessly true, true independently of whether anyone takes it to be true. It needs no bearer. It is not true for the first time when it is discovered, but is like a planet which, already before anyone has seen it, has been in interaction with other planets.[56]

Our characterization of the third world has thus far been primarily negative, i.e., we have distinguished it less by what it is than by what it is not. Third realm entities are unlike material objects in that they cannot be perceived by the senses. They are unlike mental entities in that they are ontologically independent of human consciousness. Finally, they are unlike both material and mental entities in that they are eternal and immutable. But what *are* third realm objects, and in what sense do they constitute a world? Frege, unfortunately, does not offer a detailed positive account of the third realm. And my intuitions, for the most part, balk beyond the physical and the mental. But attention to Frege's metaphors does suggest at least one positive characteristic. Thoughts, like planets, are in interaction with one another. If we consider such interaction to be logical and if we remember the second of Frege's three fundamental principles:

> never to ask for the meaning of a word in isolation, but only in the context of a proposition.[57]

then we might conclude that what binds third realm entities together as a world is their systematic logical relation to one another. For this reason, thoughts, numbers, and whatever third realm entities exist might be considered logical objects.

Mathematical Psychologism

(3) Sounds much like (2), but there is a significant difference. (2) is the thesis that the *senses* of words and sentences are third realm entities. (3) is the thesis

that the *references* of the members of a certain well-defined set of terms are third realm entities. (3) can be contrasted with what might be called "mathematical psychologism". According to one version of mathematical psychologism, numbers are properties of material objects, or objects abstracted from sense perceptions of material objects. As such, truths about numbers are ultimately dependent upon the data of sense experience. To that extent, mathematical psychologism is analogous to logical psychologism. Had our experience been different, our arithmetical truths might have been other than what they in fact are. And our experience is incomplete. Hence, the certainty of our arithmetical beliefs is suspect. Such beliefs, like any other belief founded upon sense perception, are subject to revision in the light of further empirical evidence. Simply put, mathematical truths are nothing but inductive generalizations.

The version of mathematical psychologism sketched above is just that offered by John Stuart Mill in *A System of Logic*. There Mill "hoped to show how mathematics can yield propositions which are not merely verbal and which are certainly true of the world of experience, but which do not depend on any non-experiential sources of knowledge."[58] Toward this end, Mill characterized: (a) numbers not as things but as properties of things; (b) the basic propositions of arithmetic as definitions which assert the meanings of terms as well as observed matters of fact; and (c) the basic axioms of mathematics (e.g., "that things equal to the same thing are equal to one another") as inductive truths, the results of observation and experience, and founded on the evidence of the senses.[59]

According to (a), arithmetical statements that make no explicit reference to objects, e.g., "2 + 2 = 4", are elliptical for statements that do refer to objects:

> When we call a collection of objects, *two, three,* or *four,* they are not two, three, or four in the abstract; they are two, three, or four things of some particular kind; pebbles, horses, inches, pounds weight. What the name of number connotes is, the manner in which single objects of the given kind must be put together, in order to produce that particular aggregate.[60]

According to Mill, "all numbers must be numbers of something: there are no such things as numbers in the abstract."[61] What accounts for the generality of arithmetical truths, on this theory, is that all things possess quantity, i.e., all things consist of parts which can be numbered.[62] Given (a), the "observed matters of fact" alluded to in (b) consist of the possible and alternate aggregative formations of objects. But what makes this theory specifically psychologistic, as opposed to generally empiricistic, is Mill's reference to the possible phenomenal forms in which such collections of objects impress the senses:

> ...we may call "Three is two and one" a definition of three; but the calculations which depend on that proposition do not follow from the definition itself, but from an arithmetical theorem presupposed in it, namely, that collections of objects exist, which while they impress the senses thus, $^o o^o$, may be separated into two parts, thus, oo o.[63]

42

Hence, while, e.g., "three pebbles" and "two and one pebbles" denote the same collection of objects, their connotations differ. As Mill expresses it, "they by no means stand for the same physical fact."[64] Rather, they differ precisely in the manner in which such collections of pebbles impress the senses. Moreover, the so-called "arithmetical theorem" that collections of objects which impress the senses as three pebbles may be separated in such a way as to impress the senses as two and one pebbles is a proposition that is confirmed through observation:

> It is a truth known to us by early and constant experience: an inductive truth; and such truths are the foundation of the science of Number. The fundamental truths of that science all rest on the evidence of sense; they are proved by showing to our eyes and our fingers that any given number of objects, ten balls for example, may by separation and re-arrangement exhibit to our senses all the different sets of numbers the sum of which is equal to ten.[65]

Finally, with regard to (c), Mill wrote:

> That things equal to the same thing are equal to one another, and that two straight lines which have once intersected one another continue to diverge, are inductive truths; resting, indeed, like the law of universal causation, only on induction *per enumerationem simplicem*; on the fact that they have been perpetually perceived to be true, and never once found to be false.[66]

(a), (b), and (c) point to the inductive character of mathematics. But Mill did not deny the deductive or calculative nature of the science. Arithmetic may be a deductive science, but this is due to "the fortunate applicability to it of a law so comprehensive as 'The sum of equals are equals.' "[67] And this basic law was thought by Mill to rest on induction. So, Mill did not hold that every arithmetical truth is known in virtue of direct empirical observation. And it may even be the case that certain arithmetical truths can be known only through calculation. But according to Mill, any such calculation appeals to inductive laws and definitions which assert observed matters of fact.

Nevertheless, it might be thought that the admission of calculation is a consideration which would force Mill to admit *something* that is not empirical. Calculation may rest on laws that are known by induction, but what about the *inference* from those laws to particular cases? This is tempting, but the point to be made is that Mill regarded all inferences as inference from particular statements.[68] The inference from "John is mortal, and Mary is mortal, and Charles is mortal, etc." to "All men are mortal" is really an inference from those statements to "The next man I come across is mortal." The introduction of the general statement serves simply to abbreviate inferences already made. Such inferences are based on habit. Through his perceptual experiences man has come by habit to associate certain properties with objects of a given type. Inference occurs when man comes to expect that those properties also belong to the objects of that type of which he has not yet had perceptual experience. According to Mill, whatever inference occurs is noted in the framing of general laws. What we call "inference from general laws to particular statements" is nothing more than the deciphering of our notes.

Frege opposed mathematical psychologism with (3), the doctrine that mathematical objects are third realm entities. (3) is argued repeatedly and at length throughout *The Foundations of Arithmetic*. Insofar as (3) holds that mathematical objects are third realm entities, it implies that numbers are not properties or attributes of objects, but self-subsistent objects themselves. Contrary to Mill, "2 + 2 = 4" needs to make no reference, implicit or otherwise, to any objects other than 2 and 4 to express a thought. But the question whether numbers are objects or concepts is really tangential to Frege's anti-psychologism. What is essential to (3) is that numbers are *third realm* objects. Whereas (3) characterizes numbers as self-subsistent objects, it denies that these objects are either spatio-temporal, and hence material ("like Mill's piles of pebbles and gingersnaps"[69]), or mental entities like ideas[70]:

> In the spatial sense they (numbers) are, in any case, neither inside nor outside either the subject or any object. But, of course, they are outside the subject in the sense that they are not subjective. Whereas each individual can feel only his own pain or desire or hunger, and can experience only his own sensations of sound and colour, numbers can be objects in common to many individuals, and they are in fact precisely the same for all, not merely more or less similar mental states in different minds.[71]

There are two distinct theses here denied by (3): (a) numbers are material or spatio-temporal entities; (b) numbers are mental entities. Frege associates (a) with Mill's philosophy of arithmetic. But Mill, in fact, characterized numbers as *properties* of objects. In any event, it might be thought that (a) is not psychologistic in that it characterizes numbers not as mental entities but as objects of the first world, i.e., physical entities. And this, at least, is a characterization of numbers as objective insofar as spatio-temporal objects are not dependent upon the mind for their existence. But here there are two questions concerning objectivity to be distinguished. The first concerns the objectivity of the ontological status of numbers; the second concerns the objectivity of our *knowledge* of numbers, i.e., the justification of our statements concerning numbers. Frege thought that "objectivity cannot ... be based on any sense-impression, which as an affection of our mind is entirely subjective"[72]:

> ...I understand objective to mean what is independent of our sensation, intuition and imagination, and of all construction of mental pictures out of memories of earlier sensations, but not what is independent of the reason...[73]

Any epistemology which restricts the sources of knowledge to sensuous intuition of material objects would thus result in psychologism. So even if numbers were material objects and ontologically objective, our knowledge of arithmetical statements would still be subjective in that it would be based upon sensuous intuition of such material objects. Relegation of numbers to the third realm thus insures the objectivity of arithmetical knowledge. Regardless of whether numbers are objects or concepts, third realm entities cannot be perceived through the senses. Any knowledge of such entities is thus independent of sensation, intuition, and imagination.

It might seem that part of the impetus for (3) is a concern for the autonomy of mathematics, in this case arithmetic. If numbers were ideas or mental constructions, then arithmetic would be psychology.[74] Analogously, if numbers were material objects or properties of material objects, arithmetic would be physics. In neither instance would there cease to be a science of arithmetic. But arithmetic would be subject to the basic laws of psychology or physics in the same way in which optics is subject to the basic laws of physics and biology and chemistry is thought reducible to physics. But closer examination reveals that it is not so much the autonomy of arithmetic as its objectivity that is at stake. Or are we to suppose arithmetic to be more autonomous for its being reducible to logic?

Psychology, according to Frege, cannot provide the foundations of arithmetic not because airthmetic is autonomous, but because the subject matter of psychology is ontologically distinct from that of arithmetic. Here the issue turns on the dichotomy between what is objective and what is subjective. Psychology, on Frege's view, deals with ideas in the subjective sense, entities which are of a sensible, pictorial character. But numbers are more akin to ideas in the objective sense, i.e., entities which are in principle nonsensible. And ideas in the objective sense belong to logic, not psychology.[75] Here we can glean one relationship between anti-psychologism and logicism. An idea in the objective sense belongs to logic. If such ideas are the subject matter of arithmetic, but not psychology, then arithmetic must be related to logic in a way in which psychology is not. But that there *is* a distinction between ideas in the objective sense and ideas in the subjective sense cuts to the very heart of the psychologism/anti-psychologism debate. For as Frege acknowledges, the distinction between ideas in the objective sense and ideas in the subjective sense stands or falls with that between logic and psychology.[76] In other words, the distinction between ideas in the objective sense and ideas in the subjective sense is part and parcel of the distinction between psychology and logic. And if there is no distinction between psychology and logic, if logic is just a branch of psychology, then the distinction between such ideas falls. But that there is a distinction between psychology and logic is precisely what psychologistic logicians deny. Hence, the thesis that the subject matter of arithmetic is ontologically distinct from that of psychology is not the ground or argument for anti-psychologism, but just another statement of the position.

Why should anyone think that numbers are third realm entities (ideas in the objective sense)? According to Frege's semantic theory, a sentence has truth value only if each name that occurs in that sentence has a reference. The referents of names are, of course, objects. Hence, if the statements of arithmetic have truth value, then numbers must be objects. But even given Frege's semantic theory, the question still remains: what kind of objects are numbers? Frege argued that if numbers were mental entities, then arithmetic would be hopelessly subjective. We would, on that account, be unable to speak of *the* number one, but only of my number one and your number one:

> If the number two were an idea, then it would have straight away to be private to me only. Another man's idea is, *ex vi termini*, another idea. We should then have it might be many millions of twos on our hands. We should have to speak of my two and your two, of one two and all twos.[77]

More exactly, each individual would have on his hands only those twos that exist in his mind. Numbers that exist in the minds of other individuals would be, quite literally, different objects. And, strictly speaking, there would be no reason to think such numbers similar in any respect other than their names. If, on the other hand, numbers were spatio-temporal objects, then what facts we know about numbers would, on a radically empiricist account like Mill's, be dependent upon sense experience. As such, our arithmetical knowledge would, on Frege's view, again be hopelessly subjective. Since sense perceptions are private to the individual who has them, we would be unable to ascertain whether and to what extent an individual's perception of the number two corresponds to another individual's perception of the number two — let alone to the number two itself. In either case, we could only attain an empirical certainty of arithmetical truths. If numbers were spatio-temporal objects or mental constructions thereof, we could not say with absolute certainty that $2 + 2 = 4$. We would have to look and see, and look again. In this way, our knowledge of arithmetic would be, as Mill thought, built up by induction from particular instances. We would have recourse to no purely general laws[78] and arithmetical statements would be knowable only *a posteriori*. But while experience might tell us that $2 + 2 = 4$, it could never tell us that $2 + 2$ *must* equal 4. Hence, the necessity associated with arithmetical truths would be a matter for speculation.

For these reasons, Frege identified numbers as third realm entities, as objects that are apprehended not through the senses but by the reason. Contrary to Mill, Frege held that our knowledge of arithmetic (and mathematical knowledge is general) is not *a posteriori* and based on induction from sense experience, but *a priori* and derivable from general laws which are independent of particular facts.

This doctrine, that mathematical knowledge is *a priori*, should not be thought a mere consequence of mathematical anti-psychologism. Rather, it provides the cornerstone for the thesis. While we have here restricted our discussion to arithmetic, Mill's psychologism and Frege's anti-psychologism apply to geometry as well. Insofar as this is concerned, mathematical anti-psychologism *must* be distinguished from logicism, i.e., the thesis that arithmetic is reducible to logic. On the one hand, the objects of geometry, a science Frege did not think reducible to logic, were thought to be third realm entities. On the other hand, Frege's rejection of logicism did not lead him to adopt an empiricist theory of arithmetic. While Russell's Paradox led Frege to recognize that the existence of objects cannot be derived from the logical source of knowledge, he continued to maintain that "arithmetic does not need to appeal to sense perceptions in its proof."[79] Here, Frege was led to distinguish between three sources of knowledge for mathematics and physics: (a) sense perception; (b) the geometrical source of knowledge; and (c) the logical source of knowledge:

> The last of these is involved when inferences are drawn, and thus is almost always involved. Yet it seems that this on its own cannot yield us any objects. From the geometrical source of knowledge flows pure geometry. In the case of arithmetic, just as in the case of geometry, I exclude only sense perception as a source of knowledge. Everyone will grant that there is no largest whole number, i.e. that there are infinitely many whole numbers. This doesn't imply there has ever been a time at which a man has grasped infinitely many whole numbers. Rather, there are probably infinitely many whole numbers which no man has ever grasped. This knowledge cannot be derived from sense perception, since nothing infinite in the full sense of the word can flow from this source. Stars are objects of sense perception. And so it cannot be asserted with certainty that there are infinitely many stars. Since probably on its own the logical source of knowledge cannot yield numbers either, we will appeal to the geometrical source of knowledge. This is significant because it means that arithmetic and geometry, and hence the whole of mathematics flows from one and the same source of knowledge – that is the geometrical one. This is thus elevated to the status of the true source of mathematical knowledge, with, of course, the logical source of knowledge also being involved at every turn.[80]

Mill's philosophy of mathematics is not the only version of mathematical psychologism to be found in the literature. The so-called "mathematical intuitionism" associated with L.E.J. Brouwer might also be called psychologistic in that it conceives of mathematical proofs as mental operations. According to intuitionism, one cannot separate the inquiry into the foundations of mathematics from the discussion of the conditions by which the mathematical activity of the mind is brought about. But whereas Brouwer wrote:

> The...point of view that there are no non-experienced truths and that logic is not an absolutely reliable instrument to discover truths, has found acceptance with regard to mathematics much later than with regard to practical life and to science. Mathematics rigorously treated from this point of view, and deducing theorems exclusively by means of introspective construction, is called intuitionistic mathematics.[81]

intuitionism should not be thought empirical in the Millian sense that mathematical truths are based on inductive generalizations.

Nevertheless, Brouwer's philosophy of mathematics may be considered empiricist in at least two other senses. Heyting, for example writes:

Intuitionist mathematics consists in mental constructions; a mathematical theorem expresses a purely empirical fact, namely the success of a certain mental construction.[82]

According to Heyting, "2 + 2 = 3 + 1" *means* "I have effected the mental constructions indicated by '2 + 2' and by '3 + 1' and I have found that they lead to the same result."[83] And Parsons writes:

Brouwer insisted that mathematical constructions are *mental*. The possibilities in question derive from our perception of external objects, which is both mental and physical.[84]

Intuitionism is psychologistic in both an ontological and an epistemological sense. Ontologically, it conceives of the existence of mathematical objects as dependent on *our* ability to construct such objects. Concerning the notion of construction, Parsons writes:

A consideration of existential propositions connects the broad philosophical notion of constructivity with the general mathematical notion. Roughly, a proof in mathematics is said to be constructive if wherever it involves the mention of the existence of something, it provides a method of "finding" or "constructing" that object. It is evident that the constructivist standpoint implies that a mathematical object exists only if it can be constructed; to say that there exists a natural number x such that Fx is to say that sooner or later in the generation of the sequence an x will *turn up* such that Fx.[85]

Insofar as Brouwer thought that such constructions are mental operations, the existence of mathematical objects is dependent upon the existence of minds in which such constructions are actualized. Epistemologically, intuitionism construes the truth of a mathematical statement as dependent on the construction of a proof for that statement. Whereas classical mathematics is based on the assumption that mathematical statements are true or false regardless of our ability to recognize their truth values, intuitionism collapses the distinction between being true and being known to be true by relating the truth value of a statement to the construction of a proof for that statement. As Parsons writes:

...whatever one may think of the notion of form of intuition, Brouwer's position is based on a limitation, in principle, on our knowledge: constructivism is implied by the postulate that no mathematical proposition is true unless we can in a non-miraculous way *know* it to be true.[86]

So according to Brouwer, we are justified in asserting "p" only if we are able to construct a proof of "p". But this is not simply a criterion regarding the justified assertion of a mathematical statement. What is being denied is that mathematical statements are timelessly true or false. Rather, the truth of a mathematical statement is given in the temporal construction of its proof.

But this has direct implications for some of the basic statements of classical mathematics. Parsons, for example, writes:

48

This point of view leads immediately to a criticism of the basic notions of logic, particularly negation and the law of the excluded middle. That "(x)Fx" is true if and only if it can be proved does not mean that "(x)Fx" is a statement about certain entities called proofs in the way in which, on the usual interpretation, it is statement about the totality of natural numbers. According to Brouwer we can *assert* "p" only if we have a proof; the hypothesis that (x)Fx is the hypothesis that *we have* a proof, and it is a reasonable extrapolation to deny that we can say more about what "(x)Fx" asserts than is said in specifying what is a proof of it. The explanation of "-(x)Fx" as "(x)Fx cannot be proved" does not satisfy this condition. Brouwer said instead that a proof of "-p" is a construction which obtains an absurdity from the supposition of a proof of "p".[87]

But for a given statement "p", there is no reason to suppose that we will ever be able to give a proof of "p" or derive an absurdity from the supposition of a proof of "p". Hence, the law of the excluded middle, i.e., that for all "p", either "p" is true or "-p" is true does not hold. So intuitionism does not only deny that mathematical statements are timelessly true or false, it also necessitates a revision of classical mathematics.

Brouwer, incidentally, offered a psychological explanation of the belief that the law of the excluded middle is *a priori* valid:

The long belief in the universal validity of the principle of the excluded third in mathematics is considered by intuitionism as a phenomenon of history of civilization of the same kind as the old-time belief in the rationality of π or in the rotation of the firmament on an axis passing through the earth. And intuitionism tries to explain the long persistence of this dogma by two facts: firstly the obvious non-contradictoit of the principle for an arbitrary single assertion; secondly the practical validity of the whole of classical logic for an extensive group of *simple everyday phenomena*. The latter fact apparently made such a strong impression that the play of thought that classical logic originally was, became a deep-rooted habit of thought which was considered not only as useful but even as *aprioristic*.[88]

We should not, however, rush to the conclusion that Brouwer was a conventionalist. As Beth writes:

... while investigators such as Carnap join to the linguistic conception the so-called "tolerance principle", Brouwer from his standpoint rightly resists the "delusion of the *freedom* of logic", thereby agreeing with the view of the realists. For, from both Brouwer's and the realistic point of view, logic has a definite subject-matter even though an intuitionist such as Brouwer seeks this subject-matter in another area than a realist such as Frege.[89]

It is not very clear whether or to what extent Brouwer regarded mathematical knowledge as *a priori* valid.[90] But it is clear that intuitionism denies: (a) that mathematical entities are third realm objects;[91] and (b) that being true (at least in mathematics) is distinct from being known to be true. Frege, of course, did not directly address the question of mathematical intuitionism. But insofar as (a) and (b) are just the fundamental tenets of mathematical anti-psychologism, it is reasonable to assume that Frege would have found intuitionism no more palatable than Mill's empiricist account of mathematics.

Epistemological Psychologism

(4) Concerns the task and scope of epistemology. It is, in effect, a thesis about what epistemologists should be doing. According to (4), epistemology is concerned with the justification of cognitive claims and scientific theories, and with neither the facts concerning their discovery nor the extra-logical factors influencing their acceptance or rejection. (4), of course, assumes that the extra-logical factors influencing the discovery, acceptance, or rejection of a theory are irrelevant for the justification of that theory. The directive that epistemology orient itself toward questions of justification thus reflects the predominant anti-psychologistic concern for objectivity. The methods of justification, being modelled on the valid inference forms of classical logic, are accessible to all and the same in all cases. But the psychological, historical, and sociological factors which influence the discovery, acceptance, or rejection of a theory are thought to be subjective and variable from case to case. Hence, the extra-logical facts concerning the discovery, acceptance, or rejection of a theory can never be pertinent to the justification of that theory.

We can contrast (4) with what might be called "epistemological psychologism". According to epistemological psychologism, the consideration of extra-logical factors which influence the discovery, acceptance, or rejection of a scientific theory is a proper concern for epistemology. There are, however, different reasons for this contention. Most philosophers have given up hope for the development of a logic of discovery, i.e., a set of objective rules whose systematic use would inevitably result in the generation of scientific theories. As Reichenbach writes:

> The act of discovery escapes logical analysis; there are no logical rules in terms of which a "discovery machine" could be constructed that would take over the creative function of the genius. But it is not the logician's task to account for scientific discoveries; all he can do is to analyze the relation between given facts and a theory presented to him with the claim that it explains these facts.[92]

Nevertheless, there is reason to think both that the context of discovery bears weight on the context of justification, and that epistemology should be concerned with the extra-logical factors which influence the acceptance or rejection of a theory as well as the factors which pertain to the justification of that theory. On the one hand, some philosophers have argued that, contrary to popular belief, valid deductive arguments do not conclude with inferences at all. So the soundness of an argument does not justify an inference, for properly speaking there is no inference there to be justified. On the other hand, philosophers have recognized that the acceptance or rejection of a theory is not simply a function of its justification. So even if we admit a distinction between the context of discovery and the context of justification, any understanding of scientific progress, conceptual change, and the growth of knowledge requires that we consider factors concerning the acceptance or rejection of a theory as well as those concerning its justification.

The distinction between questions of discovery and questions of justification is a familiar parcel of the analytic methodology of inquiry. Nevertheless, there remain problems concerning its interpretation. One major problem concerns the strength of the distinction. Given that questions of discovery are distinct from questions of justification, the question arises whether and to what extent questions of discovery are relevant to questions of justification. On one interpretation, the distinction merely disclaims *interest* in the psychological genesis of theories. On this interpretation, the distinction merely notes the obvious: that the question "How did you come to believe that p?" is different from the question "What is the justification of P?" Here, intuition is that we often believe propositions which are in fact true for reasons which fall short of justification. And often, the reasons for which a thought first dawns on us have nothing to do with its justification. But here there is no denial that questions of discovery may sometimes be relevant for the justification of a claim. And such an interpretation would allow the following possibility: that our belief that snow is white is justified by sense perceptions of white snow. In other words, we come to believe that snow is white by visual perception, and it is the visual perception of white snow that justifies the statement "snow is white". But on this interpretation, there would be little controversial about the distinction. It would be little more than a warning against the pitfalls of fallacious reasoning. And it is, of course, possible that this is all that Frege and others ever intended by the distinction. But there is another and stronger interpretation according to which questions of discovery have no bearing whatsoever on the justification of a statement. On this interpretation, statements can be justified only by other statements. Specifically, intuitions, be they sense perceptions or *a priori* cognitions, provide no basis or justification for propositions. In what follows, we will interpret the distinction between discovery and justification as saying that questions of discovery are never relevant to the justification of a statement, i.e., that intuitions, sensuous or otherwise, provide no justification for propositions. Not only is this the more interesting interpretation, it is also the interpretation adopted by Popper. So our discussion of it here will provide a basis for our discussion in later chapters.

The issue of epistemological psychologism deals with the question of what constitutes a rational justification. To that extent, it is intricately related to the issue of logical psychologism. Just as logicians debate whether the subject matter of their science are the facts concerning how humans reason or the norms concerning how they should reason, epistemologists debate whether their study concerns the facts of how theories are accepted or the norms concerning how theories should be accepted. Earlier we remarked that philosophers have long been prone to equate rationality with logicality. Acceptance of this equation leads to a concept of justification as logical proof. If rationality is equated with logicality, then to give a rational justification of a statement is to demonstrate that statement as the conclusion of a deductively valid argument with true premises. For such philosophers, statements cannot be justified by intuitions —

for intuitions are simply not statements and hence cannot serve as premises in a logical proof.

In *The Foundations of Arithmetic* Frege writes:

> It not uncommonly happens that we first discover the content of a proposition, and only later give the rigorous proof of it, on other and more difficult lines; and often this same proof also reveals more precisely the conditions restricting the validity of the original proposition. In general, therefore, the question of how we arrive at the content of a judgement should be kept distinct from the other question, Whence do we derive the justification for its assertion.[93]

This distinction between questions of discovery and questions of justification seems to have played a catalytic role in Frege's clarification of Kant's epistemological categories. At least, the question whether a truth is *a priori, a posteriori,* analytic, or synthetic, according to Frege, turns on the epistemic status of the premises in its proof:

> Now these distinctions between *a priori* and *a posteriori,* synthetic and analytic, concern, as I see it, not the content of the judgement but the justification for making the judgement. Where there is no such justification, the possibility of drawing the distinctions vanishes. An *a priori* error is thus as complete a nonsense as, say, a blue concept. When a proposition is called a posteriori or analytic in my sense, this is not a judgement about the conditions, psychological, physiological and physical, which have made it possible to form the content of the proposition in our consciousness; nor is it a judgement about the way in which some other man has come, perhaps erroneously, to believe it true; rather, it is a judgement about the ultimate ground upon which rests the justification for holding it to be true.
>
> This means that the question is removed from the sphere of psychology, and assigned, if the truth concerned is a mathematical one, to the sphere of mathematics. The problem becomes, in fact, that of finding the proof of the proposition, and of following it up right back to the primitive truths. If in carrying out this process, we come only on general logical laws and on definitions, then the truth is an analytic one, bearing in mind that we must take account of all propositions upon which the admissibility of any of the definitions depend. If, however, it is impossible to construct a proof without making use of truths which are not of a general logical nature, but belong to the sphere of some special science, then the proposition is a synthetic one. For a truth to be *a posteriori,* it must be impossible to construct a proof of it without including an appeal to facts, i.e., to truths which cannot be proved and which are not general, since they contain assertions about particular objects. But if, on the contrary, its proof can be derived exclusively from general laws, which themselves neither need nor admit of proof, then the truth is *a priori.*[94]

Frege's footnote to this passage is also of interest here:

> If we recognize the existence of general laws at all, we must also admit the existence of such primitive laws, since from mere individual facts nothing follows, unless it be on the strength of a law. Induction itself depends upon the general proposition that the inductive method can establish the truth of a law, or at least some probability for it. If we

deny this, induction becomes nothing more than a psychological phenomenon, a procedure which induces men to believe in the truth of a proposition, without affording the
slightest justification for so believing.[95]

From these passages it is clear that Frege construed the justification of a statement on the model of logical proof. But whether the statement is analytic, synthetic, *a priori*, or *a posteriori* depends not simply on the validity of the proof,
but also on the character of its premises. Moreover, premises which do not actually *entail* the statement to be justified (e.g., an inductive argument that does
not appeal to primitive laws[96]) provide no justification at all. While Frege does
speak of "the justification for making a judgement" and "the justification for
holding it to be true", this conception of justification removes the issue of justification from the mind of the knowing subject. So *a priori* truths may be
known *a posteriori* by certain individuals. But this does not affect their cognitive
value.

Now (4) bears a similarity in spirit to Frege's *Begriffsschrift*. There Frege
thought he could abstract from the thought expressed by a sentence to focus on
its logical relations to other sentences. With this in mind, he developed a canon-
ical notation that replaced whole sentences with sentential letters. The impetus
behind the replacement of sentences by sentential letters (aside from the convenience of perspicuity in deduction) was the belief that the senses of sentences
exert a psychological and distorting influence on the human mind which obscures the logical relations between sentences. By replacing sentences with sentential letters, Frege hoped that the influence of predilections which obscure the
logical relations between sentences could be avoided. In like manner, Frege
thought that he could abstract from the sociological, historical, and psychological factors which influence the acceptance or rejection of a theory and thereby focus on the ultimate grounds for its justification.

From the Fregean perspective, epistemological psychologism is mistaken
not because extra-logical factors never play a role in the acceptance or rejection
of a theory. Unfortunately, all to the contrary. And it may even be possible to
construct a syllogism appealing to general psychological, historical, and sociological laws that would entail the acceptance or rejection of a theory. But this
would miss the point. Frege's quarrel with epistemological psychologism is that
psychologistic epistemologists confuse the acceptance or rejection of a theory
with its justification. The reasons for the acceptance or rejection of a theory are
relative to the individual or community that accepts or rejects it. But the justification of a theory concerns its ultimate grounds and is completely independent
of any individual or community. The two issues are completely distinct. Unjustified and unjustifiable theories have been accepted. And justifiable theories
have been rejected. To confuse justification with acceptance is to render justification a matter of consensus. And this, needless to say, is to threaten the possibility of critical science and objective knowledge.

But the distinction between questions of discovery and questions of justification is not meant to demean the significance of the psychological, historical,

and sociological factors which influence the acceptance or rejection of scientific theories. Rather, it asserts only that the study of such factors has no significance *for epistemology*. This is what was meant when we said that (4) concerns the task and scope of epistemology. And this point, I think, deserves emphasis. There is, in contemporary philosophy, a tendency to conflate anti-psychologism with what might be called "anti-psychology-ism", i.e., the view that psychology, as an empirical science, can yield no positive knowledge. But Frege, even in his most anti-psychologistic moments, never denigrated the value of psychological inquiry. Rather, he claimed simply that such inquiry can contribute nothing to the justification of logical laws. A study of the extra-logical factors which lead to the acceptance or rejection of a scientific theory might well be of interest to historians of science. And a consideration of such factors falls well within the bounds of a study of human nature. Eventually, such a study might lead to a psychological theory of discovery. And such a theory might even yield successful predictions concerning the construction or "discovery" of new scientific theories. So we might, in the future, have reason to *expect* the introduction of new scientific theories given the existence of certain psychological, historical, and sociological conditions. And such investigations might even yield predictions concerning the concepts to which successful new theories might appeal. But if the business of epistemology is the justification of cognitive claims and justification is construed on the model of logical proof, then the consideration of such extra-logical factors is, by definition, of interest to epistemology only as curiosity.

The most blatant example of epistemological psychologism can, perhaps, be found in the philosophy of David Hume. In discussing the possibility of an infinite chain of reasoning in a justifying argument, Hume writes, "you must at last terminate in some fact, which is present to your memory or senses; or must allow that your belief is entirely without foundation".[97] But it should not be thought that Hume thereby *confused* justification with discovery. Rather, he argued for psychologistic justification because he thought purely rational justification, i.e., justification of statements only by other statements, impossible.[98] But John Stuart Mill's views on the justification of cognitive claims provides a more subtle and interesting example of epistemological psychologism. And again, it should not be thought that Mill *confused* the acceptance of a theory with its justification. If he had, he would never have argued that the inconceivability of a proposition does not render it unjustifiable. Rather, Mill challenged the notion that the validity of an argument is an *essential* ingredient in justification. According to Mill:

> We say of a fact or statement, that it is proved, when we believe its truth by reason of some other fact or statement from which it is said to *follow*. Most of the propositions, whether affirmative or negative, universal, particular, or singular, which we believe, are not believed on their own evidence, but on the ground of something previously assented to, from which they are said to be inferred.[99]

But Mill denied that valid deductive arguments are instances of real inference.

According to Mill, an inference in the proper sense of the term occurs when "we set out from known truths, to arrive at others really distinct from them".[100] But this, Mill argued, does not occur with deductive arguments:

> It must be granted that in every syllogism, considered as an argument to prove the con-
> clusion, there is a *petitio principii*. When we say,
>
> All men are mortal,
> Socrates is a man,
> therefore
> Socrates is mortal;
>
> it is unanswerably urged by the adversaries of the syllogistic theory, that the proposition,
> Socrates is mortal, is presupposed in the more general assumption, All men are mortal:
> that we cannot be assured of the mortality of all men, unless we are already certain of
> the mortality of every individual man: that if it be still doubtful whether Socrates, or
> any other individual we choose to name, be mortal or not, the same degree of uncertain-
> ty must hang over the assertion, All men are mortal: that the general principle, instead
> of being given as evidence of the particular case, cannot itself be taken for true without
> exception, until every shadow of doubt which could affect any case comprised with it,
> is dispelled by evidence *aliunde*; and then what remains for the syllogism to prove?[101]

According to Mill, nothing ever was, or can be, proved by syllogism, which was not known, or assumed to be known, before.[102]

Mill's argument here is at once ironic and indicative of one of the deepest disputes in philosophy. At base, what is at issue is the philosophical value or worth of deductive methods. Philosophers have traditionally recognized two types of inference. Deductive reasoning has traditionally been recognized as inference from general statements to particular statements. Inductive reasoning, on the other hand, has traditionally been construed as inference from particular statements to general statements. Now there are problems with this characteriza-tion of induction stated thus simply. For the premises of an inductive argument may well include general statements. Still, from the EP_1 perspective, deduction was considered epistemologically superior to induction. This judgment was based on the fact that the validity of a deductive argument insures the truth of its con-clusion given the truth of its premises. But the truth of the premises of an in-ductive argument is consistent with the falsity of its conclusion. Hence, in-ductive inference has, at least since Hume, been thought problematic. Now these considerations were instrumental in the EP_1 characterization of the valid deduc-tive argument as the paradigm for justification. And it is ironic that Mill's criticism of deduction rests on the very reasons for which deduction has tradi-tionally been prized.

Mill held that all inference is from particular statements to particular state-ments. General statements are merely registers of inferences already made, and short formulae for making more[103]:

> When ... we conclude from the death of John and Thomas, and every other person we
> ever heard of in whose case the experiment had been fairly tried, that the Duke of
> Wellington is mortal like the rest; we may, indeed, pass through the generalization, All

men are mortal, as an intermediate stage; but it is not in the latter half of the process, the descent from all men to the Duke of Wellington, that the *inference* resides. The inference is finished when we have asserted that all men are mortal. What remains to be performed is merely deciphering our own notes.[104]

But if deduction is merely the deciphering of notes, then the rigorous deduction advocated by Frege can be nothing more than the deciphering of notes — carefully.

Mill, it is interesting to note, offered something of an historical explanation of the belief that deduction is real inference:

> So long as what are termed Universals were regarded as a peculiar kind of substances, having an objective existence distinct from the individual objects classified under them, the *dictum de omni* (that whatever can be affirmed (or denied) of a class, may be affirmed (or denied) of everything included in the class) conveyed an important meaning; because it expressed the intercommunity of nature, which it was necessary on that theory that we should suppose to exist between those general substances and the particular substances which were subordinated to them. That everything predicable of the universal was predicable of the various individuals contained under it, was then no identical proposition, but a statement of what was conceived as a fundamental law of the universe. The assertion that the entire nature and properties of the *substantia secunda* formed part of the nature and properties of each of the individual substances called by the same name; that the properties of Man, for example, were properties of all men; was a proposition of real significance when man did not *mean* all men, but something inherent in men, and vastly superior to them in dignity. Now, however, when it is known that a class, an universal, a genus or species, is not an entity *per se*, but neither more nor less than the individual substances themselves which are placed in the class, and that there is nothing real in the matter except these objects, a common name given to them, and common attributes indicated by the name; what, I should be glad to know, do we learn by being told, that whatever can be affirmed of a class, may be affirmed of every object contained in the class?[105]

Nevertheless, it should not be thought that Mill thought deduction worthless. On the contrary, Mill regarded deductive logic (the logic of consistency) as a necessary auxiliary to inductive logic (the logic of truth).[106] But according to Mill, deduction provides a test, rather than a justification, of our cognitive claims.[107] This notion, incidentally, bears a striking similarity to Popper's notion of falsifiability — albeit with an inductivist twist. Just as Popper thinks that a particular statement can falsify a general statement, Mill wrote:

> When ... we argue from a number of known cases to another case supposed to be analogous, it is always possible, and generally advantageous, to divert our argument into the circuitous channel of an induction from those known cases to a general proposition, and a subsequent application of that general proposition to the unknown case. This second part of the operation, which, as before observed, is essentially a process of interpretation, will be resolvable into a syllogism or a series of syllogisms, the majors of which will be general propositions embracing whole classes of cases; every one of which propositions must be true in all its extent, if the argument is maintainable. If, therefore, any fact fairly coming within the range of one of these general propositions, and consequently

56

asserted by it, is known or suspected to be other than the proposition asserts it to be, this mode of stating the argument causes us to know or to suspect that the original observations, which are the real grounds of our conclusion, are not sufficient to support it.[108]

But if all inference is from particulars to particulars, and truth can be known only through inference and intuition[109] (e.g., bodily sensations and mental feelings[110]), then the justification of a cognitive claim must ultimately concern the particular statements from which it is inferred. So ultimately, justification must appeal to truths known through intuition. And here it becomes clear that on Mill's view questions of discovery *are* pertinent to questions of justification.[111]

In this chapter we have given brief expositions of four specific anti-psychologistic theses which can be found in the philosophical writings of Gottlob Frege. In doing so we have in each case sketched one or more of their psychologistic counterparts. There are, of course, interrelations between these four theses. The distinction between questions of discovery and questions of justification, for example, would have little point were logic a science descriptive of the way in which humans actually reason. And to the extent to which logical and mathematical truths and their proofs are expressed in language, the thesis that meanings are third realm entities seems to underlie each of the other positions. To a large extent, each of these anti-psychologistic theses are motivated by a concern to provide the prerequisites for the sort of justification thought necessary from the EP$_1$ perspective. But the common thread that runs through these four specific anti-psychologistic theses ia a denial that truth is, in any way, dependent upon the judging subject. This we have characterized as the hub of Frege's anti-psychologistic thought. It is also the thesis that motivated Frege's conception of the third realm:

Surveying the whole question, it seems to me that the source of the dispute lies in a difference in our conceptions of what is true. For me, what is true is something objective and independent of the judging subject; for psychological logicians it is not. What Herr B. Erdmann calls 'objective certainty' is merely a general acknowledgment on the part of the subjects who judge, which is thus not independent of them but susceptible to alteration with the constitution of their minds.

We can generalize this still further: for me there is a domain of what is objective, which is distinct from that of what is actual, whereas the psychological logicians without ado take what is not actual to be subjective.[112]

But in this passage, Frege slides from his conception of objective truth to Erdmann's conception of objective certainty. Nevertheless, the psychologistic tendency toward subjectivism is not without its own claims. And it is interesting to note that Mill pointedly listed as two *a priori* fallacies: (1) the natural prejudice of mistaking subjective laws for objective laws; and (2) the natural prejudice of ascribing objective existence to abstractions.[113]

Ironically, Frege's belief that *truth* is independent of the judging subject, and even his belief in the third realm are not inconsistent with any of the versions of psychologism discussed. Truth may well be independent of the judging subject, it may well be eternal and unconditioned, but it is *knowledge* with which we are primarily concerned. Frege wrote:

> If we want to emerge from the subjective at all, we must conceive of knowledge as an activity that does not create what is known but grasps what is already there.[114]

But this is just indicative of the problem. Throughout our discussion we have been running up against the question whether psychologism and anti-psychologism are epistemological or metaphysical theses. In what follows, we will address that issue.

NOTES AND REFERENCES

1. Carnap, Rudolf; *Logical Foundations of Probability*; University of Chicago Press (Chicago, 1950) p. 581.

2. *Op. cit.*; Wild; p. 20.

3. Frege, of course, did not identify the meaning of a proper name with its sense. Rather, he thought the sense of a proper name to be one component of that name's meaning. To that extent, Frege did not characterize the *meaning*, but the *sense* of a proper name as a third realm entity. Frege did, however, regard the thought (the sense of an indicative sentence) as the bearer of truth value. (See: Frege, Gottlob; "On Sense and Reference"; in *Translations from the Philosophical Writings of Gottlob Frege*; ed. by Peter Geach and Max Black; Basil Blackwell (Oxford, 1970) pp. 56-78.)

4. Sober distinguishes between three versions of psychologism: (1) epistemological psychologism, i.e., the view that there is no question of justifying a logical rule or epistemological maxim above and beyond the question of whether it is in fact followed in practice; (2) metaphysical psychologism, i.e., the view that the laws of logic and characterizations of rationality that epistemology seeks to formulate are *about* human mental activity; and (3) what we will call "the psychological reality thesis", i.e., the view that the laws of logic and maxims of epistemology are the psychological laws of cognition and, as such, have psychological reality. (See: Sober; pp. 166-168.) While Sober thinks that Frege opposed all three of these views, we will argue later that he was not opposed to the psychological reality thesis. What we here call "logical psychologism", "linguistic psychologism", and "mathematical psychologism" seem to be instances of what Sober calls "metaphysical psychologism". We distinguish them here because they seem to emerge as separate theses in Frege's writings.

5. Husserl, Edmund; "Philosophie als strenge Wissenschaft"; *Logos*, Volume 1 (1910) pp. 289-314. Translated by Quentin Lauer as "Philosophy as Rigorous Science"; in Edmund Husserl, *Phenomenology and the Crisis of Philosophy*; Harper & Row (New York, 1965) pp. 91-92. For a discussion of the links between empiricism and psychologism, see: Husserl, Edmund; *Logische Untersuchungen*; M. Niemeyer (Halle, 1900). Translated by J.N. Findlay as Edmund Husserl, *Logical Investigations*; Humanities Press (New York, 1970) Volume 1, pp. 111-117.

6. Toulmin, Stephen; *Human Understanding*; Princeton University Press (Princeton, 1972) p. 44. One of Toulmin's programmatic aims is to dismantle this equation between rationality and logicality. Toulmin thinks such a dismantling is necessary if philosophy is to progress past the rejection of the *a priori*.

7. Mill, John Stuart; *A System of Logic*; ed. by J.M. Robson; University of Toronto Press (Toronto, 1973) Book II, chapter vii, section 5; pp. 277-278.

8. See: Mill, John Stuart; *An Examination of Sir William Hamilton's Philosophy*; ed. by J.M. Robson; University of Toronto Press (Toronto, 1979) p. 376.

9. *Ibid.*; p. 373.

10. *Ibid.*

11. *Ibid.*; pp. 380-381.

12. *Ibid.*; pp. 382-383.

13. *Op. cit.*; Mill; *A System of Logic*; Book II, chapter v, section 6; pp. 236-251.

14. Frege, Gottlob; *Grundgesetze der Arithmetik, begriffsschriftlich abgeleitet*. Band I; Verlag Hermann Pohle (Jena, 1893). Translated by Montgomery Furth as *The Basic Laws of Arithmetic*; University of California Press (Los Angeles, 1967) p. 12.

15. *Ibid.*; p. 14.

16 *Ibid.*; pp. 12-13.

17. *Ibid.*; p. 13.

18. *Ibid.*; p. 15.

19. *Op. cit.*; Husserl; *Logical Investigations*; Volume 1, p. 99.

20. *Ibid.*; p. 100.

21. *Op. cit.*; Frege; *The Basic Laws of Arithmetic*; p. 14.

22. *Ibid.*

23. *Op. cit.*; Husserl; *Logical Investigations*; pp. 115-116.

24. See: Frege, Gottlob; "Der Gedanke"; *Beitrage zur Philosophie des deutschen Idealismus*, 1 (1918-1919) pp. 58-77. Translated by A.M. and Marcelle Quinton as "The Thought: A Logical Inquiry"; in *Philosophical Logic*; ed. by P.F. Strawson; Oxford University Press (New York, 1967) pp. 17-18.

25. Frege wrote that "A property of a thought will be called inessential which consists in, or follows from the fact that, it is apprehended by a thinker." (See: *Ibid.*; p. 37.)

26. Here, of course, we are referring to our theoretical knowledge (knowledge that) as opposed to our practical knowledge (knowledge how). (See, e.g., Ryle, Gilbert; "Knowing

How and Knowing That"; *Collected Papers*; by Gilbert Ryle; Barnes & Noble (New York, 1971) Volume II, pp. 212-225. Popper, as we shall see in later chapters, disputes the idea that knowledge necessarily consists of true propositions.

27. Locke, John; *An Essay concerning Human Understanding*; ed. by P.H. Nidditch; Oxford University Press (New York, 1975) Book I, chapter I, section 8; p. 47.

28. *Ibid.*; Book II, chapter I, sections 2-8; pp. 104-108.

29. *Ibid.*; Book II, chapter I, sections 17-18; pp. 113-115.

30. *Ibid.*; Book III, chapter II, section 2; p. 405.

31. *Ibid.*; Book III, chapter II, section 1; pp. 404-405.

32. *Ibid.*; Book IV, chapter V, section 2; p. 574.

33. *Ibid.*; Book IV, chapter I, section 2; p. 525.

34. *Ibid.*; Book IV, chapter II, section 1; p. 531.

35. *Ibid.*; Book IV, chapter III, section 6; pp. 539-543.

36. *Ibid.*; Book IV, chapter IV, sections 1-3; pp. 562-563.

37. *Ibid.*; Book IV, chapter IV, sections 1-2; pp. 562-563.

38. *Ibid.*; Book IV, chapter VIII, section 8; p. 614.

39. *Op. cit.*; Mill; *A System of Logic*; Book I, chapter ii, section 5; pp. 30-40.

40. *Ibid.*; Book I, chapter ii, section 1; pp. 24-25.

41. *Ibid.*; Book I, chapter ii, sections 13-14; pp. 74-75.

42. *Ibid.*; Book I, chapter v, section 5; p. 99.

43. *Ibid.*; Book I, chapter v, section 4; p. 98.

44. Frege, of course, considered thoughts to be the senses of indicative sentences. (See: *Op. cit.*; Frege; "The Thought: A Logical Inquiry".)

45. See: Frege, Gottlob; *Begriffsschrift, eine der arithmetischen nachgebildete Formelsprache des reinen Denkens*; Halle a/S., (1879). Translation in J. van Heijenoort, ed.; *Source Book in Mathematical Logic, 1897-1931*; Harvard University Press (Cambridge, Mass., 1966).

46. Frege, Gottlob; "Über Sinn und Bedeutung"; *Zeitschrift für Philosophie und philosophische Kritik*, 100 (1892) pp. 25-50. Translated by Max Black as "On Sense and Reference"; in *Translations from the Philosophical Writings of Gottlob Frege*; ed. by Peter Geach and Max Black; Basil Blackwell (Oxford, 1970) p. 56. It may seem strange that in discussing Frege's *Begriffsschrift* views, I here quote from "On Sense and Reference". Nevertheless, this passage seems to be Frege's most explicit statement concerning his reasons for adopting the *Begriffsschrift* theory that identity is a relation between the names of objects. Indeed, in

what immediately precedes this passage, Frege writes:

EQUALITY gives rise to challenging questions which are not altogether easy to answer. Is it a relation? A relation between objects, or between names or signs of objects? In my *Begriffsschrift* I assumed the latter. The reasons which seem to favour this are the following...

("On Sense and Reference"; p. 56.)

47. *Ibid.*; p. 57.

48. *Ibid.*; p. 59.

49. The discussion of ideas in "On Sense and Reference" is sketchy. But Frege elaborates on the distinction between sense and idea in "The Thought: A Logical Inquiry" (especially pp. 26-29). We will return to this distinction later in our discussion.

50. The antecedent of this conditional should not be taken for granted. Frege, however, offers no in depth discussion of his theory of communication.

51. See: Wittgenstein, Ludwig; *Philosophical Investigations*; Trans. by G.E.M. Anscombe; Macmillan (New York, 1953).

52. We will return to Frege's concept of truth later in our discussion.

53. *Op. cit.*; Frege; "The Thought: A Logical Inquiry"; p. 29.

54. *Ibid.*

55. *Ibid.*; p. 29.

56. *Ibid.*

57. Frege, Gottlob; *Die Grundlagen der Arithmetik, eine logisch-mathematische Untersuchung über den Begriff der Zahl*; Verlag Wilhelm Koebner (Breslau, 1884). Translated by J.L. Austin as *The Foundations of Arithmetic*; Basil Blackwell (Oxford, 1953) p. x^e.

58. Schneewind, J.B.; "John Stuart Mill"; in *Op. cit.*; *Encyclopedia of Philosophy*; Volume 5; p. 317.

59. *Op. cit.*; Mill; *A System of Logic*; Book III, chapter xxiv, section 4; p. 609.

60. *Ibid.*; Book III, chapter xxiv, section 5; p. 611.

61. *Ibid.*; Book II, chapter vi, section 2; p. 254.

62. *Ibid.*; p. 255.

63. *Ibid.*; p. 257.

64. *Ibid.*; p. 256.

65. *Ibid.*; p. 256.

66. *Ibid.*; Book III, chapter xxiv, section 4; p. 609.

67. *Ibid.*; Book III, chapter xxiv, section 5; p. 613.

68. We will consider this in greater detail in our discussion of epistemological psychologism.

69. *Op. cit.*; Frege; *The Foundations of Arithmetic*; p. 38^e.

70. Ideas, of course, are not self-subsistent, but depend upon the mind for their existence. So the characterization of numbers as self-subsistent objects in itself denies that numbers are mental entities.

71. *Op. cit.*; Frege; *The Foundations of Arithmetic*; p. 105^e.

72. *Ibid.*; p. 38^e.

73. *Ibid.*; p. 36^e.

74. *Ibid.*; p. 37^e.

75. *Ibid.*

76. *Ibid.*

77. *Ibid.* Husserl, it is no surprise, echoes similar concerns about the generality of number:
We ought of course to exclude from factual laws such general assertions as merely apply pure conceptual propositions — which state universally valid relations on a basis of pure concepts — to matters of fact. If $3 > 2$, then the three books on this table also exceed the two books in this cupboard, and so for any things whatever. But our pure proposition of number does not refer to things, but to numbers in their pure generality — it is *the* number 3 that is greater than *the* number 2 — and it applies not merely to individual, but to 'general' objects, e.g. to species of colour or sound, to types of geometrical figure and to such-like timeless generalities.
(Husserl; *Logical Investigations*; pp. 107-108.)

78. Frege seems to have regarded what is objective in an intuition as what is subject to laws (See: Frege; *The Foundations of Arithmetic*; p. 35^e). But in distinguishing subjective ideas from objective ideas Frege writes: "An idea in the subjective sense is what is governed by the psychological laws of association." (Frege; *The Foundations of Arithmetic*; p. 37^e.) Perhaps what is at issue here is the types of laws to which an intuition is subject.

79. Frege, Gottlob; *Nachgelassene Schriften*; ed. by H. Hermes, F. Kambartel, and F. Kaulbach; Felix Meiner (Hamburg, 1969). Translated by Peter Long and Roger White as *Gottlob Frege: Posthumous Writings*; The University of Chicago Press (Chicago, 1979) p. 279.

80. *Ibid.*; p. 280.

81. Brouwer, L.E.J.; "Consciousness, Philosophy, and Mathematics"; in *Philosophy of Mathematics*; ed. by Paul Benacerraf and Hilary Putnam; Prentice-Hall (Englewood Cliffs, N.J., 1964) p. 78.

82. Heyting, A.; *Intuitionism: An Introduction*; North-Holland Publishing Company (Amsterdam, 1956) p. 8.

83. *Ibid.*

84. Parsons, Charles; "Foundations of Mathematics"; in *Encyclopedia of Philosophy*; Volume 5; p. 204.

85. *Ibid.*

86. *Ibid.* Appropos to our discussion of linguistic psychologism, Dummett cites Wittgenstein's doctrine that meaning is use as part of the philosophical basis for intuitionism (See: Dummett, Michael; "The Philosophical Basis of Intuitionist Logic"; in *Truth and Other Enigmas*; by Michael Dummett; Harvard University Press (Cambridge, 1978) p. 216.

87. *Op. cit.*; Parsons; pp. 204-205.

88. *Op. cit.*; Brouwer; p. 82.

89. Beth, Evert W.; *Mathematical Thought*; Reidel (Dordrecht, Holland, 1965) pp. 76-77.

90. Brouwer might be taken to affirm the *a priori* character of mathematical knowledge in: Brouwer, L.E.J.; "Intuitionism and Formalism"; in *Philosophy of Mathematics*; ed. by Benacerraf and Putnam.

91. Intuitionism denies that mathematical entities are third realm objects at least in the Fregean sense in which the third realm is construed as completely independent of the human mind.

92. Reichenbach, Hans; *The Rise of Scientific Philosophy*; University of California Press (Berkeley, 1951) p. 231.

93. *Op. cit.*; Frege; *The Foundations of Arithmetic*; pp. 3-4[e].

94. *Ibid.*

95. *Ibid.*

96. The footnote of Frege's cited above does allow that induction might establish "some probability" for a law. And it might be thought that this compromises my characterization of Frege as an EP_1 philosopher. Now this footnote is one of the few passages in which Frege mentions probability, though he does distinguish, at least implicitly, between empirical and *a priori* certainty (See: Frege; *The Foundations of Arithmetic*; p. ix[e]; see also: chapter 6 of this work.) Nevertheless, I do not think the acknowledgment of probability is inconsistent with the EP_1 perspective. On the one hand, the proposition that a statement has a certain probability value, a proposition which can be established *deductively* upon the recognition of general laws of probability, is consistent with the proposition that that statement is false. But this simply means that an EP_1 philosopher might acknowledge induction as establishing not the truth of a statement, but the *probability* of the truth of a statement. In other words, it is not the statement but the probability of the statement (i.e., of its truth) that the EP_1 philosopher would regard as justified, though certain probability values might be construed as providing justification for *believing* that a statement is true. On the other hand, an EP_1 philosopher might acknowledge that certain *statements* can only be justified probabilistically, but regard such justification as of an inferior nature.

97. Hume, David; *An Enquiry Concerning Human Understanding*; ed. by Eric Steinberg; Hackett (Indianapolis, 1977) p. 30.

98. We will return to Hume's views on justification in greater detail in our discussion of Popper.

99. *Op. cit.*; Mill; *A System of Logic*; p. 158.

100. *Ibid.*; Book II, chapter i, section 3; p. 158.

101. *Ibid.*; Book II, chapter iii, section 2; p. 162.

102. *Ibid.*; Book II, chapter iii, section 1; p. 183.

103. *Ibid.*; Book II, chapter iii, section 3; p. 193.

104. *Ibid.*; p. 187.

105. *Ibid.*; Book II, chapter ii, section 2; pp. 174-175.

106. *Ibid.*; Book II, chapter iii, section 9; p. 208.

107. *Ibid.*; Book II, chapter iii, section 5; pp. 196-199.

108. *Ibid.*; pp. 197-198.

109. *Ibid.*; p. 6.

110. *Ibid.*; p. 7.

111. Popper, we should note, explicitly links psychologism with inductive methodology. Popper distinguishes between the psychology of knowledge, which deals with empirical facts, and the logic of discovery, which deals only with logical relations. In so doing, Popper writes that "the belief in induction is largely due to a confusion of psychological problems with epistemological ones." (Popper; *The Logic of Scientific Discovery*; p. 30.) According to Popper, the view that inductive inference provides justification for cognitive claims depends on the view that statements can be justified by sense perceptions. We will return to this point later in our discussion. For now, suffice it to say that on Popper's view, any position which conceives of induction as providing a justification for cognitive claims would be guilty of psychologism.

112. *Op. cit.*; Frege; *The Basic Laws of Arithmetic*; pp. 15-16.

113. *Op. cit.*; Mill; *A System of Logic*; Book V, chapter iii, section 2, 4; pp. 747-757.

114. *Op. cit.*; Frege; *The Basic Laws of Arithmetic*; p. 23.

4. THE LOGIC OF PHILOSOPHICAL TAXONOMY

Are psychologism and anti-psychologism primarily epistemological or meta-physical positions? An answer to this question bears on our discussion in that it delimits the sorts of considerations pertinent to the evaluation of these theses. But in a certain sense of "metaphysics", there is no real distinction to be drawn. If philosophical statements are not based upon or justified by the data of sense experience, then all philosophy is metaphysics. Ethics is the metaphysics of moral norms and judgments; aesthetics is the metaphysics of art and art criticism; epistemology is the metaphysics of cognition and the justification of cognitive claims; etc. But then, what we are referring to as "metaphysics" in our question is just the metaphysics of ontology, i.e., that body of thought concerned with what and how things exist.

Paul Benacerraf has, in effect, classified philosophies of mathematics into two groups: those inspired by ontological considerations, and those inspired by epistemological considerations.[1] But there is nothing peculiar here about philosophies of mathematics. The same division can be made with respect to, e.g., theories of meaning. But the difficulty with this classification is that ontological and epistemological considerations have so many points of interdependency that it is often difficult to clearly demarcate their boundaries. And interdependency here is not coincidental. Earlier we likened philosophy to the game of chess, saying that good philosophers, like good chess players, usually hold one position to protect another. Here the relationship between epistemology and metaphysics illustrates the point. For philosophers often, if not usually, maintain whatever ontological positions they do in order to protect or support the epistemological theses they consider more primary to their philosophy. Classical empiricism, for example, denied the existence of innate ideas. But this denial resulted not simply from a concern for an accurate index of what there is. Rather, innate ideas provided philosophers with a shelter from criticism. If a belief is innate in the traditional sense, then it is in no need of further justification. Hence, the empiricists' denial of innate ideas was part and parcel of their opposition to dogmatism, an attitude buttressed by the assumption of truths not subject to criticism. Analogously, when classical rationalism asserted the existence of *a priori* valid statements, it was in an effort to provide the prerequisites for the objective certainty rationalism thought essential for knowledge. So our question here is not motivated by any scholastic concern for philosophical taxonomy. Rather it is asked to determine what, if anything, hangs on psychologism.

Consider an instance of the interrelation between ontology and epistemology that is pertinent to our discussion. Frege's famous distinction between the sense and reference of proper names is a distinction drawn in semantics, the theory of meaning (or the metaphysics of language). The ontological claim Frege made is that there exist senses of names that are distinct from both the names themselves and the objects to which those names refer. But as we noted earlier, the distinction between sense and reference, in Frege's case, was drawn only when it became apparent that failure to draw it would render all true identity statements either tautologous or informative of language alone – results both of which Frege wished to avoid. In short, it was Frege's epistemological belief that certain true identity statements of the form "a=b" are genuinely informative and express real knowledge not knowable *a priori* that provided much of the impetus for the distinction.[2]

Another distinction drawn in Frege's theory of meaning, and a distinction more pertinent to his anti-psychologism, also illustrates this interdependency. This is the distinction between senses and ideas. Frege's characterization of senses as third realm entities, eternal and independent of the knowing subject, was proposed to protect the possibility of objective knowledge and critical science.

The distinction between sense and idea is drawn in "On Sense and Reference", but its discussion is there curtailed. What little is said indicates that the distinction is drawn to explain the possibility of communication. In speaking of the essential subjectivity of ideas, Frege writes:

> This constitutes an essential distinction between the idea and the sign's sense, which may be the common property of many and therefore is not a part or a mode of the individual mind. For one can hardly deny that mankind has a common store of thoughts which is transmitted from one generation to the next.[3]

It would be tempting here to infer a connection between the possibility of communication and the possibility of objective knowledge. It is necessary that we be able to communicate our thoughts if we are to engage in a common science. If knowledge is objective in a subject-independent sense, then it is necessary that the objects of knowledge – thoughts – also be so objective. And if senses were mental entities, and mental entities are private to the individual consciousness that bears them, then there would not even be the possibility of communication, let alone a common science.

But inference here is unnecessary. The connection between the doctrine that thoughts are third realm entities and the possibility of objective knowledge is explicit in "The Thought: A Logical Inquiry":

> I now return to the question: is a thought an idea? If the thought I express in the Pythagorean theorem can be recognized by others just as much as by me then it does not belong to the content of my consciousness, I am not its bearer; yet I can, nevertheless, recognize it to be true. However, if it is not the same thought at all which is taken to be the content of the Pythagorean theorem by me and by another person, one should not really say 'the Pythagorean theorem' but 'my Pythagorean theorem', 'his Pythagorean theorem' and these would be different; for the sense belongs necessarily to the sentence. Then my thought can be the content of my consciousness and his thought the

content of his. Could the sense of my Pythagorean theorem be true while that of his was false? I said that the word 'red' was applicable only in the sphere of my consciousness if it did not state a property of things but was supposed to characterize one of my sense-impressions. Therefore the words 'true' and 'false', as I understand them, could also be applicable only in the sphere of my consciousness, if they were not supposed to be concerned with something of which I was not the bearer, but were somehow appointed to characterize the content of my consciousness. Then truth would be restricted to the content of my consciousness and it would remain doubtful whether anything comparable occurred in the consciousness of others.

If every thought requires a bearer, to the contents of whose consciousness it belongs, then it would be a thought of this bearer only and there would be no science common to many, on which many could work. But I, perhaps, have my science, namely, a whole of thought whose bearer I am and another person has his. Each of us occupies himself with the contents of his own consciousness. No contradiction between the two sciences would then be possible and it would really be idle to dispute about truth, as idle, indeed almost ludicrous, as it would be for two people to dispute whether a hundred-mark note were genuine, where each meant the one he himself had in his pocket and understood the word 'genuine' in his own particular sense. If someone takes thoughts to be ideas, what he then recognizes to be true is, on his own view, the content of his consciousness and does not properly concern other people at all.[4]

That there is a distinction between senses and ideas is an ontological thesis. This thesis concerns the nature of senses and thoughts. Ultimately, it concerns the nature of truth. And this thesis is one locus of Frege's anti-psychologism. It might even be argued that, insofar as it asserts that truth is independent of the knowing subject, this thesis just *is* Frege's anti-psychologism. So it might be thought that anti-psychologism is clearly and essentially an ontological thesis. But the point I wish to emphasize is that what hangs on this ontological thesis pertains to epistemology. The hypothesis of the third realm is not held in isolation. If its only concern was to describe the ontological status of truths and meanings, then it would have about as much significance as a theory of the ontological status of toothbrushes. But this is not the case. The third realm is significant because the possibility of objective knowledge in the EP_1 sense hangs on its being there. Alternately, the possibility of such knowledge is its *raison d'être*.

Here we can glean criteria for the evaluation of anti-psychologism. So long as the ontological thesis is considered in isolation, we are not sure how to move. The realization of its epistemological connections provides a direction. So long as we acknowledge the possibility of objective knowledge in the EP_1 sense, a third realm must be recognized. But while the subject-independence of truth is a necessary condition for the possibility of such knowledge, it is not sufficient. For it might be the case that it is impossible for *men* to apprehend the third realm despite its existence. Alternately, it might be the case that the process of apprehension alters or compromises the objectivity, i.e., the subject-independence, of the thoughts apprehended. Now Frege himself seems to have recognized this problem:

And yet! What value could there be for us in the eternally unchangeable which could neither undergo effects nor have effect on us? Something entirely and in every respect inactive would be unreal and non-existent for us. Even the timeless, if it is to be anything for us, must somehow be implicated with the temporal. What would a thought be for me that was never apprehended by me? But by apprehending a thought I come into a relation to it and it to me. It is possible that the same thought that is thought by me today was not thought by me yesterday. In this way the strict timelessness is of course annulled. But one is inclined to distinguish between essential and inessential properties and to regard something as timeless if the changes it undergoes involve only its inessential properties. A property of a thought will be called inessential which consists in, or follows from the fact that, it is apprehended by a thinker....[5]

But what if one such "inessential property" were that the process of apprehension renders apprehended thoughts essentially private to the individual consciousness that bears them? Frege's failure to explain the mechanics of apprehension makes his hypothesis of the third realm less plausible, and thus weakens his anti-psychologism. The apprehension of a thought may be without effects for the objectivity and timelessness of that thought. But it may effect the value that such objectivity and timelessness has *for us*. This might be the case if, for example, apprehension were thought analogous to sense perception. Our sense perception of material objects presumably has no effects on the objectivity of those objects. Only the most radical of empiricists would think that material objects cease to exist when not perceived. But despite the objectivity of material objects, the ideas via which they are perceived are essentially private. If apprehension is analogous to sense perception, then similar problems might arise. And if apprehension is not analogous to sense perception, then what *is* it like?

But even were it made clear exactly how thoughts can be apprehended without compromising their objectivity *for us*, the question still remains how the truth values of such thoughts are recognized. The apprehension of a thought and the recognition or judgment of its truth value are entirely different matters.[6] But both are required for knowledge. Frege's failure to give a clear account of how objective truths are apprehended is thus significant for an evaluation of his anti-psychologism. If the primary reason for holding that senses are third realm entities is to insure the possibility of communication and objective knowledge, then the ontological thesis, by itself, fails. If the third realm cannot be apprehended, then it is without value for us — even if it does in fact exist. One might well speculate on the existence of all sorts of objects that cannot be perceived through the senses while at the same time restricting the sources of human knowledge to sensuous intuition. And if the third realm can be apprehended, but only in a way that compromises the objectivity of thoughts (for us), then it is difficult to see how it would make a significant advance over the theory that thoughts are mental entities. So simply put, without a theory of apprehension, the third realm becomes a third wheel that turns nothing.

I am not alone in stressing this point. Susan Haack has also criticized Frege for failing to offer a theory of apprehension:

Frege's objections to psychologism are quite complex, and I shall only consider the argument which is most relevant to the position I have defended. This argument runs as follows. Logic has nothing to do with mental processes; for logic is objective and public, whereas the mental, according to Frege, is subjective and private. This is why Frege is so concerned to stress ... that the sense of a sentence is not an idea (a mental entity), but a thought (*Gedanke*: an abstract object, a proposition). Since ideas are mental, they are, Frege argues, essentially private; you can no more have my idea than you can have my headache. If the sense of a sentence were a private, mental entity, an idea in Frege's sense, there would be a mystery about the relation between one person's idea and another's.... Propositions, however, are public; you and I can both 'grasp' the same proposition, and this is what makes it possible for there to be objective, public knowledge.

This argument could be questioned on more than one score: e.g. why does Frege assume that everything mental is subjective and private? Is it relevant that the psychology with which he was familiar was introspectionist? But it is, anyway, pretty clear that the argument does *not* oblige one to divorce logic from mental processes in the way Frege supposes. For the postulation of propositions will only guarantee the publicity of knowledge if propositions are not only *objective*, but also *accessible*, if we can 'grasp' them; and this is just what the Platonist version of the argument for weak psychologism requires.

In fact, however, Frege has nothing very substantial to say to mitigate the mysteriousness of our supposed ability to 'grasp' his *Gedanken*.... [7]

To round out the point: it was, in part, the mysteriousness of our supposed ability to 'grasp' objective and timeless truths that led empiricists to limit the sources of human knowledge to sensuous intuition in the first place.

Frege, of course, did not think that communication and objective knowledge (in the EP_1 sense) were merely *possible*. And it is this point – that we can and do have objective knowledge – that is the fundamental assumption of anti-psychologism. It is, as it were, its ground. But being the ground of anti-psychologism, it is only asserted and never positively supported. We are told what must exist if such knowledge is possible, and we are warned that failure to postulate third realm entities results in the extreme subjectivism of a private language. But all this argues only for what must be the case *if* communication and objective knowledge in the EP_1 sense are possible. It does not argue that communication and objective knowledge in this sense are possible. And this is important for understanding the ground of psychologism.

Anti-psychologists, and Frege is no exception, often write as if psychologism were the result of a confusion, of an inconsistency on the part of psychologistic philosophers. Their arguments proceed as if it is expected that once psychologistic philosophers recognize the inconsistency in, e.g., holding that both meanings are mental entities and objective knowledge is possible, they would be led to reject psychologism. Now this might well be the case for some psychologistic philosophers. But it depends, on the whole, on the self-gratuitous assumption that psychologistic philosophers hold the possibility of objective knowledge in the EP_1 sense as more certain than the doctrine that meanings are mental entities. More often than not, psychologism reflects not a confusion or an inconsistency, but an adherence to a different position concerning the nature and limits of knowledge. In other words, one reason why a psychologistic philosopher might hold that meanings are mental entities is that he regards objective knowledge in the EP_1 sense as impossible.

Consider the example of linguistic psychologism. The doctrine that meanings are mental entities is inconsistent with the possibility of communication — provided that communication involves the apprehension of an ontologically identical thought by different individuals. But was this *Locke's* theory of communication? Locke thought that words can properly and immediately signify nothing but the ideas that are in the mind of the speaker. Nevertheless, Locke recognized that men, in their thoughts, give them a secret reference to two other things:[8]

> *First, they suppose their words to be Marks of the* Ideas *in the Minds also of other Men, with whom they communicate*: For else they should talk in vain, and could not be understood, if the Sounds they applied to one *Idea*, were such, as by the Hearer, were applied to another, which is to speak two Languages. But in this, Men stand not usually to examine whether the *Idea* they, and those they discourse with have in their Minds, be the same: But think it enough, that they use the Word, as they imagine, in the common Acceptation of that Language: in which case they suppose, that the *Idea*, they make it a Sign of, is precisely the same, to which the Understanding Men of that Country apply that Name.
>
> *Secondly*, Because *Men* would not be thought to talk barely of their own Imaginations, but of Things as really they are; therefore they *often suppose their Words to stand also for the reality of Things*. But this relating more particularly of Substances, and their Names, as perhaps the former does to simple *Ideas* and Modes, we shall speak of these two different ways of applying Words more at large, when we come to treat of the Names of mixed Modes, and Substances, in particular: Though give me leave here to say, that it is a perverting the use of Words, and brings unavoidable Obscurity and Confusion into their Signification, whenever we make them stand for any thing, but those *Ideas* we have in our own Minds.[9]

Locke, of course, explicitly and repeatedly draws the connection between epistemology and the theory of meaning. But while he seems generally less confident than Frege about the extent of our communication, he does not conclude that his doctrine that words signify ideas entails a private language. Ironically, Locke does write:

> But if it should happen, that any two thinking Men should really have different *Ideas*, I do not see how they could discourse or argue one with another.[10]

But Locke seems to take the fact that men do discourse with one another to indicate not that thoughts are third realm entities, but that we share the same ideas. But here I take it that what Locke means by "same ideas" is not what Frege means. By "same ideas" Locke means not the ontologically singular object, but objects that are comparatively similar in quality.[11]

Here, what separates Frege and Locke is not their characterization of ideas, but their theories of communication. Frege thought that communication involves the apprehension of a single object by different individuals. For Frege, I

communicate with you when I use words in such a way as to get you to apprehend the same object, i.e., the thought, that I apprehend. Here, thoughts cannot
be ideas because the privacy of ideas is such as to prohibit their common apprehension by different individuals. But Locke held that communication occurs
when men succeed in using words, which properly signify only the ideas in their
own minds, to *excite* in the minds of others ideas which are qualitatively similar.
And this point is significant. Frege writes as if the private language follows
simply from the doctrines: (a) that meanings are mental entities; and (b) that
mental entities are private to the individual consciousness that bears them. What
Frege takes for granted is his theory of communication. But one way to avoid
the private language while maintaining both (a) and (b) is to maintain a different
theory of communication. And this is exactly what Locke does. Locke is labor-
ing under no *confusions*. He clearly recognizes the problems with his theory and
addresses them. The point to be made, however, is that an empiricist would find
the inference from the apparent success of communication to the qualitative
similarity of ideas far more plausible than that to the existence of a third realm.
If Locke were confronted with Frege's anti-psychologistic arguments, they
would come as no great surprise. But rather than altering his theory of meaning,
Locke, I suspect, would reply, "Yes Gottlob, you've understood my point.
There are no such things as communication and objective knowledge – at least
not in your sense!"

Consider another example. In criticizing Mill's mathematical psychologism,
Frege charged Mill with misinterpreting arithmetical propositions by holding,
e.g., that the identity statement "1 = 1" could be false because a one pound
weight does not always weigh precisely the same as another:

> Mill always confuses the applications that can be made of an arithmetical proposition,
> which often are physical and do presuppose observed facts, with the pure mathematical
> proposition itself.[12]

But it is Frege who is here confused. Mill held that the condition that 1 = 1
underlay all arithmetical ratiocination. It would be too naive to consider Mill a
Platonist. But Mill did, at least implicitly, distinguish between "1 = 1" qua statement of pure number and "1=1" qua statement of quantity. Even in calling the
condition that 1 = 1 into question, Mill wrote:

> It is certain that 1 is always equal in *number* to 1; and where the mere number of ob-
> jects, or of the parts of an object, without supposing them to be equivalent in any other
> respect, is all that is material, the conclusions of arithmetic, so far as they go to that
> alone, are true without mixture of hypothesis.[13]

Now I do not pretend that this distinction is clearly, or even consistently drawn.
When Mill speaks of "pure number" he seems to be suggesting that we can
abstract the property of number from material quantities and, when our purposes warrant it, speak of that property alone. But Mill explicitly denies that
there are numbers in the abstract:

> All numbers must be numbers of something: there are no such things as numbers in the abstract. *Ten* must mean ten bodies, or ten sounds, or ten beatings of the pulse. But though numbers must be numbers of something, they may be numbers of anything. Propositions, therefore, concerning numbers, have the remarkable peculiarity that they are propositions concerning all things whatever; all objects, all existences of every kind, known to our experience. All things possess quantity; consist of parts which can be numbered; and in that character possess all the properties which are called properties of numbers.[14]

What Mill is denying here is that numbers are objects. Rather, numbers are properties of objects. Perhaps what Mill means when he speaks of truths which relate to "pure number" are those in which the nature of the quantity that is numbered is left unspecified, i.e., those in which no reference is made explicitly to material objects and the statement can be interpreted as concerning any object at all. Whether or not this can be consistently held with the denial of Platonism is unclear. But the distinction is significant because it leads Mill to allow that there are certain mathematical truths that have more than a mere certainty of inference.

It would, of course, be fair to say that Mill was far more concerned with the applications of statements of pure number than with such statements themselves. But Mill denied that true arithmetical statements, qua statements of pure number, could be false. Considered as a statement of pure number, "$1 + 1 = 2$" is always true. But "how can we know that one pound and one pound make two pounds, if one of the pounds may be troy, and the other avoirdupois?"[15] Perhaps a chemical reaction may occur to alter the expected weight. So while Mill thought it certain that 1 is always equal to 1 in number, he thought it an entirely different matter whether *that* certainty would always be of practical aid when specific physical quantities were under consideration. With this in mind, Mill bifurcated the class of mathematical truths with respect to certainty:

> What is commonly called mathematical certainty, therefore, which comprises the two-fold conception of unconditional truth and perfect accuracy, is not an attribute of all mathematical truths, but of those only which relate to pure Number, as distinguished from Quantity in the more enlarged sense; and only so long as we abstain from supposing that the numbers are a precise index to actual quantities. The certainty usually ascribed to the conclusions of geometry, and even to those of mechanics, is nothing whatever but certainty of inference. We can have full assurance of particular results under particular suppositions, but we cannot have the same assurance that these suppositions are accurately true, nor that they include all the data which may exercise an influence over the result in any given instance.[16]

Now Mill may be confused in thinking that he can distinguish between truths which relate to pure number and truths which relate to quantity (given everything else he has said). But far from *confusing* the applications that can be made of an arithmetical proposition with the pure arithmetical proposition in holding that "$1 = 1$" could be false, Mill's position seems more akin to Einstein's: "As far as the laws of mathematics refer to reality, they are not certain; and as far as they are certain, they do not refer to reality."[17]

I would suppose that Frege would disagree with Mill's position regarding geometrical certainty. For Frege held geometry to be *a priori* synthetic. But I do not think that Frege would much oppose Mill's doctrine concerning arithmetical certainty, though Frege might deny that what Mill calls statements of quantity are really mathematical statements. But here the issue seems to concern more the emphasis than the substance of the doctrine.

What separates Frege and Mill on the issue of arithmetical certainty involves a difference in focus. And what separates Frege and Locke on the issue of the ontological status of thoughts involves a difference in their theories of communication. In either case, to accuse the psychologistic philosopher of inconsistency and confusion is to beg rather than meet the question.

This point is pertinent especially to the extent to which psychologism is related to empiricism. Husserl, for example, writes:

> One might almost say that it is only inconsistency that keeps psychologism alive: to think it out to the end, is already to have given it up, unless extreme empiricism affords an example of the greatly superior strength of ingrained prejudices to the most certain deliverances of insight. What we have said in objection to this logical position – that on it logical truths must lose their *a priori* guarantee, and their wholly exact, purely conceptual character, and must become more or less vague probabilities resting on experience and induction, concerned with matters of fact in the mental life of man – all this, if we ignore its emphasis on vagueness, is what empiricism expressly teaches.[18]

But the point to be made here is that this *is* what empiricism expressly teaches. And it would be callow to fault empiricists with confusion or inconsistency on these points. Of course empiricism denies the possibility of absolute certainty of universal generalizations ranging over infinite domains. Of course empiricism denies the *a priori* character of logical truths. But this seems to be the point, not the fault, of empiricism.

Finally, it is somewhat ironic that Husserl accuses empiricism of having ingrained prejudices – if only because this is exactly the charge Mill levels against the *a priorists*. In his autobiography Mill writes that the doctrine that we have intuitive and infallible knowledge of the principles governing ourselves and the outside world is:

> the great intellectual support of false doctrines and bad institutions. By the aid of this theory, every inveterate belief and every intense feeling, of which the origin is not remembered, is enabled to dispense with the obligation of justifying itself by reason, and is erected into its own all-sufficient voucher and justification. There never was such an instrument devised for consecrating all deep seated prejudices.[19]

We have been discussing the interrelationship between the metaphysical and the epistemological. The point of this discussion is to show that the ontological theses of psychologism and anti-psychologism need to be evaluated on epistemological grounds. Later, I will suggest an even stronger relation between anti-psychologism and epistemology. The epistemological thesis to be discussed is fallibilism. My claim is not that fallibilism is inconsistent with anti-psychologism, but that fallibilism, at least in a justificationist programme, renders anti-psychologism insignificant. In effect, my claim is that justificationist anti-psychologism is held not simply to insure the possibility of objective knowledge, but to underscore claims to objective certainty in particular domains. Simply put, anti-psychologism involves a claim to cognitive authority.

NOTES AND REFERENCES

1. See: Benacerraf, Paul; "Mathematical Truth"; *The Journal of Philosophy*, Volume LXX, No. 19 (November 8, 1973) pp. 661-679.

2. This is contrary to Geach, who claims that the motivations for Frege's descriptivist theory of sense could not have been epistemological. We will return to this point in greater detail in Chapter 6. Of course, the logical analysis of intensional contexts provided Frege with an independent motivation for the theory of sense and reference.

3. *Op. cit.*; Frege; "On Sense and Reference"; p. 59.

4. *Op. cit.*; Frege; "The Thought: A Logical Inquiry", pp. 28-29. There is one clause in this passage that is curious. I have no idea what Frege means by "the sense belongs necessarily to the sentence."

5. *Ibid.*; p. 37.

6. *Ibid.*; pp. 19-22.

7. Haack, Susan; *Philosophy of Logics*; Cambridge University Press (New York, 1978) pp. 239-240.

8. *Op. cit.*; Locke; *An Essay concerning Human Understanding*; p. 406.

9. *Ibid.*; pp. 406-407.

10. *Ibid.*; p. 180.

11. Compare this with the distinction between "same token object" and "same type object" in the next chapter.

12. *Op. cit.*; Frege; *The Foundations of Arithmetic*; p. 13^e.

13. *Op. cit.*; Mill; *A System of Logic*; Book II, chapter vi, section 3; p. 258.

14. *Ibid.*; Book II, chapter vi, section 2; pp. 254-255.

15. *Ibid.*; p. 258.

16. *Ibid.*; p. 259.

17. Einstein, Albert; "Geometry and Experience"; in *Readings in the Philosophy of Science*; ed. by Herbert Feigl and May Brodbeck; Appleton-Century-Crofts, Inc., (New York, 1953) p. 189.

18. *Op. cit.*; Husserl; *Logical Investigations*; p. 111.

19. Mill, John Stuart; *Autobiography*; ed. by Jack Stillinger; Houghton Mifflin (Boston, 1969) p. 134.

5. FREGE AND THE PSYCHOLOGICAL REALITY THESIS

Why has psychology been thought to block the path of scientific progress? Rorty's answer, "Fear of ghosts", is teasing:

> The thought that by countenancing the mental, even temporarily, we are losing the scientific spirit, comes from two sources. The first ... is the confusion of the post-Cartesian conception of "consciousness" with the pre-philosophical notion of the soul as what leaves the body at death.[1]

But such fear and confusion should not be attributed to Frege. Or are we to suppose third realm entities to be ontologically more comforting than souls? Rorty's second source is more apt:

> The second is the epistemological argument that introspectibility carries with it privileged access, and that since epistemic privilege must be based on an ontological difference (mental entities being intrinsically better known to their possessors than anything physical could be known to anyone), we must deny the existence of the mental-qua-introspectable on pain of making part of our knowledge of reality depend upon unverifiable reports.[2]

Here, the answer to our question rests on philosophical underpinnings concerning the nature of scientific knowledge, the methodology of psychological inquiry, and the epistemic status of statements concerning mental states. But at base is the attitude that only scientific statements can lay valid claim to cognitive authority.

If the methodology of psychological inquiry is introspection of mental states, and mental states are private to the individual consciousness that bears them, then psychological statements are closed to the possibility of public testing. Here, two dogmas concerning cognitive authority come into conflict. The first is that the cognitive authority for scientific statements is, in part, a result of their capacity for public empirical verification or falsification. The second is that an individual is the sole and ultimate authority for statements concerning his own conscious states. This conflict does not quite entail that we deny the *existence* of mental states. But if the possibility of public empirical testing is the mark of the scientific, then psychological statements based on introspection cannot be considered scientific. So if psychology is to be considered a science, then its methodology of inquiry cannot be introspection, regardless of whether or not mental states exist. But the classification of psychological statements as unscientific would be merely a matter of epistemological taxonomy were it not for the thesis that only scientific statements can lay valid claim to cognitive authority. Here, the denial of scientific content is tantamount to the denial of cognitive content, and ultimately to the denial of the value of psychology.

I have given reasons to explain why philosophers have regarded psychology as a block in the road of scientific inquiry. But in this century attempts have been made to vindicate psychology. The replacement of introspectionism with behaviourism as the methodology of psychology was an attempt to replace the private reports of introspection which had been thought to provide the data base for psychological theories with public and empirically testable observation reports regarding human behaviour. Elliott Sober, for example, writes:

> Behaviorism, Freudianism, and Gestalt psychology were principally focused on the discovery of cross-subject *invariance*. For these programs, the discovery that an ostensible psychological property of one subject fails to generalize across many or all subjects was strong evidence for thinking that the property was either of minor importance or wholly an experimental artifact.[3]

But Brentano wrote that "psychology" literally means "science of the soul", though some psychologists have defined it as "the science of mental phenomena".[4] So one might wonder why a science of behaviour should be considered a *psychology*. Nevertheless, the shift toward behaviourism (and other more public methodologies of inquiry) has challenged, or at least rendered moot, the privileged access theory of mental states. Even if first-person introspection reports are considered, in some sense, incorrigible, they are not to be admitted into the data base for psychological theories.

I am inclined to agree with Sober that the historical impetus for the replacement of introspectionism with other more "objective" methodologies of inquiry was a concern to provide psychology with general laws. But I have reservations about the unimportance of psychological properties that fail to generalize across subjects. Sober writes:

> The fact that introspective reports of mental images are idiosyncratic while linguistic behavior is invariant should lead us to conclude that such introspective reports are either false or wholly irrelevant to the explanation of such invariances. This is merely a consequence of the maxim which advises us to posit similar causes for similar effects.[5]

But I have no idea what he means by saying that linguistic behaviour is invariant. Disregarding the obvious problem of different languages, does he mean that everyone responds similarly to the same questions? Or that we all use the same greetings and oaths? Or that everyone calls the same objects by the same names? Or what? If there is one thing that seems variant to me, it is linguistic behaviour. Nevertheless, the advice to posit similar causes for similar effects seems sound — so long as there is no reason to posit dissimilar causes. But idiosyncratic introspective reports of mental states *may* be just such a reason. Anyone who has participated in a political demonstration knows that invariance of behaviour cannot always be attributed to invariance of motive. And murder mysteries are based on the possibility that different motives can account for the same actions. Taking this advice too seriously may well result in the framing of laws that are so general as to be of little interest.

Nevertheless, the "objectification" of psychology is sometimes thought to have positive implications for psychologism. Sober, in claiming that Frege opposed a variant of psychologism called "the psychological reality thesis", writes:

> Although Frege's subsistence argument leaves this form of psychologism untouched, his *variability argument* is so sweeping in its scope that it seeks to undermine both metaphysical psychologism and the view that rules of correct reasoning have psychological reality. This argument of Frege's succeeded in locating one of the central difficulties in the way psychology was done during the time Frege was writing. The positivists expanded upon the variability argument, but by the time they adopted it, the view of psychology it presupposed had become anachronistic.[6]

The variability argument, Sober argues, presupposes an introspectionist psychology. But as such, it cuts more against introspectionism than against the psychological reality thesis. Sober's suggestion is that the replacement of introspectionism with a more objectivist methodology of inquiry removes theoretical objections to psychologism. At least, Frege's variability argument must be reexamined once the methodology of inquiry it presupposes is altered. Contrary to Sober, I will argue: (a) that Sober's formulation of the variability argument misrepresents what is crucial to Frege's position; (b) that Frege's variability argument was not directed against the psychological reality thesis; and (c) that there are versions of the psychological reality thesis that Frege might well have accepted.

Initially, it is important to clarify terminology. According to the psychological reality thesis, "the laws of logic and the maxims of epistemology are (among other things) the laws of cognition. This is the view that the rules of correct reasoning that logicians and epistemologists try to describe have *psychological reality*."[7] By "metaphysical psychologism" Sober means "the view that the laws of logic and the characterization of rationality that epistemology seeks to formulate are *about* human activity".[8] By "the subsistence argument" Sober means the argument Frege used to maintain that the laws of logic and the truths of arithmetic are independent of knowing subjects, i.e., "even if human psychology were different − even if there were no thinking creatures at all − 2 + 3 would still equal 5."[9] And by "the variability argument" Sober means just that argument Frege used to maintain that meanings are not mental entities, i.e., "if communication is to be possible, the speakers of a language must associate the same, or nearly the same, meanings with the terms they use. But the mental images that people associate with terms vary enormously from person to person. Images vary, but meanings cannot, so meanings are not mental images."[10]

Now I really don't know why Sober should think that the variability argument cuts against metaphysical psychologism. The laws of logic and the characterization of rationality that epistemology seeks to formulate may be *about* human activity even if meanings are third realm entities. Reasoning is a human activity. And if logic is a normative science, then the laws of logic are about how humans should reason, i.e., in accordance with these laws. But whether or not this normative thesis should be considered a variant of psychologism is another question. I am not sure whether Sober has considered the normative thesis or whether he would classify it as a form of metaphysical psychologism. But Susan Haack has considered the normative thesis and has classified it as psychologistic. In *Philosophy of Logics* Haack distinguishes between the theses:

  (i)   logic is descriptive of mental processes (it describes how we *do* or perhaps how we *must* think)
  (ii) logic is prescriptive of mental processes (it prescribes how we should think)
  (iii) logic has nothing to do with mental processes.[11]

Haack labels these positions "strong psychologism", "weak psychologism", and "anti-psychologism", respectively. And she goes on to say that Frege held (iii). But earlier we argued that part of Frege's anti-psychologism is the claim that the laws of logic are normative rather than descriptive of human reasoning. There we showed that Frege thought that psychologistic logicians cannot consistently appeal to logical laws as norms.[12] The dispute whether (ii) should be called "weak psychologism" or "anti-psychologism" is merely verbal and fruitless. But the dispute whether or not Frege held (ii) is not. Here I take it that Haack is simply mistaken in saying that Frege denied (ii). And if this is correct, then Frege's affirmation of (ii) suggests that he did not intend his variability argument to undermine all versions of what Sober calls "metaphysical psychologism".

Now the replacement of introspectionism with a suitably objectivist methodology of inquiry may make psychology acceptable as an empirical science. But Frege's anti-psychologism was not simply anti-introspectionism. A psychology based on behaviourism (or any other *empirical* methodology) would have been found just as objectionable. Nor should Frege's anti-psychologism be confused with anti-psychology-ism. Frege seems to have had no opposition to psychology (introspectionist or otherwise) as an empirical science. What he denied is that any empirical psychology could serve as the foundation for logic, regardless of its methodology of inquiry. It is true that Frege argued against the private language associated with the thesis that meanings are mental entities. But his primary concern in arguing against psychologism was to account for the presumed objectivity, universality, and incorrigibility of the laws of logic. To that extent, Frege would have opposed any account that renders the laws of logic knowable only *a posteriori*. Were the logical laws knowable only *a posteriori*, then their strict universality could never be asserted with certainty and they would always be subject to revision in the light of further empirical evidence. From the EP_1 perspective, they simply would not be considered objective knowledge.

Here I want to consider two questions raised by reflection on Sober's paper: (1) Does the variability argument undermine the psychological reality thesis?

and (2) What is the relation between the psychological reality thesis and the sorts of psychologism opposed by Frege?

The variability argument, as far as I can see, is primarily an argument about communication, and ultimately an argument about the possibility of objective knowledge. Simply put: communication must be possible if we are to have a common science. The variability argument concerns what must be necessary if communication is possible. Frege seems to have held what might metaphorically be called "the clothesline theory of communication". According to the clothesline theory, a necessary condition for communication is that the persons communicating grasp or apprehend the same object of meaning. The material objects, e.g., sound waves, ink blots, raised dots, etc. that are words are not themselves meanings, but the clothing, or "material garments", of meanings. In order to communicate, a person takes a meaning, dresses it up in its material garments, hooks it to the clothesline, and sends it over to the person with whom he wishes to communicate. That person takes the clothed meaning off the clothesline, undresses it, and apprehends the meaning. Exactly what the process of apprehension is like is, as noted earlier, unspecified. And the metaphor of the clothesline may be misleading in that it represents meanings as moving. But the reason why ideas cannot be meanings, according to Frege, is not simply that "mental images that people associate with terms vary enormously from person to person". For it is very possible, according to Frege, that the *senses* that people associate with terms vary from person to person. The reason why meanings cannot be mental entities is that mental entities are *private* to the individual consciousness that bears them. In Fregean vernacular, senses are apprehended, but ideas are had. And two people simply cannot have the same idea. Metaphorically, ideas never make it to the clothesline.

We've said that Frege thought that a necessary condition for communication is that the persons communicating apprehend the *same* object of meaning. Ideas are "essentially idiosyncratic" in that they are private. To that extent, they are separate objects. But we often use "same object" to refer to separate objects that are alike in all respects pertinent to the similarity we wish to note. Communication, for Frege, is a sort of pointing. Now I can point, e.g., at my tennis racket, or I can point at a tennis racket that is just like mine and indistinguishable from it at least to the extent that neither you nor I would be able to tell whether or not it is mine. In pointing at the racket I might say, "That is the same racket I use." And here I might mean: (1) that that racket just *is* the racket I use; or (2) that that racket is a racket that is *just like* the racket I use, i.e., that it is indistinguishable from my racket in make, color, weight, grip size, stringing, etc. Both uses of "same" as proper. But the sense in which Frege thought my ideas are not the same as yours is (1) and not necessarily (2). (To facilitate expression we will henceforth use "same token" to refer to "same" in the sense of (1), and "same type" to refer to "same" in the sense of (2).) In other words, the ideas I associate with terms *may* be the same type as the ideas you associate with those terms. But the ideas I associate with terms *cannot* be the same tokens as the ideas you associate with those terms. But whether or not the ideas you and I associate with terms are the same type is indeterminable. And this is just the other side of the doctrine that mental entities are private to the individual consciousness that bears them. To conclude from this doctrine that our ideas are not the same type would be like concluding that God does not exist from the fact that we cannot prove that he does.

The crux of the variability argument is not that ideas vary enormously from person to person, but that ideas are essentially private to the individual consciousness that bears them. But here the word "private" is importantly ambiguous. My ideas may be private to me in the sense of belonging essentially to me; i.e., if a is an idea of mine, then it is necessarily such. Therefore, if b is an idea of yours, necessarily b $\neq$ a. This sense of the privacy of ideas might be called "grammatical". Another sense of "private" is epistemological; i.e., if a is an idea of mine, then only I can be acquainted with it.[13] Now it is important to realize that grammatical privacy does not imply epistemological privacy. Ideas may be grammatically private, but epistemologically public — if, for example, the privileged access thesis is false. And if ideas were grammatically private but epistemologically public, then it would be possible to determine whether or not different individuals share the same type ideas.

It might be thought that Frege held that grammatical privacy alone disqualifies ideas as meanings. But it is difficult to see how the grammatical privacy of ideas would, alone, impede communication. If I had access to the contents of your consciousness, then I would be able to compare my ideas with yours and determine whether and to what extent they are similar. In that case, I could determine whether the idea I associate with "tennis racket" is the same type as the idea you associate with "tennis racket". And were I to determine that the idea I associate with "tennis racket" is not the same type as yours, I would be able to substitute an idea that was in order to understand you. Nor would grammatical privacy have any significant implications for the possibility of a common science. Suppose we were to debate the question whether a hundred-mark note is genuine, where we each meant the hundred-mark note in our own pockets and had grammatically private ideas associated with "genuine". Were we able to compare the hundred-mark notes and our ideas associated with "genuine", then the debate would not be so ludicrous.

Frege held that ideas need a bearer, and that no two men have the same idea.[14] And this suggests that he held ideas to be grammatically private. But Frege is explicit that it is impossible for us as men to compare another person's ideas with our own:[15]

... when the word 'red' does not state a property of things but is supposed to characterize sense-impressions belonging to my consciousness, it is only applicable within the sphere of my consciousness. For it is impossible to compare my sense-impression with that of someone else. For that it would be necessary to bring together in one consciousness a sense-impression, belonging to one consciousness, with a sense-impression belonging to another consciousness. Now even if it were possible to make an idea disappear

from one consciousness and, at the same time, to make an idea appear in another consciousness, the question whether it were the same idea in both would still remain un-
answerable.[16]

But if Frege held that ideas are private in the grammatical sense alone, then the
question whether it was the same idea in both consciousnesses *would* be answerable. Here we need not worry whether it is the same token or the same type idea
in question. Grammatical privacy entails that the ideas are distinct in virtue of
their being in different consciousnesses.

Now the psychological reality thesis is consistent with the variability argument, and not just because introspectionism has been rejected as the methodology of psychology. Rather, it is because the question whether or not we are
determined to reason in accordance with certain logical laws has nothing to do
with whether or not meanings are mental entities. When Sober says that "the
mental images people associate with terms vary enormously from person to
person", he seems to be saying that most people do not have the same type
ideas. And that people do not share the same type ideas implies that they do
not share the same token ideas. But that people do not share the same token
ideas does not imply that they do not share the same type ideas. And so long as
we hold ideas to be epistemologically private, whether or not people share the
same type ideas simply cannot be determined. Specifically, it is not determined
by different descriptions of mental images. Descriptions of mental images are
not themselves mental images.

Here we can round off the point. Sober seems to suppose that the psychological reality thesis would be true if everyone associated the same type ideas
with the terms of the language, and that introspection shows that everyone
does not associate the same type ideas with the terms of the language. Let's
suppose that he is right. Now Frege held that for communication to be possible,
it is necessary that it is possible for people to associate the same token meaning
with, e.g., "green". But if mental entities are private to the individual consciousness that bears them, then it is impossible that different people associate the
same token idea with "green". And this is significant. Given Frege's theory of
communication, the doctrine that meanings are mental entities entails a private
language, while the doctrine that meanings are third realm entities makes communication *possible*. Nevertheless, it is possible that, albeit indeterminable
whether, different people associate the same type ideas with "green". Now suppose that all the speakers of a language associate the same type ideas with the
terms of that language. We might even suppose that with the logical terms the
association is, in some sense, necessary. If this were the case, and it is impossible
to know that it's not, then the psychological reality thesis would, on Sober's
view, be true. But given Frege's theory of communication, the variability argument would still hold. We may all associate the same type idea with "green". But
communication demands that we all associate the same token idea with "green".
And that, so long as we hold that mental entities are private to the individual
consciousness that bears them, is impossible.

But was Frege even interested in undermining the psychological reality thesis? And what is the relation between the psychological reality thesis and the sorts of psychologism Frege opposed? These are the more important questions for our discussion. The psychological reality thesis claims that the valid rules of inference are psychological laws of cognition, i.e., that human beings are so constituted that it is psychologically necessary that they reason in accordance with these rules of inference. This is a thesis usually attributed to Kant. Sober, for example, writes:

> Kant reached the conclusion that rules of correct reason have psychological reality by returning again and again to the defense of a conditional: If an organism of a certain kind is to have experience, then that organism must use principle P.[17]

And Kant himself writes:

> Logic is a science of reason not only as to mere form but also as to matter; a science *a priori* of the necessary laws of thinking, not, however, in respect of particular objects but all objects generatim; it is a science, therefore, of the right use of the understanding and of reason as such ...[18]

But Kant also argued against the thesis that the laws of logic are empirical generalizations. And it is this latter thesis that Kant called "psychologism" (*Psychologismus*). For example, in what immediately follows the passage last cited, Kant continues:

> ... not subjectively, i.e. not according to empirical (psychological) principles of how the understanding thinks, but objectively, i.e. according to *a priori* principles of how it ought to think.[19]

More explicitly:

> Some logicians presuppose *psychological* principles in logic. But to bring such principles into logic is as absurd as taking morality from life. If we took the principles from psychology, i.e. from observations about our understanding, we would merely see *how* thinking occurs and *how* it *is* under manifold hindrances and conditions; this would therefore lead to the cognition of merely *contingent* laws. In logic, however, the question is not one of *contingent* but of necessary rules, not how we think, but how we ought to think. The rules of logic, therefore, must be taken not from the *contingent* but from the *necessary* use of the understanding, which one finds, without any psychology, in oneself. In logic we do not want to know how the understanding is and thinks, and how it hitherto has proceeded in thinking, but how it ought to proceed in thinking. Logic shall teach us the right use of the understanding, i.e. the one that agrees with itself.[20]

Now if Kant did hold the psychological reality thesis, then it would, at least, be interesting that he should also hold that logic is a normative science. If the laws of logic are psychologically necessary in the sense that humans cannot reason in any other way but in accordance with them, then what sense does it make to say that humans *ought* to reason in accordance with them? Insofar as this is concerned, when Kant says that logic is occupied with the universal and necessary laws of thinking in general,[21] he may well mean "universal and necessary laws of thinking" in a legislative sense. But regardless of whether or not Kant held a version of the psychological reality thesis, he should not for that reason alone be regarded as a psychologistic logician.[22]

I wish neither to affirm nor deny the most general statement of the psychological reality thesis, i.e., that in which the logical laws claimed to be psychologically necessary are unspecified. For it may be the case that there are logical laws psychologically necessary to human beings that are not identical with the laws of classical logic. If some of the laws of classical logic are not psychologically necessary to human beings, it does not follow that none of the laws of classical logic are psychologically necessary to human beings. And even if none of the laws of classical logic are psychologically necessary to human beings, it may still be the case that there are other more basic and heretofore unstated logical laws that are.

When stated in this weak form, it might be thought that the psychological reality thesis implies that some one (though perhaps not *this* one) system of logic is psychologically necessary to human beings. In other words, it might be thought that the psychological reality thesis implies that the psychologically necessary logical laws are unique. But even if this weakened version of the thesis does imply that the psychologically necessary logical laws are unique, it is not, in itself, inconsistent with the existence and use of deviant rules of inference. Psychological necessity may hold only at a very deep level of the logical structure. So the use of deviant inference rules consistent with a base logic that is psychologically necessary to human beings is consistent with the psychological reality thesis. Intuitionist and quantum logics differ from classical logic. But each of these systems may be consistent with some more basic system of logic that has psychological reality. And if the laws of this base logic are general enough, the use of any number of different "surface logics" may be consistent with this form of psychologism.

But why should this weakened version of the psychological reality thesis prohibit a plurality of base logics? Might not base logics have psychological reality and be psychologically necessary to *subsets* of human beings? Perhaps human beings need to be subclassified according to the logical laws psychologically necessary *to them*. The prevalent belief in the uniqueness of logic might well be a consequence of a philosophical tradition governed by white male intellectuals. Political laws might need amendment to protect against logical discrimination. Rights would be granted to all regardless of race, creed, color, or logic!

But when stated in its strong form in which the logical laws claimed to be psychologically necessary are identified as just those laws of classical logic, exactly what is meant by "psychologically necessary" will need explication. For whatever else may be the case, it is clear that human beings *do* reason according to inference forms that deviate from the valid forms of classical logic. Such "deviations" abound, the affirmation of the consequent, perhaps, being the most common. Indeed, this "fallacy" has even found some degree of sanction in the methodology of confirmation. Such deviations may, of course, be labelled "mistakes". But if mistakes are possible, then in what sense are the laws of classical logic claimed to be psychologically necessary? Kant seems to have recognized this problem:

> How error in the formal meaning of the word, however, is possible, that is, how a form of thinking contrary to the understanding is possible, that is difficult to understand; as indeed how any force should deviate from its own essential laws cannot be comprehended at all.[23]

One might rather think that if the laws of classical logic were truly psychologically necessary, then there would be no mistakes. There would be no need to *teach* classical logic, and there would be no sense in the notion of logic as a normative science. But even if mistakes are allowed, there still remains the difficulty of determining if and when inferences reflect mistakes or deviant but psychologically real logical laws. Mistakes may be possible, but that alone will not help us determine who's making them!

Nevertheless, it has been suggested that the psychological reality thesis admits of proof. The suggested "proof" is the construction of a model that postulates certain logical laws as psychologically necessary and which is able to account for all pertinent human behaviour. But the construction of such a model is an entirely different question from that of its truth. The point is mundane. There may be two different and incompatible models which each account for all the relevant data. This simply points to the underdetermination of theories by evidence. Obviously, the two theories cannot both be true — not, unless we are to accept a radically deviant logic! So the mere construction of such a model does not serve as its proof (though it may pose a powerful psychological argument!). Moreover, the failure to construct such a model does not imply that such a model *cannot* be constructed — not, unless there is some other reason to think that such a model cannot, in principle, be constructed. So the failure to find such a model does not imply that such a model does not exist, and hence does not imply that the psychological reality thesis is false.

But what is curious about this psychological reality thesis is that the burden of the traditional question of the uniqueness of the logical laws, a question with which Frege was deeply concerned, is here reversed. According to the strong version of the psychological reality thesis, the logical laws claimed to be psychologically real are also claimed to be unique. They are just the laws of classical logic. And if this is psychologism, then the use of a non-classical logic would be a reason to think psychologism wrong. But Frege's arguments claim just the opposite. According to Frege, psychologism results in a vindication of inference forms that differ from those of classical logic. And this is one reason to oppose psychologism. Frege's anti-psychologism argued that such deviant inference forms must be rejected as irrational.[24] So on the Fregean view, it is the anti-psychologist, and not the psychologistic logician, who claims uniqueness for the laws of logic. So unless Frege's arguments are to be rejected as *non sequiturs*, we must interpret them as directed against a different form of psychologism.

Frege regarded the laws of logic as laws of thought.[25] But he distinguished laws of thought from psychological laws of thinking. Thoughts, for Frege, were third realm entities, senses of sentences and bearers of truth. But thinking, for Frege, was a mental phenomenon. So as to avoid the danger of "mixing different things up", Frege preferred to call the logical laws "laws of truth". As we've suggested earlier, Frege understood the laws of truth to be laws concerning what is, and not just what ought to be:

> The word 'law' is used in two senses. When we speak of laws of morals or the state we mean regulations which ought to be obeyed but with which actual happenings are not always in conformity. Laws of nature are the generalization of natural occurrences with which the occurrences are always in accordance. It is rather in this sense that I speak of laws of truth. This is, to be sure, not a matter of what happens so much as of what is. Rules for asserting, thinking, judging, inferring, follow from the laws of truth.[26]

So Frege thought the laws of thought to be both descriptive and normative. But Frege explicitly denies that logic is descriptive of the mental processes of thinking and the psychological laws in accordance with which thinking takes place:

> Perhaps the expression 'law of thought' is interpreted by analogy with 'law of nature' and the generalization of thinking as a mental occurrence is meant by it. A law of thought in this sense would be a psychological law. And so one might come to believe that logic deals with the mental process of thinking and the psychological laws in accordance with which it takes place. This would be a misunderstanding of the task of logic, for truth has not been given the place which is its due here.[27]

Nevertheless, the strong version of the psychological reality thesis is not inconsistent with Frege's anti-psychologism, nor does Frege deny the possibility of its truth. The laws of thinking may well be co-extensive with the laws of logic. But in order to know that, we must first be able to determine, on grounds independent of empirical psychology, exactly what the laws of logic are:

> The assertion both of what is false and of what is true takes place in accordance with psychological laws. A derivation from these and an explanation of a mental process that terminates in an assertion can never take the place of a proof of what is asserted. Could not logical laws also have played a part in this mental process? I do not want to dispute this, but when it is a question of truth possibility is not enough. For it is also possible that something not logical played a part in the process and deflected it from the truth. We can only decide this after we have discerned the laws of truth; but then we will probably be able to do without the derivation and explanation of the mental process if it is important to us to decide whether the assertion in which the process terminates is justified.[28]

The assertion of both what is false and what is true takes place in accordance with psychological laws. But it should not be thought that Frege opposed psychologism because he feared it might result in the assertion of what is false. For the assertion of what is false might also take place in accordance with logical laws. Logical laws cannot guarantee the truth of what is asserted in accordance with them (how simple life would be!). The task of logic is to set up laws according to which a judgment is justified by others, irrespective of whether these are themselves true.[29] But following the laws of logic can guarantee the truth of a judgment only insofar as our original grounds for making it, reside in judgments that are true.[30] So the logical laws guarantee the truth of the conclusion of a valid argument, *provided the truth of its premises*. Logical laws *preserve* truth, they do not insure it.

But what is interesting in the above passage is that Frege does not deny that logical laws may play a part in the mental process of inference. Going one step further, logical laws and only logical laws could play a part, could play the only part, in all processes of mental inference. In this case, the laws of logic would be identical (or at least the same type) with the laws of thinking, and the strong version of the psychological reality thesis would be true. But what Frege denies is that this question could be decided prior to the determination, on grounds independent of psychology, of the laws of logic. Whether or not something non-logical has played a part in the mental process and deflected it from its logical course can be decided only after we have discerned the laws of truth. In other words, it is necessary to know which laws are logical in order to know which are not. So while the strong version of the psychological reality thesis is not inconsistent with Frege's anti-psychologism (provided it can be amended in some way to account for mistakes), it can be known to be true only *a posteriori*.

Of course, the strong version of the psychological reality thesis might be true without the laws of logic being, in Frege's sense, objective. For the psychological reality thesis does not, in itself, imply the existence of a third realm — indeed, it is usually proposed to explain how we can get by without one. But suppose the psychological reality thesis is true but the third realm does not exist. Then, if arithmetic were reducible to logic (as Frege thought it was), the subsistence argument would not work. So, far from cutting against the psychological reality thesis, the variability argument is needed to explain how the subsistence argument could be true.

Nevertheless, it might be thought that, ignoring ontological considerations, the laws of logic referred to in the strong version of the psychological reality thesis *might as well be objective*. While the laws of logic may be ontologically dependent upon the existence of human beings, they are not ontologically dependent upon the existence of any particular human being. This, of course, is to conflate objectivity with universality. The laws of logic may be objective (ontologically independent of the human mind) without thereby being universal (true for all human beings). And they may, of course, be universal without thereby being objective. And isn't it really the universality of the logical laws with which Frege is really concerned?

Frege was undoubtedly concerned with the universality of logic and arithmetic. He would have found little solace in the claim that $2 + 3 = 5$ is objective but not universal. Or are we really to suppose that the point of the subsistence argument concerns what would be the case if humans never existed? If nobody existed, nobody would much care what $2 + 3$ equals! Truth may be eternal, but there must be minds to apprehend it temporally if it is to be meaningful. The sort of subjectivity Frege really opposed is that which would render the truth of a thought relative to its thinker – the sort of subjectivity in which the truth of $2 + 3 = 5$ would be seriously challenged by anyone who thought $2 + 3 = 6$. It is this sort of subjectivity that obliterates standards for judgment. And it is the obliteration of objective standards for judgment that endangers the possibility of a common and critical science. But this is just the sort of subjectivity denied by the strong version of the psychological reality thesis. So insofar as the psychological reality thesis maintains that the laws of logic are universal, it is completely consistent with Frege's anti-psychologism – regardless of whether or not it postulates a third realm.

Or is it?

NOTES AND REFERENCES

1. Rorty, Richard; *Philosophy and the Mirror of Nature*; Princeton University Press (Princeton, 1979) p. 218.

2. *Ibid.*

3. *Op. cit.*; Sober; "Psychologism".

4. *Op. cit.*; Brentano; *Psychology from an Empirical Standpoint*; pp. 3-19.

5. *Op. cit.*; Sober; "Psychologism".

6. *Ibid.*

7. *Ibid.*

8. *Ibid.*

9. *Ibid.*

10. *Ibid.*

11. *Op. cit.*; Haack; *Philosophy of Logics*; pp. 238-242.

12. See our discussion of Frege's logical anti-psychologism, Chapter 3.

13. I owe this distinction to Charles D. Parsons.

14. *Op. cit.*; Frege; "The Thought: A Logical Inquiry"; pp. 27-28.

15. *Ibid.*; p. 27.

16. *Ibid.*

17. *Op. cit.*; Sober.

18. Kant, Immanuel; *Logik*; ed. by Gottlob Benjamin Jasche; Friedrich Nicolovius (Konigsberg, 1800). Translated by Robert Hartman and Wolfgang Schwarz as *Kant's Logic*; Bobbs-Merrill (New York, 1974) p. 18.

19. *Ibid.*

20. *Ibid.*; p. 16.

21. *Ibid.*; p. 17.

22 Buchner, in *A Study of Kant's Psychology*, supports this view:
Kant is, also, as stringent in his demand that there shall be a wide gap between logic and psychology. Indeed, on the former disparateness of psychologic 'opinion' and 'metaphysical' science rose the whole structure of Criticism itself; while the divergence of logic from psychology provided the foundations of that edifice on the former science. Having once determined what the 'sure' science of Criticism required, Kant looked about for some corner stone which should have the inherent potency of shaping the structure, and not merely the kindliness of a propadeutic. Accordingly, this was to be had in the logic of Aristotle which 'has not had to retrace a single step; so that to all appearance, it may be considered as completed and perfect.' Logic, in itself, deals with the 'necessary rules' of the understanding. It answers the question, not how we *do* think, but how we *must* think. General logic is either 'pure or applied,' 'analytic or dialectic,' 'elementary logic or an organon' of a particular science. In a passage recommending certain rules to logicians there is expressed the specific difference between logic and psychology: "1. As general logic it takes no account of the contents of the knowledge of the understanding nor of the difference of its objects. It treats of nothing but the mere form of thought. 2. As pure logic it has nothing to do with empiric principles and borrows nothing from psychology (as some have imagined, i.e., of the influence of the senses, the play of imagination, the laws of memory, the force of habit, the inclinations, and therefore, the sources of prejudice also), because psychology has no influence whatever on the canon of understanding. It proceeds by way of demonstration and everything in it must be completely *a priori*." The transformation of this general logic into absolute universality gave the 'Transcendental Logic' whose explication resulted in the medley of philosophical divisions which the *Critique of Pure Reason* really represents.
(See: Buchner, Edward Franklin; *A Study of Kant's Psychology*; in *The Psychological Review*, No. 4, January, 1897; The Macmillan Company (New York, 1897; pp. 25-26.) Buchner, incidentally, goes on to give a psychologistic critique of Kant's position.

23. *Op. cit.*; Kant; *Kant's Logic*; p. 59.

24. *Op. cit.*; Frege; *The Basic Laws of Arithmetic*; p. 14.

25. *Op. cit.*; Frege; "The Thought: A Logical Inquiry"; p. 17.

26. *Ibid.*

27. *Ibid.*

28. *Ibid.*; pp. 17-18.

29. *Op. cit.*; Frege; *Gottlob Frege, Posthumous Writings*; p. 175.

30. *Ibid.*

6. TRUTH, RECOGNITION, AND COGNITIVE AUTHORITY

Throughout our discussion we have stressed the epistemological significance of the psychologism/anti-psychologism debate. While this debate may ultimately reduce to an ontological question concerning the existence of *a priori* truths, the significance of that question concerns the possibility of objective knowledge in the EP_1 sense. This concern for objective knowledge is explicit in Frege's work, and it might be thought that the point is obvious and wholly uncontroversial. But this, unfortunately, is not the case. There is a myth common among philosophers that Frege was not concerned with epistemological issues. This myth is pernicious in that it impedes our recognition of the scope of Frege's thought and, ultimately, of the target of his anti-psychologism. Nevertheless, the myth is widespread and has several sources. In what follows we will explore these sources in an attempt to explode this myth.

One source of the myth is, undoubtedly, the fact that Frege never articulated a detailed epistemology. To that extent, very little is known about his epistemological views. In general outlook, he seems to have been a Kantian with parochial quibbles.[1] He accepted Kant's epistemological divisions, but offered what he intended to be a clarification. And he believed in the possibility of *a priori* synthetic knowledge, but thought Kant wrong in his classification of arithmetic as such. Late in his life, frustration with Russell's Paradox led Frege to abandon the view that arithmetic does not need to appeal to intuition and to attempt a reduction of arithmetic to geometry.[2] But here Frege stressed the difference between sense perception and the geometrical source of knowledge, characterizing the latter as outside the domain of psychology and involving an *a priori* mode of cognition that does not have to flow from purely logical principles.[3] Russell's Paradox forced Frege to acknowledge that, contrary to appearances, the logical source of knowledge is not infallible and that even logicians have to struggle against language.[4] But to the extent to which there are geometrical axioms and these axioms are derived from the geometrical source of knowledge, the geometrical source of knowledge, unlike sense perception and the logical source of knowledge, was thought to provide objective certainty:

> The *axioms* are truths as are the theorems, but they are truths for which no proof is needed. It follows from this that there are no false axioms, and that we cannot accept a thought as an axiom if we are in doubt of its truth; for it is either false and hence not an axiom, or it *is* true but stands in need of proof and hence is not an axiom.[5]

Axioms, Frege held, are relative to systems. It is possible for a truth to be an axiom in one system and not in another.[6] But this, we should hasten to add, does not mean that Frege held it possible for a thought to be true in one system and not in another. Truth, for Frege, was absolute. Insofar as this is concerned, Frege regarded the choice between Euclidean and non-Euclidean geometry as a choice between truth and untruth, and seems to have considered non-Euclidean geometry an historical curiosity.[7]

Nevertheless, what we know of Frege's epistemology is admittedly sketchy and only serves to underscore the kernel of truth that engenders the myth: Frege did not consider it his task to articulate a detailed epistemology. But the fact that Frege never articulated a detailed epistemology does not imply that he was not *motivated* by epistemological considerations. Or are we to suppose that a person cannot be motivated by sexual considerations unless he has articulated a detailed theory of sex? Geach, however, in discussing Frege's motivations for his descriptivist theory of proper names, writes:

> Frege's reasons for adopting the disguised-description theory of proper names cannot have been, as Russell's reasons were, epistemological; for it is certain that he wholly rejected an epistemological approach to philosophical problems. (His life-long attitude was: First settle what is known, and how these known truths are to be analysed and articulated – and only then can you profitably begin to discuss what makes these truths dawn upon a human being; if you try to *start* with a theory of knowledge, you will get nowhere.)[8]

But contrary to Geach, I know of no place in the Fregean corpus where Frege rejects an epistemological approach to philosophical problems. What Frege eschews is a *psychological* approach to philosophical problems, i.e., "the predominance in philosophy of psychological methods of argument."[9] Indeed, Frege hoped that the results of *The Foundations of Arithmetic* might lead some empiricist to "reexamine afresh the principles of his theory of knowledge."[10] It is only if we construe epistemology as concerned solely with questions of discovery (or the psychological genesis of knowledge) that we can justifiably say that Frege was unconcerned with epistemology. Apropos to this, Dummett writes:

> ... the general contention that Frege wanted to extrude everything epistemological from logic or from the theory of meaning is quite misconceived: he wanted to extrude everything psychological; but that was for him a quite different matter.[11]

Now Geach goes on to say that he does not know how Frege's adoption of the disguised description theory is to be explained. Of course, if we ignore epistemological considerations! Frege argued that if proper names did not have senses then it would be difficult to see how true identity statements could differ in cognitive value. But if the introduction of senses is to provide an explanation, then it is necessary that the sense of an expression uniquely determines the referent of that expression. And if the sense of an expression uniquely determines the referent of that expression, then it is difficult to see how such a sense could fail to be identical with the sense of *some* definite description. But the point to be made is that sense, for Frege, is a cognitive notion. Dummett, incidentally, supports this view:

> ... the distinction between sense and reference is introduced precisely in order to explain how certain sentences can have a cognitive value (can be informative), and we can find no place for the notion of sense, as distinct from that of reference, save as embodying the manner common to speakers of a language in which they apprehend the semantic roles of the expressions of the language. Analyticity and apriority are, for Frege, cognitive notions also: the status of a sentence, as analytic, synthetic a priori or a posteriori, relates to the means that exist whereby the sentence may be known to be true (though not to the means whereby we happen, in practice, to know that it is true, if we know this at all). To this extent, the sense of a sentence determines its status, independently of the way the world is: a sentence, if analytically true, or true a priori, is so of necessity, in virtue of its sense alone.[12]

That Dummett should stress the cognitive character of the notion of sense is, at least, ironic. For a second source of the myth that Frege was not concerned with epistemology is the view that Frege's work replaced epistemology with logic as the primary philosophical discipline. And this is a view most often expressed by Dummett:

> From the time of Descartes until very recently the first question for philosophy was what we can know and how we can justify our claim to this knowledge, and the fundamental philosophical problem was how far scepticism can be refuted and how far it must be admitted. Frege was the first philosopher after Descartes totally to reject this perspective, and in this respect he looked beyond Descartes to Aristotle and the Scholastics. For Frege, as for them, logic was the beginning of philosophy; if we do not get logic right, we shall get nothing else right. Epistemology, on the other hand, is not prior to any other branch of philosophy; we can get on with philosophy of mathematics, philosophy of science, metaphysics, or whatever interests us without first having undertaken any epistemological inquiry at all. It is this shift in perspective, more than anything else, which constitutes the principle contrast between contemporary philosophy and its forebears, and from this point of view Frege was the first modern philosopher.[13]

Initially, we must acknowledge that the view that Frege replaced epistemology with logic as the fundamental philosophical discipline does not, in itself, imply that Frege had no interest in epistemological issues. Nevertheless, I find this often repeated theme of Dummett's curious. Sluga, for example, in challenging Dummett's view that Frege was of the opinion "that logic could be approached independently of any prior philosophical substructure", writes:

> It is of course true that Descartes had spoken contemptuously of logic and had considered his own epistemological considerations a separate issue, and it is also true that for the empiricists epistemological problems were problems of perception and of the nature of mental processes rather than purely logical problems, but it is quite wrong to find a general conflict between logical and epistemological considerations. Leibniz, as has been said, had criticized the Cartesian separation of the two. And later on Kant saw epistemology and logic as intertwined. Frege's interest in logic shows not a lack of concern

with epistemology but rather a particular anti-empiricist (or anti-naturalistic) epistemological viewpoint.[14]

For Sluga, Frege is decidedly an epistemological logician. But even were
Dummett using "epistemology" to refer to theories of psychological genesis,
which does not seem the case, we must recognize that he uses "logic" and
"philosophy of logic" to refer to theories of meaning.[15] And this is significant.
Sluga not withstanding, even so "ancient" and empiricist a philosopher as Locke,
despite his order of exposition, recognized the dependence of epistemology on
the theory of meaning:

> Having thus given an account of the original, sorts, and extent of our *Ideas*, with several
> other Considerations, about these (I know not whether I may say) Instruments, or
> Materials, of our Knowledge, the method I at first proposed to my self, would now
> require, that I should immediately proceed to shew, what use the Understanding makes
> of them, and what Knowledge we have by them. This was that, which, in the first general
> view I had of this Subject, was all that I thought I should have to do: but upon a nearer
> approach, I find, that there is so close a connexion between *Ideas* and Words; and our
> abstract *Ideas*, and general Words, have so constant a relation one to another, that it is
> impossible to speak clearly and distinctly of our Knowledge, which all consists in Propo-
> sitions, without considering, first, the Nature, Use, and Signification of Language...[16]

Nor was Locke the only empiricist after Descartes and prior to Frege to recognize the significance of theory of meaning for epistemology. John Stuart Mill
seems to have held that epistemology (the science of Belief) is dependent upon
logic (the science of Proof, or Evidence) at least to the extent to which justified
belief is dependent on proof:

> The object of logic ... is to ascertain how we come by that portion of our knowledge
> (much the greatest portion) which is not intuitive: and by what criterion we can, in
> matters not self-evident, distinguish between things proved and things not proved,
> between what is worthy and what is unworthy of belief.[17]

But if Mill thought epistemology dependent on logic, he also thought logic dependent on an analysis of language. Mill underscored this point in the first chapter of *A System of Logic*, a chapter entitled "Of the Necessity of Commencing
with an Analysis of Language". Here Mill's remarks provide a challenge to
Dummett's historical claim. Far from claiming any novelty for his approach, Mill
wrote that it is the established practice of writers on logic to commence their
treatises with an analysis of language, and that the practice is recommended by
considerations "far too obvious to require a formal justification".[18] Nevertheless, Mill did offer an explanation for his approach. And it is not, perhaps, too
surprising that Mill's reasons for beginning with the theory of meaning are in
accord with those Dummett attributes to Frege:

> Logic is a portion of the Art of thinking: Language is evidently, and by the admission

of all philosophers, one of the principal instruments or helps of thought; and any imperfection in the instrument, or in the mode of employing it, is confessedly liable, still more than in almost any other art, to confuse and impede the process, and destroy all ground of confidence in the result. For the mind not previously versed in the meaning and right use of the various kinds of words, to attempt the study of methods of philosophizing, would be as if some one should attempt to become an astronomical observer, having never learned to adjust the focal distance of his optical instruments so as to see distinctly.[19]

Simply put: Mill thought that if we do not get logic right, then we will get nothing else right; and if we do not get theory of meaning right, then we will not get logic right.

So the tradition that epistemology is prior to logic is perhaps not as unanimous as Dummett suggests. Nevertheless, it is certainly a very influential strand in modern philosophy, and we have yet to show that Frege does not reject it. Now Dummett is certainly right that as a result of Frege's work philosophers began to focus more sharply on logic, and epistemological problems, as traditionally conceived, became of secondary interest. But that Frege did not reject this tradition is really quite obvious. For Frege held that in order to get logic right, we must *first* recognize that the results of empirical psychology can contribute nothing to the science of logic. Getting the epistemology of logic right is thus important for getting logic right. And Frege held that so long as psychologistic logicians attempt to abstract the laws of logic from empirical observations, they run the risk of getting logic wrong. Now getting the epistemology of logic right does not imply that one must preface his logical theory with a detailed and articulated theory of knowledge. But it does mean that one must first resolve questions concerning the source and ultimate justification of the logical laws. For Frege, anti-psychologism was just such a resolution: the laws of logic neither have their source in nor can be justified by sense impressions.

But why this reference to *sources* of knowledge? It is often said that Frege had little concern for generative epistemology. Such theories, Frege thought, are irrelevant in that they contribute nothing toward answering questions concerning the justification of cognitive claims. Insofar as Frege considered such theories psychological, this disinterest was simply part and parcel of his epistemological anti-psychologism. But here we must be careful — *insofar as Frege considered such theories psychological*. But is there any reason to think that Frege considered all generative epistemologies psychological? Or that we should? Frege construed psychology as dealing with the affections of the soul. But here, his primary focus was on sense impressions and the mental images abstracted from sense impressions. Radical empiricism insists that sense perception is the *only* source of human knowledge. And it was *this* generative epistemology that Frege considered psychologistic. But sense impressions, according to Frege, are not the only source of knowledge. So there seems to be no reason to think that he considered all generative epistemologies psychologistic. Indeed, Frege was explicit that the logical and geometrical *sources* of knowledge lay outside the domain of psychology. If today we have come to consider such sources psychological, it is only because we have broadened our conception of psychology.

Epistemologies that focus on *a priori* modes of cognition may not be psychologistic. But it would be too naive to think that they are not generative. Epistemology has always dealt with the justification of cognitive claims. But unless justification is to regress infinitely, it must ultimately appeal to a source of knowledge. And here, the cutting edge of justification is the reliability of the source. Frege held that restricting the sources of knowledge to psychology made objective certainty impossible. But this is because he held the sense impressions of psychology unreliable as a measure of external reality. It is not for naught that in discussing sense perception as a source of knowledge, Frege focused on "sense illusions".[20] Perhaps a more accurate statement of Frege's significance in the history of philosophy is that he replaced psychology with logic as the primary focus of epistemology. This he did by conceiving of justification as logical proof, and by insisting that such proof requires *a priori* truths – truths he originally thought derived from the logical source of knowledge.

But if this is correct, then Dummett's contrast between the Cartesian and Fregean approaches to philosophy seems less than convincing. Once we recognize questions concerning the epistemic status of statements as a proper concern of epistemology, Frege's epistemological motivations become clear. One of the major themes of *The Foundations of Arithmetic* is that arithmetical truths are analytic, and hence knowable *a priori*. But the impetus toward logicism was, at base, an attempt to insure the certainty of arithmetic. As Susan Haack writes:

> It is sometimes said that the laws of logic are certain, and so, unalterable, because they are *self-evident*. A view of this kind apparently underlay Frege's logicism; for the logicist programme, to express the axioms of arithmetic in purely logical terms, and to derive them from purely logical truths, draws its epistemological importance from the idea that, in this way, the certainty of logic will be transmitted to arithmetic.[21]

That Frege held the laws of logic to be self-evident is clear from the passage Haack cites:

> I have never disguised from myself its (e.g., the axiom of abstraction's) lack of self-evidence that belongs to the other axioms and that must properly be demanded of a logical law.[22]

But Haack is surprised by this appeal to self-evidence:

> This is puzzling, in a way: for self-evidence is presumably a psychological property, and elsewhere Frege enthusiastically combats psychologism.[23]

Contrary to Haack, this appeal to self-evidence in no way compromises Frege's anti-psychologism. For the self-evidence Frege appeals to has nothing to do with the sense perceptions of empirical psychology, but was thought to be derived solely from the logical source of knowledge. To that extent, Frege considered self-evidence an objective rather than a psychological property, though such a construal of self-evidence would not withstand criticism today. But we should not think that this attempt to insure the certainty of arithmetic was peculiar to the logicist programme. As we've already noted, the discovery of Russell's Paradox did not lead Frege to question the certainty of arithmetic, but to an attempt to ground it in the geometrical source of knowledge.

But if Frege's life-long task was to insure the certainty of arithmetic, then his philosophy seems to fall well within the bounds of the Cartesian tradition. At least, it has definite implications for the question how far scepticism can be refuted and how far it must be admitted. Insofar as this is concerned, Haack seems to align Frege with the Cartesian justificationist tradition:

> One line of argument in favour of (1) points to the failure of 'justificationist' pro-
> grammes – e.g. Descartes', Frege's, or Carnap's attempt to provide certain of our beliefs
> with respectively, an indubitable, or self-evident, or epistemologically prior, founda-
> tion.[24]

And Haack is not alone in this conception. Sluga, for example, writes:

> Throughout his writings Frege seems much more concerned with epistemological ques-
> tions concerning the nature and status of mathematical truth (than with ontological
> questions).[25]

And Gregory Currie has written that Frege's objectivism, a tendency we've linked with anti-psychologism, began as an epistemological theory. Frege's arguments for the objectivity of numbers, according to Currie, are arguments about the sort of knowledge we can have of these entities.[26] Agreeing with Sluga, Currie writes:

> We should remember that Frege's most significant philosophical concerns were epistemo-
> logical rather than ontological. His logicist programme was, after all, an attempt to save
> our mathematical knowledge from sceptical doubt, and his antipsychologism was de-
> signed to avoid relativism and subjectivism; two doctrines which, as he saw it, threatened
> knowledge as much as did outright scepticism.[27]

Now such passages can be recited at length, but I think the point has been made. The point is that Dummett's characterization of Frege's significance in the history of philosophy needs qualification. Contrary to Dummett, Frege's programme might better be seen as an attempt to salvage the quest for certainty from its empiricist spoilers. Here, what distinguishes the Fregean and Cartesian programmes is not the goal of certainty, but the extent to which it is claimed and the means thought necessary to achieve it. Here, it was Frege's insight that the success of logicism required the construction of a *Begriffsschrift*. For if logicism is really to save arithmetical knowledge from sceptical doubt, then the certainty of logical laws is not enough. There must also be some way to insure that there are no gaps or oversights in the derivation of arithmetical truths from the logical laws. What is, perhaps, most impressive about Frege's justificationist programme is that he not only required a *Begriffsschrift*, he actually produced one. But we should not lose sight of the forest for the trees. Ultimately, it was Frege's logical anti-psychologism which gave the *Begriffsschrift* its justificationist bite. The rigorous derivation of arithmetic from logic might show that arithmetic has as solid a foundation as logic. But this would only reduce the question of the certainty of arithmetical truths to that of the logical laws. But here, logical anti-psychologism would guarantee that the question would not reiterate since it maintained that the logical laws are true and unique, certain in virtue of their assumed self-evidence.

A final source of the myth that Frege was not concerned with epistemological issues is that he framed his anti-psychologism in terms of "laws" and "truths" rather than "beliefs". And this is fundamental to anti-psychologism: being true is distinct from being believed to be true. Now Frege held truths to be thoughts that are true, and laws, in the logical sense, to be truths that are self-evident and, hence, certain. But what, exactly, does it mean to be true?

In "The Thought: A Logical Inquiry?" Frege discussed the nature of truth and concluded that every attempt to define "truth" must fail:

> For in a definition certain characteristics would have to be stated. And in application to any particular case the question would always arise whether it were true that the characteristics were present. So one goes round in a circle. Consequently, it is probable that the content of the word 'true' is unique and indefinable.[28]

But this does not prevent Frege from assuming the absolute character of truth. Now when we say of something that it is absolute, we may mean a number of different, albeit related, things. We may mean: (1) that the thing does not, in itself, stand in relation to anything else; or (2) that the thing has reached its extreme limit, that it is complete and that there is no further improvement or advance possible; or (3) that the thing is without qualifications or conditions.[29] Frege's notion of truth is absolutist in each of these senses. For Frege, (1), (2) and (3) are, as it were, true of truth.

Fregean semantics is notorious for its characterization of truth values as the referents of meaningful indicative sentences. And to say that truth values are the referents of such sentences is to say that they are objects. This, needless to add, is usually regarded as one of the weakest and most unintuitive features of Frege's theory of meaning. Nevertheless, the characterization of the True and the False as objects is not simply the consequence of a consistent semantics. Rather, it is part and parcel of Frege's absolutist conception of truth. Here, it is significant that Frege rejects the correspondence theory of truth on the grounds that correspondence is a relation. That truth is a correspondence:

... is contradicted, however, by the use of the word 'true', which is not a relation-word and contains no reference to anything else to which something must correspond. If I do not know that a picture is meant to represent Cologne Cathedral then I do not know with what to compare the picture to decide on its truth. A correspondence, moreover, can only be perfect if the corresponding things coincide and are, therefore, not distinct things at all. It is said to be possible to establish the authenticity of a banknote by comparing it stereoscopically with an authentic one. But it would be ridiculous to try to compare a gold piece with a twenty-mark note stereoscopically. It would only be possible to compare an idea with a thing if the thing were an idea too. And then, if the first did correspond perfectly with the second, they would coincide. But this is not at all what is wanted when truth is defined as correspondence of an idea with something real. For it is absolutely essential that the reality be distinct from the idea. But then there can be no complete correspondence, no complete truth. So nothing at all would be true; for what is only half true is untrue. Truth cannot tolerate a more or less.[30]

To say that truth is not a relation implies that it is absolute in the sense of (1). And to say that truth cannot tolerate a more or less is to say that it is absolute in the senses of (2) and (3). It is to say that what is true is complete and without qualifications in its truth.

The doctrine that truth is absolute also implies that it is independent of the judging subject. If truth were dependent on the judging subject, then truth would be a relation after all. Instead of saying that a statement is true, we could only say that it is true for so-and-so. Moreover, the doctrine that truth is absolute implies that it is eternal and immutable. For otherwise, truth would once again be a relation. Truth then would be relative to time, and instead of saying that a statement is true, we could only say that it is true at T_1, or true at T_2. What is true today might then be false tomorrow, or false yesterday. It is sometimes said that Aristotle partly exempted future contingents from the law of the excluded middle by holding that it is not (now) either true or false that there will be a naval battle tomorrow, but that it is (now) true that either there will be a naval battle tomorrow or not. But Frege held that if a statement is true then it is so timelessly, regardless of our ability to recognize its truth. A tensed sentence uttered at different times may express different thoughts. But reference to time is included in the thought. So the fact that a *sentence* can be now true, now false in no way challenges the timelessness of truth.

It follows that if truth is eternal and immutable, then it must be an object of the third realm. For the objects of the first and second realms are decidedly temporal and changing. And since thoughts are the bearers of truth, thoughts too must be objects of the third realm. Earlier we showed that Frege based the third realm status of thoughts on the possibility of communication:

If the content of the sentence 2 + 3 = 5 is exactly the same, in the strictest sense, for all those who recognize it to be true, this means that it is not a product of the mind of this person and a product of the mind of that person, but that it is grasped and recognized as true by both equally.[31]

But this argument always seemed problematic. Ignoring problems with Frege's theory of communication, it seems to presuppose: (a) that mental entities are private to the individual consciousness that bears them; and (b) that products of the mind are, for that reason, mental entities — for why else would the fact that a thought is the product of a person's mind imply that it cannot be grasped by others? Now I do not wish to quarrel with (a). But (b) seems more troublesome. The fact that some x is a *product* of some mind does not imply that that x is, itself, mental — no more than the fact that some x is a product of some human implies that it is human. Here we can see that what really argues for the existence of the third realm is the doctrine that truth is absolute. The variability argument at best implies the existence of a realm of immaterial and non-mental objects. It does not imply that those objects are not the products of the human mind. But if the objects of the third realm were products of the human mind, then they would not be eternal. And if thoughts are both bearers of truth value and objects of *this* third realm, there would no longer be any reason to think that truth is absolute.

Here it would be tempting to characterize psychologism as the denial that truth is absolute. But this must be avoided. As we've already noted, the existence of a Fregean third realm is fully consistent with psychologism. But here we can go one step further. The psychologistic logician need not even deny that third realm objects can be apprehended by humans without compromising their objectivity. It is sufficient for psychologism to claim that the truth value of apprehended thoughts cannot be *recognized* via any route other than sense perception. In other words, the psychologistic logician need only deny the existence of *a priori* modes of cognition.[32] Here we have arrived at the crux of the issue. But what are the connections between absolute truth, objective certainty, and a prioricity?

Initially, we must stress that Frege did not restrict his doctrine that truth is absolute to any particular subset of the set of truths. According to Frege, all truths are absolute, be they truths of logic or truths of biology. But if all truths are absolute, then no truth is uncertain. For to say that a truth is uncertain is to say that it is subject to revision. And this would be to qualify truth after all. But this simply means that certainty is not a property of truths. Now we often do say that some truths are subject to revision, and that others are not. But here "truth" is eliptical for "belief". What we mean is that our *belief* that a thought is true may or may not be subject to revision.

Now when Frege says that "in apprehending a scientific truth we pass, as a rule, through various degrees of certitude,"[33] the certitude of which he speaks seems to apply to our apprehension of the truth rather than to the truth itself. But even this is misleading. A truth is nothing more than a thought that is true. And thoughts can be apprehended without *recognition* of their truth. We could never be justifiably certain of our belief that a thought is true unless truth were absolute. For otherwise, certainty *would* be a property of truths, and the certainty of a belief would be relative to the certainty of the truth of the thought believed. But the doctrine that truth is absolute would be of little solace to the scientist unless there were some way to apprehend a thought and recognize its truth with certainty. Many a sceptic has admitted the absolute character of truth only to maintain our inability to recognize the truth of any thought with certainty. Hence, the connection between absolute truth and objective certainty is this: absolute truth is a necessary but not a sufficient condition for objective certainty.

We noted earlier that Frege held the epistemological categories — the distinctions between *a priori* and *a posteriori*, analytic and synthetic — to apply not to the content of a judgment, but to the ultimate justification for making it:

> Where there is no such justification, the possibility of drawing the distinctions vanishes. An a priori error is thus as complete a nonsense as, say, a blue concept.[34]

But this last statement seems ambiguous. At first glance, it might suggest a special relation between a prioricity and certainty, i.e., if the truth of a thought can be recognized *a priori*, then it can, in virtue of that, be known with certainty. Now I do not wish to deny this. But the context of the passage suggests that Frege would regard an *a posteriori* error to be as complete a nonsense as an *a priori* error. Simply put: if a thought cannot be justified, then it can be justified neither *a priori* nor *a posteriori*. Adoption of the first interpretation immediately clarifies the connection between a prioricity and objective certainty: the one implies the other. But if we opt for the second interpretation, then we must look further. For then, there is no reason to think that a thought justified *a priori* carries any greater certainty than one justified *a posteriori*.

Nevertheless, Frege seems to have distinguished (at least implicitly) between *a priori* and empirical certainty:

> ... the rigour of the proof remains an illusion, even though no link be missing in the chain of our deductions, so long as the definitions are justified only as an afterthought, by our failing to come across some contradiction. By these methods we shall, at bottom, never achieve more than an empirical certainty, and we must really face the possibility that we may still in the end encounter a contradiction which brings the whole edifice down in ruins.[35]

And the issue becomes clear once we recall that Frege regarded the laws of logic as strictly universal and necessary — as boundary stones set in an eternal foundation, which our thought can overflow but never displace. But what is true with strict universality and necessity has, at least since Kant, been associated with the *a priori*:

> Experience teaches us that a thing is so and so, but not that it cannot be otherwise. First, then, if we have a proposition which in being thought is thought as necessary, it is an *a priori* judgment; and if, besides, it is not derived from a proposition except one which also has the validity of a necessary judgment, it is an absolutely *a priori* judgment. Secondly, experience never confers on its judgments true or strict, but only assumed and

comparative *universality*, through induction. We can properly only say therefore, that, so far as we have hitherto observed, there is no exception to this or that rule. If, then, a judgment is thought with strict universality, that is, in such a manner that no exception is allowed as possible, it is not derived from experience, but is valid absolutely *a priori*. Empirical universality is only an arbitrary extension of a validity holding in most cases to one which holds in all, for instance, in the proposition, 'All bodies are heavy'. When, on the other hand, strict universality is essential to a judgment, this indicates a special source of knowledge, namely, a faculty of *a priori* knowledge. Necessity and strict universality are thus sure criteria of *a priori* knowledge, and are inseparable from one another.[36]

It may be the case that Frege regarded statements justified *a posteriori* as every bit as certain as statements justified *a priori*. But strictly universal and necessary statements cannot be justfied as such *a posteriori*. And if our grounds for believing a statement to be strictly universal and necessary are not *a priori*, then its strict universality and necessity is only assumed. It is only an arbitrary extension of a validity holding in most cases to one which holds in all. And here, we have achieved nothing more than an empirical certainty. Ironically, it was Russell's derivation of a contradiction from Frege's axioms regarding classes that led to the fall of logicism. This contradiction demonstrated that Frege's Basic Law (V) is not strictly universal and, hence, that the notion of class is not properly a logical notion. Simply put, Frege was shown to have had only an empirical certainty of Basic Law (V).

Here I think, we can glean the connection between a priority and certainty. Frege thought that the aim of a proof is twofold. On the one hand, it places the truth of a proposition beyond all doubt. On the other, it affords us insight into the dependence of truths one upon another.[37] But for Frege, these two aims were interrelated. In order to know whether a truth is *a priori* or *a posteriori* it is necessary to know whether it depends for its justification on an appeal to facts or on an appeal solely to general laws. Now Frege held that facts are truths that cannot be proved.[38] But the general laws that provide the foundation for *a priori* truths do not *need* proof. And this is because Frege regarded them as self-evident, and hence certain. Now if the truths of arithmetic are to be known to be strictly universal and necessary, then they must be *a priori*, i.e., they must be derivable exclusively from self-evident general laws. But if the proof of a proposition is rigorous, then the truth of the self-evident laws from which it is derived is preserved in the proof. And in that case, a priority presupposes and insures certainty. If we are certain of the general laws, as we must be if they do not need proof, then the logical rigour of a proof will insure our certainty of the propositions derived from them.

Here we can round out the point. Absolute truth is a necessary but not a sufficient condition for cognitive certainty. And strict universality and necessity are sufficient conditions for a priority. But since a priority involves the rigorous derivation of a proposition from self-evident general laws, a priority is a necessary and sufficient condition for the cognitive certainty of strictly universal and necessary truths. *Truths* knowable only *a posteriori* are every bit as eternal, objective, and perhaps even certain, as truths knowable *a priori*. But truths that are strictly universal and necessary can be known to be so only *a priori*.

This point, that a prioricity implies certainty, is not new. On the contrary, Kant is explicit in the *Critique of Pure Reason* that:

> Any knowledge that professes to hold *a priori* lays claim to be regarded as absolutely necessary. This applies still more to any *determination* of all pure *a priori* knowledge, since such determination has to serve as the measure, and therefore as the (supreme) example, of all apodeictic (philosophical) certainty.[39]

So if a statement is knowable *a priori*, then it is, for that reason, apodeictically certain. But what is, perhaps, more interesting is that Kant appealed to apodeictic certainty as a measure of a prioricity. In the *Prolegomena to Any Future Metaphysics* Kant continually bases his claim that a proposition is *a priori* on his assumption that it is apodeictically certain:

> ... this intuition must be pure and given *a priori*, else the proposition could not hold as apodeictically certain but would have empirical certainty only. In that case it could only be said that it is always found to be so and holds good only as far as our perception reaches. That complete space (which is not itself the boundary of another space) has three dimensions and that space in general cannot have more is based on the proposition that not more than three lines can intersect at right angles in one point. This proposition cannot at all be shown from concepts, but rests immediately on intuition, and indeed on pure intuition *a priori* because it is apodeictically certain.[40]

To claim that a proposition is *a priori* valid is to claim that it is apodeictically certain. But this is not simply because a prioricity *implies* certainty. Rather, it is because the claim that a proposition is *a priori* valid is itself based on the intuition that it is apodeictically certain.

Any statement, if true, is eternally so. So no *truth*, be it justified *a priori* or *a posteriori*, is subject to revision. If a statement is subject to revision, then what is corrigible is not the truth of that statement, but our belief about the truth of that statement. Part of the difference between general statements knowable *a priori* and those knowable only *a posteriori* lies in the quality of certainty with which the truth of such statements can be recognized. Our beliefs about the latter, but not the former, must always be held corrigible in the light of further empirical evidence. But this is simply to say that *a posteriori* knowledge of general statements is fallible.

When we say of statements, laws, truths, etc. that they are fallible, what we mean is that they are liable to error, i.e., that their truth is not certain. So long as we maintain truth as a regulative ideal for belief, fallibilism implies corrigibilism. But here we must be humble. For to say that a *truth* is fallible or corrigible is really to misplace the blame. It is *we* who are liable to error, and our beliefs that are subject to revision. Now Frege clearly spoke of truths and laws as being, on the psychologistic account, subject to revision. And perhaps what he intended here was a sort of *reductio ad absurdum*, a demonstration that psychologism must construe corrigibility as a property of truths. But one cannot dispose of psychologism simply by speaking an objectivist language. And the doctrine that truth is absolute will not suffice either. What is needed is an account of how the truth of a thought can be recognized with objective certainty. What I want to suggest here is that what psychologism entails and what anti-psychologism denies is fallibilism — in Frege's case, fallibilism in logic. To that extent, Frege's anti-psychologism was generated by two beliefs: the laws of psychology are fallible; the laws of logic are not. It follows immediately that logic cannot be a branch of psychology.

But what of Frege's oft repeated ontological claim, that being true is distinct from being thought to be true? Well, what of it? The fallibilist says of his beliefs that they may be mistaken. And beliefs can be mistaken only if there are some possible beliefs that are not. But here the fallibilist too must recognize that being true is distinct from being thought to be true — for otherwise, fallibilism would simply not make sense. So the Fregean sword cuts both ways, and, ironically, is exactly the response a fallibilist might make to Frege's claim that the laws of logic are *a priori* valid: being true is distinct from being thought to be true. But this simply underscores the fact that psychologism was never a claim about the ontological status of truth, but about the epistemological means available for recognizing it. Of course, a psychologistic logician might be *sceptical* of the *claim* that certain statements are absolute truths. But that's just the point!

Now suppose that Frege was an ontological anti-psychologist (truth is absolute), but an epistemological fallibilist (no truth can be recognized with certainty). In opposing psychologism, Frege argued that any being who reasoned according to laws contradicting those of classical logic should be regarded as irrational. But were Frege a fallibilist, the discovery of such beings would not issue in a charge of irrationality, but in an attempt to construct a decision procedure to determine which laws, if any, are right. In the absence of such a procedure, Peirce's social impulse advises caution. Nevertheless, suppose that the deviant logicians Frege encounters are just Brouwer and the intuitionists advocating, among other things, the rejection of the law of the excluded middle. But suppose that instead of charging Brouwer with madness, Frege himself were to convert to intuitionism with the fall of logicism. Now Frege could convert to intuitionism and still maintain that truth is absolute by interpreting the intuitionist doctrine that a statement receives its truth value via the construction of its proof as an epistemological criterion for the justified *assertion* of truth. In effect, he could maintain the principle of bivalence, but deny the law of the excluded middle as a theorem of logic. Concerning his former belief that the law of the excluded middle is a law of pure logic, Frege might say, "Well, the *laws* of logic are not subject to revision, but my *beliefs* certainly are!" And he would, of course, be right. But here our scenario breaks down. It would be as if Kant were to say, "Well, the axioms of geometry are *a priori* synthetic; I was just wrong about Euclid!" The significance of the doctrine that truth is absolute, like the significance of the claim that a truth is *a priori*, at least in a justificationist programme, is the cognitive authority it imparts to statements justified as true. And despite our counter-factual fantasies of Frege's fallibilism, it is just this cognitive authority with which he was primarily concerned. For Frege, anti-psychologism was meant to imply classical logic — come what may!

Toward the end of the last chapter we suggested that Frege's anti-psychologism might be consistent with the psychological reality thesis even if the third realm did not exist. But then we backed off. Here we can see the fundamental inconsistency between the two views. If the laws of thought were laws of thinking, but no third realm existed, then the laws of thought would not be absolute truths. But if the laws of thought were not absolute truths, then they would not be *a priori* valid and their strict universality and necessity could be recognized with only empirical certainty. In that case, they would not have cognitive authority come what may, but would always be held accountable to further empirical evidence. So any attempt to found the laws of logic on the results of empirical psychology subverts their cognitive authority by denying their *a priori* certainty. It was this erosion of the authority of logic that Frege would not allow.

NOTES AND REFERENCES

1. See: Kitcher, Philip; "Frege's Epistemology"; *The Philosophical Review*; Volume LXXXVIII, No. 2 (April 1979) pp. 235-262.

2. See: *Op. cit.*; Frege; *Gottlob Frege: Posthumous Writings*; pp. 267-285.

3. *Ibid.*; pp. 273, 277.

4. *Ibid.*; pp. 269-270.

5. *Ibid.*; p. 205.

6. *Ibid.*

7. *Ibid.*; p. 169.

8. Anscombe, G.E.M., and P.T. Geach; *Three Philosophers*; Basil Blackwell (Oxford, 1961) p. 137.

9. *Op. cit.*; Frege; *The Foundations of Arithmetic*; p. v^e.

10. *Ibid.*; p. xi^e.

11. *Op. cit.*; Dummett; *Frege: Philosophy of Language*; p. 240.

108

12. *Ibid.*; p. 632.

13. Dummett, Michael; "Frege's Philosophy"; in *Truth and Other Enigmas*; by Michael Dummett; Harvard University Press (Cambridge, 1978) p. 89. Dummett makes similar comments in *Frege: Philosophy of Language*. See, e.g., pp. xiii-xv, 665-669, 676-677.

14. Sluga, Hans; *Gottlob Frege*; Routledge & Kegan Paul (Boston, 1980) p. 44.

15. *Op. cit.*; Dummett; *Frege: Philosophy of Language*; pp. 669-673.

16. *Op. cit.*; Locke; *An Essay concerning Human Understanding*; Book II, chapter XXXIII, Section 19, p. 401.

17. *Op. cit.*; Mill; *A System of Logic*; Chapter 1, section 1, p. 20.

18. *Ibid.*; p. 19.

19. *Ibid.*; pp. 19-20.

20. See: *Op. cit.*; Frege; *Gottlob Frege: Posthumous Writings*; pp. 267-269.

21. Haack, Susan; *Deviant Logic*; Cambridge University Press (New York, 1974) p. 29.

22. *Ibid.* Haack erroneously attributes this passage to the *Grundlagen*. In point of fact, the passage is from an appendix to the *Grundgesetze*, Band II, and is reprinted in *The Basic Laws of Arithmetic*; p. 127, and in *Translations from the Philosophical Writings of Gottlob Frege*; p. 234.

23. *Ibid.*

24. *Ibid.*; p. 33.

25. Sluga, Hans; "Frege and the Rise of Analytic Philosophy"; *Inquiry*, 18, p. 477.

26. *Op. cit.*; Currie; p. 234.

27. *Ibid.*; p. 245.

28. *Op. cit.*; Frege; "The Thought: A Logical Inquiry"; p. 19.

29. *Op. cit.*; *Encyclopedia Britannica*; Volume 1; pp. 49-50.

30. *Op. cit.*; Frege; "The Thought: A Logical Inquiry"; pp. 18-19.

31. *Op. cit.*; Frege; *Gottlob Frege: Posthumous Writings*; p. 4.

32. Sluga, as we've already noted, is explicit on this point. See Sluga's "Frege's Alleged Realism"; p. 20.

33. *Op. cit.*; Frege; *Begriffsschrift*; p. 5.

34. *Op. cit.*; Frege; *The Foundations of Arithmetic*; p. 3^e.

35. *Ibid.*; p. ix^e.

36. Kant, Immanuel; *Kritik der reinen Vernunft*; Johann Friedrich Hartknoch (Riga, 1787). Translated by Norman Kemp Smith as *Immanuel Kant's Critique of Pure Reason*; Macmillan & Co. (New York, 1929) p. 44.

37. *Op. cit.*; Frege; *The Foundations of Arithmetic*; p. 2^e.

38. *Ibid.*; p. 4^e.

39. *Op. cit.*; Kant; *Critique of Pure Reason*; p. 11.

40. Kant Immanuel; *Prolegomena zu einer jeden kunftigen Metaphysik die als Wissenschaft auftreten konnen*; (Riga, 1783). Translated by Paul Carus as *Prolegomena to Any Future Metaphysics*; Hackett (Indianapolis, 1977) pp. 28-29.

7. POPPER, AND FALLIBILISTIC ANTI-PSYCHOLOGISM

In our discussion of Frege we associated psychologism with the denial of the possibility of *a priori* knowledge, i.e., *a priori* valid statements. There we argued that, from the EP_1 perspective, the significance of a prioricity is the support or authority it was thought to lend to cognitive claims, i.e., the *certainty* it claimed to guarantee for statements knowable *a priori*. To that extent, we argued that while the distinction between being true and being thought to be true is implied by fallibilism, the denial that *a priori* statements are objectively certain deprives a prioricity of its epistemological bite. Simply put: there is little point in claiming that certain statements can be known *a priori* if one simultaneously holds that all of his beliefs, including those "known" *a priori*, are fallible. Nevertheless, Karl Popper has attempted to wed anti-psychologism with a thorough going fallibilism. Popper, moreover, has appealed to a "Fregean" notion of the third realm to bolster his anti-psychologism, and has gone so far as to characterize psychologism as the result of a neglect or even denial of the third realm.[1] Like Frege, Popper opposes psychologism in order to insure the objectivity of knowledge and to avoid the descent into scepticism and relativism. But despite his references to Frege, it would be a mistake to think that Popper is anti-psychologistic in the same sense as Frege. While Frege argued that some truths must be *a priori* if scientific knowledge is to have more than a psychological justification, Popper eschews the thesis that any truths are *a priori* valid. Indeed, the hub of Popper's epistemological thought is his rejection of justification as a criterion of knowledge. Moreover, Popper's notion of the third realm and in particular his position concerning the mind-independence of third realm entities, differs from Frege's enough to alter the sense of his anti-psychologism. While Frege thought of the objects of the third realm as eternally existent and independent of the existence of human minds, Popper construes of such objects as human creations. If scientific theories are among the objects of the third realm, then scientific theories are not things to be discovered by human beings, but things to be created by them. Hence, while Popper opposes psychologism in order to provide for the objectivity of knowledge, his positions regarding the criteria of knowledge and the genesis of the third realm introduce a different and less absolutist concept of objectivity into the philosophical discussion. In what follows, I will attempt to make these intuitions explicit.

Initially, it might be thought that we can make sense of Popper's wedding of fallibilism and anti-psychologism by delineating the scope of each. Insofar as this is concerned, it is sometimes thought that Popper refuses to extend his fallibilism to logic and mathematics. Haack, for instance, writes:

112

Popper, for example, though he stresses our fallibility where scientific conjectures are concerned, nevertheless seems confident that logic is safe.[2]

Perhaps Haack has the following passage in mind:

> Thus we should (in the empirical sciences) use the full or classical or two-valued logic. If we do not use it but retreat into the use of some weaker logic — say, the intuitionist logic, or some three-valued logic (as Reichenbach suggested in connection with quantum theory) — then, I assert, we are not critical enough; it is a sign that something is rotten in the state of Denmark (which in this case is the quantum theory in its Copenhagen interpretation, as I indicated earlier).[3]

Now, Haack cites this passage in her *Deviant Logic*,[4] and it seems to imply a refusal to extend fallibilism to logic. But an examination of its context suggests that it is more of a recommendation concerning appropriate critical methodology. Popper holds that classical logic is well suited for the *criticism* of theories, but he also holds that so-called "deviant logics" may be better suited than classical logic for proving mathematical theorems:

> Now what I wish to assert is this. If we want to use logic in a critical context, then we should use a very strong logic, the strongest logic, so to speak, which is at our disposal; for we want our criticism to be *severe*. In order that the criticism should be severe we must use the full apparatus; we must use all the guns we have. Every shot is important. It doesn't matter if we are over-critical: if we are, we shall be answered by counter-criticism....
> Now let us look, by contrast, at proofs. Every mathematician knows that considerable interest lies in proving a theorem with the help of a *minimum apparatus*. A proof which uses stronger means than necessary is mathematically unsatisfactory, and it is always interesting to find the weakest assumptions or minimum means which have to be used in a proof. In other words, we want the proof not only to be sufficient — that is to say valid — but we want it if possible to be necessary, in the sense that a minimum of assumptions have been used in the proof. This, I admit, is a somewhat sophisticated view. In unsophisticated mathematics we are happy and grateful if we can prove anything, but in more sophisticated mathematics we really want to know what is *necessary* for proving a theorem.
> So if one can prove mathematical theorems with methods weaker than the full battery of classical logic, then this is extremely interesting from a mathematical point of view. Thus in proof theory we are interested in weakening if possible our classical logic, and we can, for example, introduce intuitionist logic or some other weaker logic as positive logic, and investigate how far we can get without using the whole battery.[5]

What we have deleted from the passage last cited is, of course, just the paragraph quoted by Haack in *Deviant Logic*. And I do not think that we can conclude from this that Popper refuses to extend fallibilism to logic. But nor should we conclude that he does not. In "Facts, Standards, and Truth: A Further Criticism of Relativism", Popper comes close to being explicit on the issue:

> ... the idea of error implies that of truth as the standard of which we may fall short. It implies that, though we may seek for truth, and though we may even find truth (as I

believe we do in very many cases), we can never be quite certain that we have found it. There is always a possibility of error; *though in the case of some logical and mathematical proofs, this possibility may be considered slight.*[6]

But even this falls short. The slight possibility of error in some logical and mathematical proofs may be due to our fallibility in *applying* the laws of logic, rather than to our fallibility in recognizing their truth. So I think it is best to suspend judgment on the question whether or not Popper extends fallibilism to logic.

Be this as it may. The point to be made is that Popper clearly does not restrict his anti-psychologism to logic and mathematics, but extends it generally over the entire domain of science. And since Popper is unabashedly fallibilistic with regard to natural science, any tension that exists between fallibilism and anti-psychologism will surface there — regardless of whether or not Popper extends fallibilism to logic.

In order to appreciate what separates Popper's anti-psychologism from Frege's, it is necessary to consider differences in their general epistemological outlooks that stretch well beyond the specific psychologism/anti-psychologism debate. This is because the psychologism/anti-psychologism debate is ultimately an issue concerning the foundations, limits, and sources of human knowledge, i.e., whether and to what extent the justification of human knowledge must appeal to laws of empirical psychology which are themselves grounded in sense perceptions. The differences between Popper's and Frege's conceptions of what knowledge is are reflected in the stance that each adopts on this issue, though they are not reflected in their respective *formulations* of anti-psychologism. In point of fact, Popper's formulation (or expression) of anti-psychologism is essentially identical to Frege's. Both argue for the existence of a third realm to insure the possibility of objective knowledge. And each attributes psychologism to a failure to take seriously the third realm. But these terms, "objective knowledge" and "third realm" are blank checks. It is necessary to fill them in in order to see how different the two versions really are. Here, what I want to suggest is that the senses of certain key epistemological terms in Popper's vocabulary differ radically from those in Frege's. What has occurred is a sort of terminological shift whose effect has been to camouflage Popper's true motivations for anti-psychologism.

But if this is true, then many will find it ironic. So before going any further, I want to stifle one possible criticism or confusion that might result from *my* formulation of this issue. It is my position that much of the muddle one feels in reading Popper is due to a systematic terminological shift which changes the meanings of many of the terms in which traditional philosophical problems have been posed. The irony here is that Popper sharply criticizes so-called "meaning philosophers", and disavows himself from any concern with the meanings of words. I do not intend my formulation of the problem to repudiate Popper's attack on "meaning philosophers", nor Popper for making it. At the time at which Popper made this attack, philosophical analyses which focused on the meanings of terms were generally associated with a meta-philosophical position which maintained that philosophical problems are not genuine, but mere word puzzles or linguistic confusions which can be resolved through the clarification of terms. I have chosen to talk about Popper in linguistic terms not to align myself with that tradition, but simply to facilitate exposition. It is, I think, a moot point whether the epistemological differences between Frege and Popper are differences in meanings or differences in beliefs. And I do not think that Popper would hesitate to talk about the meanings of terms so long as one was willing to acknowledge that terminological differences may have real philosophical import. Indeed, in *The Logic of Scientific Discovery*, Popper regrets his former complacency with Carnap's use of "confirmation" to translate Popper's "Bewährung", and the misrepresentation of his position which resulted.[7]

One way to approach Popper's epistemology is to consider the problem situation that motivated his thought. But here we are already engaged in controversy. Most of the early commentators on Popper's work persisted in interpreting him as a dissenting Logical Positivist whose major philosophical thrust was to replace verifiability with falsifiability as a criterion of meaning. This view, moreover, is still prevalent today — despite Popper's frequent and explicit protests:

> Owing to the manner in which it originated, my book *Logik der Forschung*, published late in 1934, was cast partly in the form of a criticism of positivism. So were its unpublished predecessor of 1932 and my brief letter to the Editors of *Erkenntnis* in 1933. Since at this time my position was being widely discussed by leading members of the Circle, and, moreover the book was published in a mainly positivistic series edited by Frank and Schlick, this aspect of *Logik der Forschung* had some curious consequences. One was that until its English publication in 1959 as *The Logic of Scientific Discovery* philosophers in England and America (with only a few exceptions, such as J.R. Weinberg) seem to have taken me for a logical positivist — or at best for a dissenting logical positivist who replaced verifiability by falsifiability. Even some logical positivists themselves, remembering that the book had come out in this series, preferred to see in me an ally rather than a critic. They thought they could ward off my criticism with a few concessions — preferably mutual ones — and some verbal stratagems. (For example, they persuaded themselves that I would agree to substitute falsifiability for verifiability as a criterion of meaningfulness.) And because I did not press my attack home (fighting logical positivism being by no means a major interest of mine) the logical positivists did not feel that logical positivism was seriously challenged.[8]

But even those philosophers who recognize Popper's distinction between a criterion of demarcation and a criterion of meaning continue, for the most part, to interpret him within the positivist framework. According to their interpretation, Popper's major philosophical points are: (1) that a criterion of demarcation is distinct from a criterion of meaning; and (2) that the correct criterion of demarcation is not verifiability, but falsifiability. Now it is true that Popper stresses both (1) and (2). But on my view, this interpretation is both simplistic and pernicious. Simplistic, because it ignores what I think is Popper's major philosophical thesis, i.e., that scientific knowledge is *not* justified true belief.

Pernicious, because so long as we conceive of Popper as a quasi-positivist we will continue to interpret him in positivist terms, and thereby ignore his terminological shift. And so long as we do this we will interpret him as addressing the question how a human being justifies his beliefs.

On my view, Popper's relationship to the Vienna Circle was incidental. Logical positivism provided him with a contemporary illustration of a philosophical view he sharply opposed. Far from motivating Popper's philosophy, logical positivism merely provided him with a ready whipping boy. To read Popper aright, I think it is necessary to look beyond the positivists to Kant, Hume, Descartes, and the great issue that separates classical rationalism from classical empiricism: whether and to what extent human knowledge depends upon sensory experience. Interestingly enough, Popper attributes the demise of positivism, in part, to its decline of interest in great issues:

> ... what I regard as the ultimate cause of the dissolution of the Vienna Circle and of Logical Positivism is not its various grave mistakes of doctrine ... but a decline of interest in the great problems: the concentration upon *minutiae* (upon "puzzles") and especially upon the meanings of words; in brief, its scholasticism.[9]

Popper's problem situation is writ large on the history of philosophy. In Popper's case, it was inherited from Hume, via Russell. The Russellian connection is interesting and, perhaps, sheds some light on Popper's understanding of psychologism. In his autobiography, Popper acknowledges his intellectual debt to Russell, the "spiritual father" of the Vienna Circle, and "perhaps the greatest philosopher since Kant".[10] And in "Conjectural Knowledge: My Solution of the Problem of Induction", Popper adopts Russell's interpretation of Hume which stresses the clash between Hume's solution of the problem of induction on the one hand, and rationality, empiricism, and scientific procedures on the others. There Popper quotes Russell that "the growth of unreason throughout the nineteenth century and what has passed of the twentieth is a natural sequel to Hume's destruction of empiricism".[11] But what sheds light on Popper's understanding of psychologism comes from Russell's *An Inquiry Into Meaning and Truth*. There Russell defines "psychological premiss" as a "belief which is not caused by any other belief or beliefs", and goes on to say that "the most obvious class of beliefs not caused by other beliefs are those that result directly from perception".[12]

Hume's rejection of *a priori* valid statements, and of induction as logically valid inference led him to (1) reject the possibility of knowledge *founded* on reason, and (2) adopt an irrationalist epistemology. The problem which Popper inherited was that of accepting Hume's rejection of *a priori* valid statements and of induction as logically valid inference without thereby embracing either his scepticism or his irrationalist epistemology. As Popper saw it, it was the problem of framing an epistemology which solves the problem of induction without clashing with either rationality, empiricism, or scientific procedures. And as Popper came to see it, it was a problem which dovetails with that of demarcation, i.e., the task of formulating a criterion which differentiates science from other cognitive endeavors, e.g., art, metaphysics, etc., where science is understood as both rational and empirical in nature.

Popper tells us that his work on the problem of demarcation was originally independent of his work on the problem of induction, and that it was only upon his solution of the latter that he recognized the significance of the former and the intricate relation between the two.[13] Nevertheless, the connections between the two problems, and between Popper's solutions of them, are obvious. Popper rejected the positivist verifiability criterion of meaning as the demarcation between science and metaphysics (between science and *Unsinn*) primarily because:

> ... *it did not exclude obvious metaphysical statements, but it did exclude the most important and interesting of all scientific statements*, that is to say, the scientific theories, the *universal laws* of nature.[14]

The universal laws of nature, of course, are not empirically verifiable, and hence not scientific according to the positivist criterion, because strictly universal statements (universal statements which quantify over infinite domains) cannot be inferred from any finite number of particular statements, no matter how large. But this, of course, is simply another way of saying that induction is not a logically valid inference form. Insofar as this is concerned, Popper, with reference to Carnap, writes:

> ... induction has always been one of the most popular criteria of demarcation for science; for the empirical sciences are, as a rule, considered to be characterized by their methods; and these, in turn, are usually characterized as *inductive.*[15]

If the rationality of science is to be understood as a methodological adherence to the laws of logic, and if empirical science is to include strictly universal laws of nature, then the inductivist verifiability criterion cannot be the correct criterion of demarcation.

The equation traditionally presupposed in the formulations of these problems identifies rational knowledge with statements justified via logically valid arguments (rationality=justification=logicality). The problem with this equation as it relates to Hume's rejection of *a priori* valid statements and of induction as logically valid inference is reflected in Frege's statement that "from mere individual facts nothing follows, unless it be on the strength of a law."[16] If general laws are prerequisite for logical inference, but our cognitive faculties are restricted to the intuition of particular facts and the consequences that can be inferred from those facts, then how can there be rational empirical knowledge at all?

Frege thought that "induction itself depends on the general proposition that the inductive method can establish the truth of a law, or at least some probability for it".[17] But this was due, in part, to the fact that Frege believed in *a priori* modes of cognition. Hume, on the other hand, was adament that inductive inference is neither logically valid nor can be made logically valid by appeal to an *a priori* principle of induction.[18] But this, needless to say, was due to the fact that Hume prohibited appeals to *a priori* principles of anything. Now, if Hume had stopped there, he would have been remembered merely as a sceptic. And in fact, this is how Hume is usually interpreted. But Hume was equally adamant that scientific laws *are* founded (psychologically) on inductive inference, and hence not on reason, but on custom or habit. The custom or habit which Hume regarded as the ultimate foundation for inductive inference was itself developed, according to Hume, by the repetition of sense perceptions and memories of sense perceptions. And here we can see that what Popper regards as Hume's irrationalist epistemology is nothing more nor less than his psychologism. What made Hume a believer in an irrationalist epistemology, as opposed to a mere sceptic, was his belief that judgments *are* justified, but justified not logically – by appeal to sufficient reason – but psychologically – by appeal to sense perceptions and memories of sense perceptions:

> ... if we proceed not upon some fact, present to the memory or senses, our reasonings would be merely hypothetical; and however the particular links might be connected with each other, the whole chain of inferences would have nothing to support it, nor could we ever, by its means, arrive at the knowledge of any real existence. If I ask, why you believe any particular matter of fact, which you relate, you must tell me some reason; and this reason will be some other fact, connected with it. But as you cannot proceed after this manner, *in infinitum*, you must at last terminate in some fact, which is present to your memory or sense; or must allow that your belief is entirely without foundation.[19]

Hume, as we've said, is remembered in the history of philosophy primarily as a sceptic, as the radical empiricist who followed his epistemological principles courageously to their logical conclusion, but failed to recognize the *reductio ad absurdum* waiting there. But such an interpretation is both simplistic and self-gratuitous. It is simplistic because it recognizes only Hume's negative achievement. It is self-gratuitous (to believers in rationalist epistemology) because it frees Hume's critics from the obligation of dealing with his more radical and challenging legacy: the thesis that knowledge is possible, albeit not rational (founded on reason). And here it is, at least, ironic that while Frege opposed psychologism as eroding the foundations of knowledge, Hume proposed it as the last possibility of providing such a foundation. For Hume, it was *anti*-psychologism which leads to scepticism. *Either* our rational justification terminates in sense perceptions or memories of sense perceptions, i.e., something not logical, but psychological, *or* we must allow that our beliefs are entirely without foundation. This, because for Hume there was no *a priori* knowledge, no third realm, and hence no third possibility. And here, it is important to recognize that Popper's anti-psychologism differs from Frege's in that it is a response not to Hume's negative thesis (his scepticism), but to his positive thesis (his irrationalist epistemology).

Here it would be tempting to identify the differences between Popper's and Frege's general epistemological outlooks as just those differences between EP$_1$ and EP$_2$, and leave it at that. Leaving it at that might even go a long way toward clarifying Popper's terminological shift. Now it is clear that Popper is an EP$_2$ philosopher. On the one hand, Popper is explicit in his denial that there are truths that are *a priori* valid. But here it is important to note that Popper is denying only that truths can be justified *a priori*, i.e., that a prioricity implies apodeictic certainty:

> When Kant said that our intellect imposes its laws upon nature, he was right — except that he did not notice how often our intellect fails in the attempt: the regularities we try to impose are *psychologically a priori*, but there is not the slightest reason to assume that they are *a priori valid*, as Kant thought.[20]

Moreover, Popper denies that *any source* of knowledge, *a priori* or otherwise, can infallibly provide cognitive authority for the certainty of statements. Popper rightly regards epistemologies which ground the justification of cognitive claims on the alleged "purity" of cognitive sources as subjectivist:

> ... it gets into the difficulty of admitting something like subjective sufficient reasons; that is, kinds of personal experience or belief or opinion which, though subjective, are certainly and unfailingly true, and can therefore pass as knowledge.
>   The difficulty is great, for how can we distinguish within the realm of beliefs? What are the criteria by which we can recognize truth, or a sufficient reason? Either by the strength of the belief (Hume), which is hardly rationally defensible, or by its clearness and distinctness, which is defended (by Descartes) as an indication of its divine origin; or, more straightforwardly, by its origin or its genesis, that is to say by the 'sources' of knowledge. In this way, the commonsense theory is led to the acceptance of some criterion of the 'given' (revealed?) knowledge; to the sense-given or sense datum; or to a feeling of immediacy, or directness, or intuitiveness. It is the purity of the origin that guarantees the freedom from error and thus the purity of the content.
>   But all these criteria are clearly spurious.[21]

According to Popper, there is in science *always* the possibility of error and hence revision. This fallibilistic attitude can be traced to Popper's rejection of the "optimistic" doctrine that *truth is manifest* and can be recognized as such once revealed.[22] Popper believes that this doctrine led to Descartes' theory of the *veracitas dei* and to Bacon's theory of the *veracitas naturae*, the former of which led to the explanation of error as sin and the latter of which led to the explanation of error as illness. Contrary to the doctrine that truth is manifest, Popper holds that "truth is often hard to come by, and that once found it may easily be lost again".[23] So while scientists may appeal to authorities in their search for truth, no authority can ever be assumed to lend a foolproof guarantee to cognitive claims.

On the other hand, Popper continues to regard scientific knowledge as rational and objective: objective, because it can be formulated and communicated in language; rational, because such formulation makes logical criticism possible. So while the methodology of conjecture and refutation (or trial and error) stresses the fallibility of scientific knowledge, it refuses to resign itself to either scepticism or an irrationalist epistemology. Not to scepticism, because Popper stresses "the fact that knowledge can grow, and that science can progress – just because we can learn from our mistakes".[24] Not to an irrationalist epistemology, because science progresses rationally through conjecture and refutation in virtue of its methodological adherence to the *Modus Tollens* of deductive logic as the organon of criticism.

Popper's strategy here is to maintain the connection between rationality and logic by shifting its emphasis from the *modus ponens* of justification to the *modus tollens* of criticism. This shift, which is ultimately the result of his rejection of induction as logically valid inference, is part and parcel of his shift from varificationism to falsificationism:

> My proposal is based upon an *asymmetry* between verifiability and falsifiability; an asymmetry which results from the logical form of universal statements. For these are never derivable from singular statements. Consequently it is possible by means of purely deductive inferences (with the help of the *modus tollens* of classical logic) to argue from the truth of singular statements to the falsity of universal statements. Such an argument to the falsity of universal statements is the only strictly deductive kind of inference that proceeds, as it were, in the 'inductive direction'; that is, from singular to universal statements.[25]

This conception of scientific knowledge as rational and objective, albeit fallibilistic, is often perceived as the central tension in Popper's philosophy. It has been described[26] as the result of a noble but misguided attempt to wed two seemingly distinct strains of thought in the philosophy of science. The first conceives of science as governed by standards and controls that are untainted by human (subjective) determinations, and are free of context or human discretion. This is Popper's anti-psychologism. The second strain of thought recognizes science as a *human* activity (or institution) that is goal-oriented and rule-governed. According to this view, which is part and parcel of Popper's fallibilism, scientists seek to promote their aims and solve their problems. And the methods to which they appeal must be adequate to the needs for critical control that arise in the diverse circumstances and contexts in which they find themselves.

Popper's attempt to wed these two strains of thought has bent contemporary philosophical intuitions to the point of snap. And this, I maintain, is in part due to the fact that contemporary philosophical intuitions straddle both EP_1 and EP_2, ignoring the conceptual slack between the two. But leaving it at this would simply render Popper's wedding of fallibilism and anti-psychologism less intelligible. The fact of the matter is that even within EP_2 Popper has effected an epistemological change of such dimensions that it might in itself be considered a paradigm shift. I am, of course, referring to his rejection of the justified true belief theory of knowledge and, in particular, to his rejection of justification as a criterion of knowledge. It is, moreover, the consequences of this shift which, more than anything else, distinguish Popperian anti-psychologism from the Fregean variety. Popper's epistemology thus has two targets. One aim is to oppose the view that knowledge is or entails objective certainty, i.e., EP_1. But the other is to construct a positive theory of objective knowledge within EP_2 which avoids both the scepticism and irrationalism associated with Hume. Insofar as this is concerned, we should note that Popper's conception of justification coincides with Frege's and is such that his rejection of justificationism follows from his conception of knowledge as fallible. Nevertheless, Popper offers distinct arguments to support his fallibilism on the one hand, and his anti-justificationism on the other. This is important because a whole tradition of philosophers (indeed, the mainstream of the analytic tradition) has accepted fallibilism – at least with regard to natural science – but has sought to maintain the justified true belief theory of knowledge by weakening its concept of justification. The difference between Popper and the philosophers in this tradition might be thought semantic and concerned merely with the meaning of "justification". But Popper's argument against the possibility of justification by reasoned argument is also targeted against those EP_2 epistemologies that appeal to such weakened concepts of justification. So it is important to distinguish EP_1 and EP_2 from the justified true belief theory of knowledge. In what follows, we will attempt to show why Popper feels that those EP_2 philosophers who wish to retain justification as a criterion of knowledge must ultimately appeal to a psychologistic notion of justification – sometimes despite their own renunciations of psychologism. Showing this will put us in a position to make sense of Popper's wedding of fallibilism and anti-psychologism, and to better appreciate the difference between Popper's anti-psychologism and Frege's.

NOTES AND REFERENCES

1.   Popper, Karl; "On the Theory of the Objective Mind"; in *Objective Knowledge* by Karl Popper; Oxford University Press (New York, 1972) p. 162.

2.   *Op. cit.*; Haack; *Philosophy of Logics*; p. 233.

3.   Popper, Karl; "A Realist View of Logic, Physics, and History"; in *Op. cit.*; *Objective Knowledge*; pp. 305-306.

4.   *Op. cit.*; Haack; *Deviant Logic*; p. 153.

5.   *Op. cit.*; Popper; "A Realist View of Logic, Physics, and History"; pp. 305-306.

6.   Popper, Karl; "Facts, Standards, and Truth: A Further Criticism of Relativism"; in *The Open Society and Its Enemies*; by Karl Popper; Princeton University Press (Princeton, 1966) Volume 2; p. 375. Emphasis mine.

7.   *Op. cit.*; Popper; *The Logic of Scientific Discovery*; pp. 251-252.

8. Schilpp, Paul Arthur, ed.; *The Philosophy of Karl Popper*; Open Court (La Salle, Illinois, 1974) Volume 1; p. 69.

9. *Ibid.*; p. 71.

10. *Ibid.*; pp. 70, 87.

11. Popper, Karl; "Conjectural Knowledge: My Solution of the Problem of Induction"; in *Op. cit.*; *Objective Knowledge*; p. 1. See also, pp. 1-5.

12. Russell, Bertrand; *An Inquiry Into Meaning and Truth*; Allen and Unwin (London, 1940) p. 132.

13. *Op. cit.*; Popper; "Conjectural Knowledge: My Solution of the Problem of Induction"; pp. 1, 29-31.

14. Popper, Karl; "The Demarcation Between Science and Metaphysics"; in *Op. cit.*; *Conjectures and Refutations*; p. 281.

15. *Ibid.*; p. 280.

16. *Op. cit.*; Frege; *The Foundations of Arithmetic*; p. 4^e.

17. *Ibid.*

18. Hume, of course, also argued that inductive inference could not, on rational grounds, establish the greater probability of a statement, i.e., that probability judgments are also based on custom or habit.

19. Hume, David; *An Inquiry Concerning Human Understanding*; ed. by Eric Steinberg; Hackett (Indianapolis, 1977) p. 30.

20. *Op. cit.*; Popper; "Conjectural Knowledge: My Solution of the Problem of Induction"; p. 24.

21. Popper, Karl; "Two Faces of Common Sense"; in *Op. cit.*; *Objective Knowledge*; pp. 76-77.

22. See: Popper, Karl; "On the Sources of Knowledge and of Ignorance"; in *Op. cit.*; *Conjectures and Refutations*; pp. 3-30.

23. *Ibid.*; p. 8.

24. *Op. cit.*; Popper; *Conjectures and Refutations*; p. vii.

25. *Op. cit.*; Popper; *The Logic of Scientific Discovery*; p. 41. This last statement is, of course, misleading. Even when the antecedent of the conditional in a *modus tollens* is a universal statement and the consequent is a singular statement, the argument proceeds from the negation of the singular statement to the negation of the universal statement. But the negation of a universal statement is an existential, and not a universal, generalization.

26. See: Lieberson, Jonathan Sears; *Critical Control and Objectivity in Popper's Theory of Scientific Method*; doctoral dissertation; Columbia University, 1978; pp. 1-2.

8. JUSTIFICATION, RATIONALITY, AND
THE GROUNDS OF PSYCHOLOGISM

Let's begin with an illustration of the problem. In *Teleology Revisited* Ernest Nagel claims that Popper and Popperian-like epistemologies invite scepticism by appealing to an arbitrary and overly restricted use of the word "knowledge":

> ... it is also frequently maintained that since general statements formulating the laws and theories of the various sciences are not entailed by any finite class of singular statements no law or theory of any empirical science can be rightly said to be *known* to be true. In short, the claim is that no statement with an empirical content can be known to be true, so that irrespective of the quantity and nature of the supporting evidence, all statements of the sciences purporting to have a factual content are always subject to revision and are never more than "conjectures". But acceptance of this claim leads easily to a pervasive scepticism concerning the competence of inquiry to yield genuine knowledge.
> However, the scepticism is not warranted, and is generated largely because the application of the word "knowledge" is restricted in an arbitrary manner. For example, it is quite correct to say that observation does not establish *demonstratively* the truth of any singular statement about what is being observed. But this is so because in the strict sense of the word "demonstratively" a necessary condition for demonstrating the truth of a statement is that it be shown to follow logically from a set of *premises* – a condition that by assumption is not satisfied by statements that are asserted on the basis of sensory observation.[1]

Now this passage deals with points fundamental to Popper's epistemology. But it seems to conflate two issues which, while closely related in that they each concern the possibility of justifying statements empirically, are better kept distinct. The first concerns the problem of induction: whether any finite class of singular statements (no matter how large) logically entails a strictly universal statement. The second concerns the problem of epistemological psychologism: whether sensory observation provides objective and rational justification for singular statements (let alone general statements). These two problems are logically distinct. One may, for example, hold that sense perceptions *do* establish the truth of singular statements, but still maintain that no finite class of singular statements entails a strictly universal generalization. And one might even hold that induction is (for some reason) logically valid inference, but that sense perceptions cannot establish the truth of any statement. Deductive inference, after all, is recognized as logically valid independent of worries concerning the justification of universal statements. But Nagel, of course, is right: Popper opposes both epistemological psychologism and the validity of inductive inference.

Nevertheless, I find it ironic that Nagel suggests that Popper's position is or leads to scepticism. Nagel, however, is not alone in this interpretation. Anthony O'Hear, for example, concludes his book *Karl Popper* with a chapter entitled "Popper's Scepticism". There, O'Hear writes:

... hovering over the picture and entering it at every point is Popper's deep scepticism. This is the other side of the rejection of justificationism. Theories are bold guesses, and what success they have cannot be underwritten. Everything, from the 'observations' of the amoeba to the theories on the basis of which we build bridges and send craft to the moon, is riddled with uncertainty.[2]

And Hilary Putnam has characterized Popper's conjectural view of knowledge as "extreme scepticism".[3] Nor should it be thought that these accusations of scepticism are issued from the EP_1 perspective and are primarily opposition to fallibilism. Putnam, after all, is one of the more vociferous critics of the view that knowledge is certain and not subject to revision. But the irony in all this is that Popper is explicit in his opposition to scepticism and relativism, and conceives of his epistemology as a means for combating those positions. Moreover, Popper is adamant that scientific inquiry is our best tool for achieving cognitive growth. Earlier, we said that Popper's epistemology has two targets: (1) to oppose the view that knowledge is or entails objective certainty, i.e., EP_1; (2) to construct a positive theory of objective and rational knowledge within EP_2. Now it is true that Popper denies that scientific statements can be known, *if to know is to know for certain.*[4] This seems to be an attempt to hit both targets at once. Regarding (1), it is a denial that to know is to know for certain. Regarding (2), it is a suggestion that objective knowledge has nothing to do with a subject that knows.[5] But Nagel, in any event, would be the last to deny that science is fallible.

This last statement, perhaps, needs qualification. In "The Quest for Uncertainty" Nagel writes:

> ... it is widely though not universally acknowledged today that *all* cognitive claims in science — no matter how securely grounded they may appear to be, and whether they are about particular occurrences or about relations between inclusive kinds of things — are *in principle* subject to further scrutiny and possible revision, so that in this sense the fallible character of scientific inquiry has become a commonplace.[6]

Nagel's emphasis on "in principle" suggests a qualification of his fallibilism. And later in the same article Nagel writes:

> ... although some questions have received either no answers thus far, or admittedly tentative answers, or answers once believed to be correct but subsequently shown to be mistaken, it is surely an exaggeration to say that *no* problems have ever been settled, or that *no* theoretical (that is strictly universal) statements are accepted in science as fully warranted. That a certain liquid substance called water expands its volume when it is under a certain pressure and is cooled to a little above its freezing temperature; that this substance decomposes under certain specifiable conditions into two identifiable gases called hydrogen and oxygen; that glowing hydrogen gas emits radiation characterized by the presence of certain distinctive spectral lines under statable circumstances, are just three examples of physical laws which no physicist today would label as "conjectures" or declare to be anything but well established.[7]

In light of this, our difficulty concerns the meaning of "in principle". "In principle", one might assume, is opposed to "in practice". And this interpretation gains credence through Nagel's comment that Popper's dictum that "almost all of the vast amount of background knowledge which we constantly use in any informal discussion will, *for practical reasons, necessarily remain unquestioned*" is by no means insignificant.[8] But here my intuitions balk. If the point of Nagel's distinction is to note that not all statements in science are actually false or even questioned, then he is fully in accord with Popper. But the sense of "fallible" that Popper uses is neither "false" nor "questioned", nor even "likely to be false" or "likely to be questioned". Rather, Popper simply means "liable to error", or "possibly false". But here, the modality of possibility which is usually thought to distinguish "in principle" from "in practice" is assumed in the very sense of "fallible". Another way of approaching this difficulty is to focus on what Nagel means by "fully warranted". If a statement is fully warranted if and only if it is demonstratively certain, then it would seem self-contradictory to say that certain statements are fully warranted but fallible — even if only in principle. If, on the other hand, "fully warranted" is interpreted in a way such that a statement could be fully warranted, but possibly false, then there would be nothing strange in the notion that a statement is both fully warranted and fallible. "Fallible" does not mean "false", but "possibly false". And a statement is *possibly* false even if that possibility is slight. So I'm not at all clear how a distinction between fallible in principle and fallible in practice would apply.

Incidentally, exactly how physicists regard scientific statements seems somehow beside the point. Or are we to suppose that we should consult working clerics to determine the status of the existence of God? No one today would seriously suggest that we should consult the writings of sixteenth century physicists to determine the nature of space and time. And this is precisely the point. On the one hand, Popper's epistemology *is* prescriptive. On the other hand, if the epistemic status of scientific statements were so clear that one need only to consult a working scientist, then there would be little disagreement among working scientists and less need to philosophize about science. And if this were the case, then scientific change would truly be miraculous.

Nagel also attributes to Popper a very restricted and arbitrary use of the word "knowledge". But this is strange. Popper everywhere asserts the existence and objectivity of scientific knowledge. At the same time, Popper everywhere acknowledges that scientific knowledge is fallible. What's so restrictive about this? What Popper does use is a strict notion of justification. For Popper, justification is logical demonstration. But there is nothing arbitrary in the notion that justification is logical demonstration. This notion is implicit in the writings of most EP$_1$ philosophers, and many EP$_2$ philosophers as well. Now Nagel's accusation of scepticism may be due to Popper's denial that scientific statements can ever be justified. But Popper also denies that scientific statements *need* to be justified to qualify as knowledge. For Popper, it is the *demand* for justification which leads to scepticism – by continually frustrating expectations. So long as one fails to take seriously Popper's denial that justification is a criterion of knowledge, the equation of justification with logical demonstration will translate out as an overly restrictive use of the word "knowledge" (overly restrictive, that is, from the EP_2 perspective). And to that extent, Popper's claim that there is objective scientific knowledge, albeit fallible, will seem paradoxical. If it can't be justified, then it can't be knowledge!

What's going on here, and why?

We can begin our explanation by focussing on the justified true belief theory of knowledge. The shift from EP_1 to EP_2 involves the abandonment of the quest for certainty, and the acceptance of fallibilism. This acceptance of fallibilism is usually premised by the rejections of (a) *a priori* valid statements, and (b) induction as logically valid inference. Arguments for the rejections of (a) and (b) are well known, and need not be rehearsed here. But what we do need to discuss is the effect that this paradigm shift has on the traditional characterization of knowledge as justified true belief.

So long as one remains within EP_1, the effect of the rejections of (a) and (b) is obvious. Science requires the statement of universal laws. And the epistemological problem which arises regarding these laws concerns the nature of their justification. Since EP_1 construes knowledge as entailing objective certainty, it requires that justification be sufficient to guarantee such certainty. Initially, philosophers thought that such certainty could be guaranteed through direct intuition and logical inference. Here, philosophers distinguished between two types of intuition, sensuous and intellectual (i.e., *a posteriori* and *a priori*), and two types of inference, deductive and inductive. But they soon recognized that inference alone is insufficient to guarantee the certainty of universal laws. Not deductive inference, because deductive inference presupposes the very universal statements here in question. Not inductive inference, because inductive inference never guarantees the truth of its conclusions. But nor can sensuous intuitions alone guarantee the objective certainty of strictly universal statements. Sense perception can tell us that such-and-such is this-and-that. But sense perception alone cannot tell us that *all* such-and-such are this-and-that (not at least, unless the class of such-and-such is finite and well determined; but then, the statement would not be *strictly* universal to begin with). Here, many philosophers appealed to intellectucal or *a priori* intuition to justify strictly universal statements. But history has not been kind to such efforts. And as claims to *a priori* knowledge became more and more suspect, the spectre of scepticism loomed ever larger on the horizon. From the EP_1 perspective, the obvious conclusion to the rejection of (a) and (b) is scepticism.

But the situation within EP_2 is very different – this, because EP_2 *begins* with the acceptance of fallibilism. Here science still requires the statement of universal laws. And the epistemological problem which arises regarding these universal laws still concerns the nature of their justificaiton. But since EP_2 *does not* conceive of knowledge as objective certainty, justification, if demanded, is no longer required to be sufficient to provide such certainty. In other words, EP_2 philosophers need not construe justification as logical demonstration. Many EP_2 philosophers, Nagel included, thus thought that the most natural way to facilitate the shift from EP_1 to EP_2 would be to retain the justified true belief theory of knowledge, but weaken the requirements for justification. But while this approach might indeed be natural, Popper thinks that it is inadequate — for there are problems with the concept of justification independent of those concerning the justification of universal laws.

Popper's response to the shift from EP_1 to EP_2 is not to weaken the concept of justification, but to abandon it as a criterion of rational knowledge. This rejection of justification as a criterion of rational knowledge is the most distinctive feature of Popper's epistemology. But while it is reflected almost everywhere in his philosophy, we should not be confused as to its ground. Whereas Popper's anti-justificationism is most often associated with his fallibilism and his falsificationist criterion of demarcation, it more clearly follows from his characterization of scientific knowledge as non-authoritarian and rational. Popper's rejection of verificationism as the criterion of demarcation was based primarily on the fact that the strictly universal laws of science cannot be empirically verified. Any criterion of demarcation that fails to account for the scientific character of scientific laws is clearly inadequate. But Popper's rejection of justification as a criterion of knowledge has more to do with general problems concerning the nature of justification *by rational or logical argument* than with specific problems concerning the justification of universal statements. In arguing against induction as logically valid inference, Popper seems primarily concerned with debunking the view that scientific knowledge is or can be objectively certain. But in rejecting justification as a criterion of knowledge, Popper seems primarily concerned with providing a positive account of knowledge as objective and rational.

According to Popper, the very idea that knowledge must be justified lays the groundwork for an authoritarian and subjectivist epistemology:

> The first, the false idea, is that we must justify our knowledge, or our theories by *positive* reasons, that is, by reasons capable of establishing them, or at least of making them highly probable; at any rate, but better reasons than that they have so far withstood criticism. This idea implies, I suggested, that we must appeal to some ultimate or authoritative source of true knowledge; which still leaves open the character of that authority — whether it is human like observation or reason, or super-human (and therefore supernatural.)[9]

In this sense, Popper considers both classical rationalism and classical empiricism to be authoritarian epistemologies: the former appealing to the authority of the intellect, the latter to the authority of the senses.[10] Contrary to classical rationalism and empiricism, Popper believes that neither observation nor reason are authorities. At least, neither are *infallible* sources of true knowledge. Intellectual intuition and imagination are most important, but they are not reliable: They may show us things very clearly and yet they may mislead us.[11] Moreover, from Popper's perspective, the very *appeal* to authority to justify cognitive claims is itself the antithesis of rationalism, which "always claimed the right of reason and of empirical science to criticize, and to reject, any tradition, and any authority, as being based on sheer unreason or prejudice or accident."[12] Finally, despite their expressed intentions to attack prejudice and traditional beliefs, Popper considers both classical rationalism and empiricism to be essentially religious doctrines, and hence subjectivist epistemologies.[13]

It is clear that Popper regards any appeal to authoritative sources of knowledge as a departure from rational methodology. But how does the demand that we justify our theories by positive reasons *imply* that we appeal to some ultimate or authoritative source of true knowledge? We can, perhaps, best illustrate Popper's thought here by considering his exposition of Fries' trilemma:

> The problem of the basis of experience has troubled few thinkers so deeply as Fries. He taught that, if the statements of science are not accepted *dogmatically*, we must be able to justify them. If we demand justification by reasoned argument, in the logical sense, then we are committed to the view that *statements can be justified only by statements*. The demand that *all* statements are to be logically justified (described by Fries as a 'predilection for proofs') is therefore bound to lead to an *infinite regress*. Now, if we wish to avoid the danger of dogmatism as well as an infinite regress, then it seems as if we could only have recourse to *psychologism*, i.e. the doctrine that statements can be justified not only by statements but also by perceptual experience.[14]

But why the demand that *all* statements be logically justified? Logical proofs function as a sort of epistemological microscope. With their aid we can evaluate the epistemic status of the conclusion of a valid argument by focussing on that of its premises — the status of the latter being transferred to the former by the validity of the argument. If justification is construed as logical proof, then the epistemological questions regarding any proposed justification concern not simply the validity of the argument, but also the truth of its premises. Hence, the analysis of the justification of a statement must ultimately involve an analysis of the justification of the statements which justify that statement. For if we thought that statements can be justified only by other statements, but did not demand logical justification of the premises of a justifying argument, then it would be difficult to see how we could consider the conclusion of that argument justified — or is it impossible for a valid argument to have false premises? But the demand that all statements be justified logically clearly leads to an infinite regress and, paradoxically, to no justification at all. Hence, the implications of the demand for logical justification lead to the rejection of that demand. And we are led to appeal to something that is *not* justified logically to serve as a foundation upon which to ground justification.

It should be clear that Fries' trilemma is simply a more explicit statement of the reasoning that led Hume to epistemological psychologism and an irrationalist epistemology. And here psychologism might be thought to be a species of dogmatism. But while both ultimately involve appeals to authority, there are subtle differences. Dogmatism involves the acceptance of statements *without* justification. But psychologism attempts to ground logical justification on statements which *are* justified, albeit not logically, i.e., not by other statements.

Dogmatism avoids the infinite regress implicit in the predilection for proofs by accepting some statements without any justification at all. From a Popperian perspective, this procedure is irrational because it requires that some statements be accepted uncritically. More generally, dogmatism renders the whole process of justification a charade. If we can only justify statements by demonstrating them as logical consequences of statements which are accepted without justification, then why the demand for justification in the first place?

Psychologism, like dogmatism, avoids the infinite regress implicit in the predilection for proofs by rejecting the demand that all statements be justified logically. But psychologism also avoids the charade of dogmatism by refusing to accept statements without justification. Rather, psychologism rejects the thesis that statements can be justified *only* by other statements, maintaining instead that statements can be justified by sense experience as well.

Here we should note that Popper regards positivist anti-psychologism as an inadequate response to Fries' trilemma and, at base, a mere masking of the problem. Whereas Fries emphasized that the (logical) relations holding between statements are very different from the relation between statements and sense experiences, the positivists tried to abolish the distinction. Either all science is made part of my knowing, "my" sense experience, or sense experiences are made part of the objective scientific network of arguments.[15] Insofar as this is concerned, Popper thinks that the positivist appeal to the formal mode of speech ultimately fails:

The view which I call 'psychologism' ... still underlies, it seems to me, a modern theory of the empirical basis, even though its advocates do not speak of experiences or perceptions but, instead, of 'sentences' – sentences which represent experiences. These are called *protocol sentences* by Neurath and by Carnap. ...

Carnap starts with a somewhat different question. His thesis is that all philosophical investigations speak 'of the forms of speech'. The logic of science has to investigate 'the forms of scientific language'. It does not speak of (physical) 'objects' but of words; not of facts, but of sentences. With this, the correct, the *'formal mode of speech'*, Carnap contrasts the ordinary or, as he calls it, the 'material mode of speech'. If confusion is to be avoided, then the material mode of speech should only be used where it is possible to translate it into the correct formal mode of speech.

Now this view – with which I can agree – leads Carnap (like Reininger) to assert that we must not say, in the logic of science, that sentences are tested by comparing them with states of affairs or with experiences: we may only say that they can be tested by comparing them with other *sentences*. Yet Carnap is nevertheless really retaining the fundamental ideas of the psychologistic approach to the problem; all that he is doing is to translate them into the 'formal mode of speech'. He says that the sentences of science are tested 'with the help of protocol sentences'; but since these are explained as statements or sentences 'which are not in need of confirmation but serve as a basis for all the other sentences of science', this amounts to saying – in the ordinary 'material' mode of speech – that the protocol sentences refer to the 'given': to the 'sense-data'. They describe (as Carnap himself puts it) 'the contents of immediate experience, or the phenomena; and thus the simplest knowable facts.' Which shows clearly enough that the theory of protocol sentences is nothing but psychologism translated into the formal mode of speech.[16]

What Popper objects to here is not that there is a causal connection between basic statements and perceptual experiences.[17] Rather, it is that this causal relation is or can be one of justification:

I readily admit that only observation can give us 'knowledge concerning facts', and that we can (as Hahn says) 'become aware of facts only by observation.' But this awareness, this knowledge of ours, does not justify or establish the truth of any statement. I do not believe, therefore, that the question which epistemology must ask is, '... on what does our *knowledge* rest? ... or more exactly, how can I, having had the *experience* S. justify my description of it, and defend it against doubt?'[18]

So it is not so much the appeal to observation that bothers Popper, but the appeal to observation to *justify* statements.

But here psychologism is, ultimately, as authoritarian an epistemology as dogmatism. Instead of accepting dogmatically the authority of statements, it accepts dogmatically the authority of sensuous experience as the source of true knowledge. This difference, however, is important for an understanding of Popper's thought. Popper opposes psychologism as an irrationalist epistemology in part because of its appeal to sense experience as an authoritative source of knowledge. But Popper also emphasizes the fact that psychologism departs from the view that statements can be justified *only* by other statements. And this calls attention to Popper's underlying commitment to the equation between rationality and logicality. Logic, Popper maintains, deals with the relationships between statements. And sense perceptions, whatever else they may be, are not statements.

Earlier we said that the equation traditionally presupposed in the formulation of Popper's problem identified rational knowledge with statements justified by logically sound arguments (rationality=justification=logicality). Popper himself cites this equation in his intellectual autobiography:

Previously, most philosophers had thought that any claim to rationality meant rational *justification* (of one's beliefs).... Thus the old philosophy linked the ideal of rationality with final, demonstrable knowledge (either proreligious or antireligious; religion was the main issue)....[19]

Explicitly: statements were considered rational knowledge to the extent to which they were justified logically. Popper has argued that this demand for logical justification leads ultimately to either infinite regress or an appeal to authority (an authoritarian epistemology). But if scientific procedures preclude appeals to authority to justify cognitive claims, then the possibility of rational knowledge demands that we abandon the above equation in favor of a new concept of rationality.

Were we to regard the appeal to the authority of sense experience as, in some sense, benign, and Popper's characterization of Hume's epistemology as irrationalist as merely pejorative, then we might be led to construe psychologism as offering a new concept of rationality. Here, the rationality of knowledge would still be linked with its justification, but justification would be understood as requiring less then *logical* demonstration. Specifically, the "justification" of statements by sense perceptions would be considered rational. It would be considered rational because it's not *crazy*. But Popper uses "rational" less in an ameliorative than in a technical sense. Popper's technical sense of "rational" plays on the linguistic link between rationality and reason (a link which construes reasons as statements, and, hence, distinct from sense perceptions). Moreover, Popper would regard any scientific knowledge justified by sense perceptions as hopelessly subjective. Hume, in any event, did not consider sense perceptions to be reasons. Rather, he maintained the distinction between reasons and sense perceptions, and used it to argue that "reason is and ought only to be the slave of the passions".[20]

Scientific knowledge, according to Popper, is rational knowledge. But scientific knowledge neither is nor can be justified. So, the rationality of knowledge, according to Popper, has nothing to do with its justification — logical or otherwise. Rather, Popper holds that rationality should be construed as rational *criticism* (of one's own theory and of competing theories).[21] And this construal of rationality is compatible with Popper's technical sense of "rational": if we cannot justify a statement with reasons (other statements) we can at least, Popper claims, condemn one. And lest Popper's characterization of rationality as rational criticism be thought circular, we should note that his rejection of the rationality=justification=logicality equation is also a recommitment to the more basic equation between rationality and logicality. *That* remains constant. What is new is Popper's replacement of justification with criticism. For Popper, rationality=criticism=logicality. What accounts for the rationality of science and scientific knowledge is its methodological adherence to deductive logic as the organon of criticism.

Here we are in a position to appreciate what is at issue in the dispute between Popper and Nagel. But in order to place that dispute in its sharpest focus, we should first emphasize the major points of agreement in their philosophies of science. As mentioned earlier, both philosophers have participated in the epistemological paradigm shift from EP_1 to EP_2. To that extent, their philosophies of science are both attempts to salvage rational knowledge in the face of uncertainty. There are, however, more specific points of agreement which unite the two. Aside from their recognition of science as a social institution, both philosophers uphold the methodological primacy of theory or speculative conjecture in opposition to the view that science progresses via the accumulation and generalization of facts (what Popper calls "the commonsense theory of knowledge", and "the bucket theory of the mind"). Insofar as this is concerned, both emphasize that science begins not with observations, but with problems — for observations must be interpreted, and interpretation involves the introduction of general ideas that are supplied by the creative imagination of the scientist:

> According to a popular view, sometimes endorsed by distinguished scientists, science starts an inquiry by collecting facts, and then passes the data through some sort of logical sieve which yields a uniquely determined formulation of a regularity between phenomena. This is a seriously misleading account of what actually takes place. For inquiry begins with a *problem*, provoked by some practical or theoretical difficulty; and in general it is not easy to know just what facts one ought to gather to resolve the problem, or whether a purported fact really is a fact. ... The scientist must therefore be selective, and concern himself only with those which are relevant. In consequence, he must adopt a preliminary hypothesis or guess as to how his specific problem may be resolved; and he must employ that hypothesis to suggest what he hopes are the relevant facts. In short, a responsibly conducted inquiry is guided by ideas that must be supplied by the investigator. Observation and experiment serve to test or control the adequacy of those ideas for the problem at hand; but observation and experiment do not provide the conceptions without which inquiry is aimless and blind.[24]

In addition, both Nagel and Popper agree that progress in science occurs not by appeal to authorities, but by a strict adherence to a critical methodology:

> It is through the operation of continual and independent criticism that scientific truth is achieved. The tradition of science is a tradition of toleration for new ideas, but a toleration qualified by a sturdy skepticism toward any notion which has not been subjected to observation and logical tests of validity — tests which are intended to be as severe as human ingenuity can devise. No one scientist engaged in this process of criticism is infallible, and each one will have his own peculiar intellectual or emotional bias. But the biases are rarely the same; and ideas which can survive the cross fire of the varied critical commentary that a large number of independently acting minds supply stand a better chance of being sound than conceptions which are alleged to be valid simply because they appear to be self-evident to some individual thinker.[25]

The above two statements of Nagel might well have been taken from the Popperian corpus. They comprise, when taken together, a fairly accurate formulation of what Popper regards as the methodology of scientific inquiry, i.e., the method of conjecture and refutation.

Nevertheless, Nagel neither eschews the need for nor possibility of justification. Nor does he *equate* the rationality of scientific inquiry with its adherence to a deductive methodology of criticism. On the contrary, Nagel rejects the identification of the rationality of science with the use of exclusively formal canons for assessing claims to knowledge. For Nagel, rationality does *not* equal logicality. Instead, Nagel characterizes a *behavior* as rational "if it regularly (or for the most part) achieves the objectives for the attainment of which the behavior is undertaken."[26] And according to Nagel, the objective for which scientists undertake the behaviour of criticism is the attainment of reliable or established knowledge:

> ... despite its deliberate cultivation of a tough-minded critical spirit, the scientific attitude is not a wholesale skepticism concerning the possibility of genuine knowledge. On the contrary, the endless criticism in which the scientific community is engaged is performed on the assumption that reliable knowledge *can* be achieved by way of just such a critical process.[27]

Finally, and again contrary to Popper, Nagel holds that the validity of a scientific theory can be established, but established *only through verifying it by experiment or observation.*[28]

Here we can return to Nagel's suggestion that Popper's epistemology is, or leads to, scepticism. Again, it is important to remember that what EP_1 scepticism denied was the possibility of objective certainty. *That* argument can be schematized as follows:

1 Rational knowledge is justified true belief.
2 Justification logically demonstrates the truth of what is justified.
3 Logical demonstration depends, ultimately, on premises which cannot, themselves, be logically demonstrated.
   Therefore:
4 Rational knowledge is impossible.

Insofar as this schematization is concerned, Popper maintains (2) and (3). But by denying (1), he attempts to avoid (4). Nagel, for his part, maintains (1) and (3).[29] But Nagel seeks to avoid (4) by denying (2). Both of these moves are part and parcel of the epistemological paradigm shift from EP_1 to EP_2. And to that extent, both Nagel and Popper seek to avoid scepticism while acknowledging the fallibility of scientific knowledge. But from the EP_1 perspective, fallibilism just *is* scepticism. And unless we accept the existence of some infallible source of knowledge, and limit scientific knowledge to just what is derived immediately from that source, the denials of (1) and (2) entail that rational knowledge is fallible. Hence, to the extent to which Popper and Nagel continue to oppose scepticism, they understand "scepticism" in some non-classical (i.e., non-EP_1) sense.

But while Nagel and Popper both use "scepticism" in a non-classical sense, they do not both use it in the same non-classical sense. Nagel, perhaps, can best be understood as using "scepticism" to describe the position that no scientific claim is *reliable.*[30] This interpretation, at least, makes some sense of Nagel's conjunction of fallibilism with the claim that some scientific statements are fully warranted. A statement need not be indubitable to be reliable. And the adequacy, or reliability, of scientific hypotheses, according to Nagel, can be achieved by way of a critical process which ultimately makes reference to matters capable of repeated public observation — this, despite the fact that *all* conclusions of scientific inquiry are corrigible in the light of future evidence.[31] But if this is what Nagel means by "scepticism", then Popper would welcome the charge. For Popper is explicit that "from a rational point of view, we should not 'rely' on any theory, for no theory has been shown to be true, or can be shown to be true":[32]

> In other words, there is no 'absolute reliance'; but since we *have* to choose, it will be 'rational' to choose the best-tested theory. This will be 'rational" in the most obvious sense of the word known to me: The best-tested theory is the one which, in the light of our critical discussion, appears to be the best so far, and I do not know of anything more 'rational' than a well-conducted critical discussion.
> Of course, in choosing the best-tested theory as a basis for action, we 'rely' on it, in some sense of the word. It may therefore even be described as the *most* 'reliable' theory available, in some sense of this term. Yet this does not say that it is 'reliable'. It is not 'reliable' at least in the sense that we shall always do well, even in practical action, to foresee the possibility that something may go wrong with our expectations.[33]

Nevertheless, it might be thought that the dispute here is merely verbal. For Nagel too would agree that there is no "absolute reliance", if "absolute reliance" means that a theory is indubitable.[34] Popper is, admittedly, targeting his denial of the reliability of scientific theories, in part, against the quest for certainty. But as we've seen, the issue here goes well beyond the fallibility of theories.

Claims about the reliability of a theory are claims about our confidence in the *future performance* of that theory. We rely upon a theory to the extent to which we have confidence that it will continue to withstand severe criticism. To that extent, the burden of justificationism, even in its weakened form in which "justified" is interpreted as "confirmed" (on the basis of past performance), is to provide rational support for our confidence that a theory will perform satisfactorily in the future. In denying inductivism, or the thesis that theories can be confirmed on the basis of past performance, Popper is denying that the past performance of a theory is ever sufficient to provide rational support for our confidence that it will perform satisfactorily in the future. And this is precisely the point at which Popper's notion of corroboration differs from the positivist notion of confirmation.

Popper discusses this divergence, and in particular the reasons for his own use of "confirmation", in a footnote to Chapter X of *The Logic of Scientific Discovery*:

> I introduced the terms 'corroboration' ('*Bewährung*') and especially '*aegree of corroboration*', ('*Grad der Bewährung*', '*Bewährungsgrad*') in my book because I wanted a *neutral* term to describe the degree to which a hypothesis has stood up to severe tests, and thus 'proved its mettle'. By 'neutral' I mean a term not prejudging the issue whether, by standing up to tests, the hypothesis becomes 'more probable', in the sense of the probability calculus. In other words, I introduced the term 'degree of corroboration' mainly in order to discuss the problem whether or not 'degree of corroboration' could be identified with 'probability' (either in a frequency sense or in the sense of Keynes, for example).
> Carnap translated my term 'degree of corroboration' ('*Grad der Bewährung*'), which

I had first introduced into the discussion of the Vienna Circle, as 'degree of confirmation'. ... I did not like this term, because of some of its associations ('make firm'; 'establish firmly'; 'put beyond doubt'; 'prove'; 'verify': 'to confirm' corresponds more closely to *'erhärten'* or *'bestätigen'* than to *'bewähren'*). I therefore proposed in a letter to Carnap (written, I think, about 1939) to use the term 'corroboration'. ... But as Carnap declined my proposal, I fell in with his usage, thinking that words do not matter. This is why I myself used the term 'confirmation' for a time in a number of my publications.

Yet it turned out that I was mistaken: the associations of the word 'confirmation' did matter, unfortunately, and made themselves felt: 'degree of confirmation' was soon used — by Carnap himself — as a synonym (or 'explicans') of 'probability'. I have therefore now abandoned it in favour of 'degree of corroboration'.[35]

The use of "corroboration" instead of "confirmation" becomes more critical in light of Popper's denial that the corroboration of a theory has anything to do with either the confirmation or the probability of that theory. And this relates precisely to the issue between Popper and Nagel. Whereas "confirmation" suggests that a theory's ability to withstand severe criticism in the past provides a warrant for our confidence that it will continue to withstand severe criticism in the future, "corroboration", at least as Popper uses it, carries no such suggestion.

According to Popper, a corroboration report of a theory is nothing more nor less than an evaluation of the past performance of that theory in withstanding criticism:

By the degree of corroboration of a theory I mean a concise report evaluating the state (at a certain time t) of the critical discussion of a theory, with respect to the way it solves its problems; its degree of testability; the severity of tests it has undergone; and the way it has stood up to these tests. Corroboration (or degree of corroboration) is thus an evaluating *report of past performance*. Like preference, it is essentially comparative: in general, one can only say that a competing theory A has a higher (or lower) degree of corroboration than a competing theory B, in the light of the critical discussion, which includes testing, *up to some time t*. Being a report of past performance only, it has to do with a situation which may lead to preferring some theories to others. But it says nothing whatever about future performance, or about the 'reliability' of a theory.[36]

And Popper goes on to emphasize this last point:

Some people thought that the phrase 'prove its fitness to survive' shows that I had here intended to speak of a fitness to survive in the *future*, to stand up to future tests. I am sorry if I have misled anybody, but I can only say that it was not I who mixed the Darwinian metaphor. Nobody expects that a species which has survived in the past will therefore survive in the future: all the species which ever failed to survive some period of time t have survived up to that time t. It would be absurd to suggest that Darwinian survival involves, somehow, an expectation that every species that has so far survived will continue to survive.[37]

Popper, as we have seen, eschews both scepticism and the thesis that scientific knowledge is reliable. So it is clear that Popper does not understand "scepticism" in the same sense as Nagel. Now Popper does characterize scepticism as a theory which is pessimistic with respect to the possibility of the growth of knowledge.[38] But since Popper argues that neither certainty nor justification are possible, this pessimism concerns neither the prospects for certainty nor the prospects for justification. Rather, Popper understands scepticism to be a pessimism concerning the prospects for a non-arbitrary *choice* between competing scientific theories. To that extent, Popper equates scepticism with relativism:

> By relativism – or, if you like, scepticism – I mean here, briefly, the theory that the choice between competing theories is arbitrary; since either, there is no such thing as objective truth; or, if there is, no such thing as a theory which is true or at any rate (though perhaps not true) nearer to the truth than another theory; or, if there are two or more theories, no ways or means of deciding whether one of them is better than another.[39]

Contrary to scepticism, Popper maintains that: (1) there is objective and absolute truth; (2) some theories have greater verisimilitude (are nearer to the truth) than others; and (3) corroboration reports can, via the elimination of false theories, help us to rationally determine whether one competing theory is better (nearer the truth) than another.

Without giving a detailed or formal account, we can introduce Popper's notion of verisimilitude. "Verisimilitude" refers generally to what Popper calls the "content" of a statement, and, in particular, to what he calls the "truth content" and "falsity content" of a statement. By "content of a statement", Popper means the consequence class of that statement, i.e., the class of all statements which follow logically from it. The class of all the non-tautological, true statements which are entailed by a statement is called the "truth content" of that statement. And the class of all the false statements implied by a statement is called the "falsity content" of that statement.[40] Concerning verisimilitude, Popper writes:

> Intuitively speaking, a theory T_1 has less verisimilitude than a theory T_2 if and only if (a) their truth contents and falsity contents (or their measures) are comparable, and either (b) the truth content, but not the falsity content, of T_1 is smaller than that of T_2, or else (c) the truth content of T_1 is not greater than that of T_2, but its falsity content is greater. In brief, we say that T_2 is nearer to the truth, or more similar to the truth, than T_1, if and only if more true statements follow from it, but not more false statements, or at least equally many true statements but fewer false statements.[41]

The truth content of tautologies consists only of tautologies. Popper sets *that* content at zero to indicate that while science aims at truth, it does not aim at tautological, or uninformative, truth.

Popper's belief that there is objective and absolute truth, while a form of absolutism, is not combined with any dogmatic or authoritarian claim to possess the truth. On the contrary, his fallibilism entails that we are *never* in a position to make such claims. So-called "fallibilistic absolutism" "merely asserts that our mistakes, at least, are absolute mistakes, in the sense that if a theory deviates from the truth, it is simply false, even if the mistake made was less glaring than that in another theory."[42] Moreover, fallibilism does not prohibit *claims* to possess absolute truth. It simply prohibits *dogmatic* claims to possess absolute truth. So it is clearly compatible with the existence of such truth. We may never know for certain whether Shakespeare or Bacon wrote *King Lear*, but it would be silly to conclude that *King Lear* had no author. For Popper, truth is decidedly *not* an illusion.[43] Fallibilism is also compatible with the claim to possess theories with greater verisimilitude than others, though such claims are, of course, always provisional. So while Popper's belief in absolute truth is admittedly meta-physical, it does play an important epistemological role. Epistemologically, absolute truth functions not as a criterion of knowledge, but as a regulative ideal for scientific inquiry. Scientific inquiry aims at truth. More exactly, scientific inquiry aims at verisimilitude. This, because: (a) science does not aim at tautol-ogies; and (b) we may prefer theories we believe to be false if we think that their truth content sufficiently exceeds their falsity content. In any event, science regulates its critical acceptance or rejection of theories with reference to their approximation of that ideal.

The fact that Nagel and Popper both oppose scepticism suggests that each is generally optimistic about the possibility of scientific knowledge. But the differ-ences in their respective uses of "scepticism" underscore the major issue between them, i.e., the nature and role of justification in the natural sciences. Whereas both philosophers maintain that strictly logical justification is impossible, Nagel, but not Popper, retains a role for non-logical justification, i.e., the justification of scientific statements by observation and sense experience. And here we can see that the basic issue that separates Popper and Nagel is, in Popper's sense, just that of psychologism. For having rejected the infinite regress implicit in the demand for strictly logical justification, and the dogmatism inherent in any claim to a prioricity (*a priori* valid statements), Nagel maintains that the reliabil-ity of a theory can be established through verification by experiment and obser-vation. And even were we to agree with Nagel that the past performance of a theory (its survival of criticism) renders it, in some sense, reliable, we would still have to concur with Popper that whatever reliability that theory has is not logical, but psychological — based on sense perceptions rather than reasons.

This psychologism, moreover, underlies any polemic concerning the validity of induction as a justification of scientific theories. Earlier we said that the prob-lem of the validity of inductive inference is logically distinct from that of psy-chologism. But there we spoke of induction only from a logical perspective. From an epistemological perspective, the validity of induction as a justification of scientific theories presupposes that statements can be justified by sense per-ceptions. For the validity of an inductive inference *as a justification* for a theory presupposes that the singular statements which serve as premises in that argu-ment are themselves justified. So even if we acknowledge that theories can be confirmed by inductive inference, we are still left with the problem of Fries' trilemma.

Nagel, as far as I can see, does not address the issue of psychologism as such.[44] But it is plain that he regards the view that statements cannot be verified by sense observation as unwarranted; provided, of course, that such "verification" is not construed as complete, i.e., as logical demonstration. To the extent to which such verification yields rational knowledge, the rational character of that knowledge is clearly not contingent upon its being justified *only by statements*. Rather, Nagel regards such attempts at purely logical justification as both otiose and the very antithesis of rationality. Rationality, for Nagel, is teleological. And the rationality of a behavior is to be assessed by its ability to achieve the goals for which it was designed. But attempts to secure complete and logical justification for scientific claims must then be irrational. For such attempts *never* achieve the ends for which they were designed. But Nagel does not think that this means that science should forsake the attempt for justification and the goal of reliable knowledge. It simply means that our concepts of justification, rationality, and reliable knowledge must be tempered by the means available to achieve approximations to those ends. And if anti-psychologism is predicated on the equation of rationality with logicality, then better we forsake *that* concept of rationality.

Apropos to these remarks, Nagel regards the "problems" with Popper's philosophy of science to stem from the latter's appeal to purely formal considerations for the evaluation of theories:

> However, much that Popper says suggests that his intent is not to offer a generalized *description* of the logic in use in science, but on the contrary to argue for a *prescription* he is recommending on how science *ought* to proceed. If his analyses are construed in this way, his prescriptions seem to me to be based ... mainly on *formal considerations*, and to presuppose a conception of what is a warranted claim to knowledge that is standard in the *formal disciplines* such as pure logic or demonstrative geometry.[45]

For Nagel, consistency is undoubtedly an ingredient in our conception of rationality. But while it may be a necessary condition for rational behaviour, it is hardly a sufficient one.[46]

The differences between Popper and Nagel have been emphasized here to provide a sharp focus on the issue of psychologism. But these differences, when viewed within the contexts of their respective philosophies of science, are subtle. So subtle, that there is a strong temptation to regard them as merely verbal. All that needs to be done is to regard corroboration reports as sufficient to warrant reliance on scientific theories, and their views might be thought virtually identical. But despite Popper's vacillation on the senses of "rely", this, I think, would be a mistake. For there are deep differences in attitude that underlie these subtle differences in epistemology. Underlying almost everything Popper writes is his deep antipathy to authority of any kind, be it the authority of religion, the past performance of theories, or the consensus of scientific belief. And while consideration of Nagel's own anti-authoritarianism might suggest that this difference is mainly one of emphasis, this difference of emphasis is important. For Popper refuses to rest content with any statement as "given", even if given by one's own sense experience. Popper's rejection of justificationism, and, in particular, psychologism, is predicated on just this refusal. And what follows upon it is a major difference in his conception of science. For while science may aim at truth, or verisimilitude, it does *not* aim at settled agreement. Rather, the research programme of all scientific inquiry includes a continual and never ending critique of all views taken as settled. But justificationism, even in its weakened form, points in the opposite direction by attempting to establish an authority for settled agreement. The research programme that follows upon Nagel's views points to the need to develop inductive logic as an instrument by which to achieve settled agreement. But any appeal to authority, even the authority of science, leads, on Popper's view, to subjectivism.

And here, finally, we can see that the target of Popper's fallibilism is not simply the rejection of the quest for certainty, but a recommitment to the quest for objective knowledge. For Popper, as much as Nagel, fully acknowledges that commonsense notion of certainty that means, briefly, 'certain enough for practical purposes'.[47] And if such commonsense claims to certainty are thought 'reasonable', then he might even acknowledge them as, in some ameliorative sense, rational. But the trouble with taking such commonsense claims to certainty as an aim of science is not that they are unattainable, but that they are purely subjective. Popper charges commonsense or practical certainty with subjectivism on at least three counts: (1) commonsense certainty is predicated of beliefs, and hence mental states, as opposed to statements, or the objective contents of statements; (2) commonsense certainty is assessed, in part, on the basis of the intensity of belief, which is variable from person to person and from time to time; and (3) commonsense certainty is relative to the *situation* in which a belief is held:

> If somebody asked me, 'Are you sure that the piece in your hand is a tenpenny piece?' I should *perhaps glance at it again* and say 'Yes". But should a lot depend on the truth of my judgment, I think I should take the trouble to go into the next bank and ask the teller to look closely at the piece; and if the life of a man depended on it, I should even try to get to the Chief Cashier of the Bank of England and ask him to certify the genuineness of the piece.
>
> What do I wish to say by this? That the 'certainty' of a belief is not so much a matter of its intensity, but of the *situation*: of our expectation of its possible consequences.[48]

Popper regards the commonsense or justified true belief theory of knowledge as inherently subjectivist at least in the sense of (1). It construes knowledge to be a species of belief, and hence a mental state. But the demand for justification by sufficient *reasons* for establishing that the item of knowledge is true with certainty was clearly an objectivist idea. Complete and logical demonstration would establish the truth of a statement regardless of anyone's belief. And Popper, I think, would even regard subjectivism in the sense of (1) as innocuous, *were such objective certainty attainable.* But in the absence of complete and logical demonstration, the inability to attain certainty without appeal to authority renders the justified true belief theory of knowledge subjectivist in the senses of both (2) and (3). For the certainty of the belief of an individual in a particular situation will always be relative to his acceptance of whatever authority is in question. Psychologism, needless to say, sins doubly against objectivism. Not only does it appeal to authority to justify cognitive claims, but the authority to which it appeals is the authority of sense perceptions, paradigmatic examples of mental states. In this way, Popper's conception of rationality as disavowing any appeal to sense experience is deeply linked to his quest for objective knowledge. In order to pursue this quest Popper found it necessary, early on, to reject justification as a criterion of knowledge. But in his later writings, Popper also found it necessary to introduce a concept of the third world — a realm of the objective contents of statements. In what follows, we will investigate this concept and, in particular, how it differs from the third realm of Frege.

NOTES AND REFERENCES

1.   Nagel, Ernest; "Philosophical Depreciations of Scientific Method"; in *Teleology Revisited*, by Ernest Nagel; Columbia University Press (New York, 1979) pp. 88-89. For a more explicit criticism of Popper's views, see: Nagel; "The Quest for Uncertainty"; in *Teleology Revisited*; pp. 64-83.

2.   O'Hear, Anthony; *Karl Popper*; Routledge & Kegal Paul (Boston, 1980) p. 205.

3.   See: Putnam, Hilary; "The 'Corroboration' of Theories"; in *Op. cit.*; *The Philosophy of Karl Popper*; Volume 1; p. 223.

4.   *Op. cit.*; Popper; *Conjectures and Refutations*; p. vii.

5.   We will return to this point later in our discussion.

6.   *Op. cit.*; Nagel; "The Quest for Uncertainty"; p. 65.

7.   *Ibid.*; p. 73.

8.   *Ibid.*; p. 69. The emphasis here is Nagel's.

9.   Popper, Karl; "On the Sources of Knowledge and of Ignorance"; in *Op. cit.*; *Conjectures and Refutations*; p. 29.

10.   *Ibid.*; p. 16.

11.   *Ibid.*; p. 28.

12.   *Ibid.*; p. 6. Popper here uses "rationalism" in a broad sense which covers not only Cartesian intellectualism, but critical empiricism too.

13. *Ibid.*; p. 15.

14. *Op. cit.*; Popper; *The Logic of Scientific Discovery*; pp. 93-94.

15. See: *Ibid.*; p. 105.

16. *Ibid.*; pp. 95-96.

17. See: *Ibid.*; p. 105.

18. *Ibid.*; p. 98.

19. *Op. cit.*; Schilpp; *The Philosophy of Karl Popper*; p. 119.

20. *Op. cit.*; Hume; *A Treatise on Human Nature*; p. 415.

21. *Op. cit.*; Schilpp; *The Philosophy of Karl Popper*; p. 119.

22. See, e.g.: *Op. cit.*; Popper; *Objective Knowledge*; pp. 341-361.

23. Nagel, Ernest; "Modern Science in Philosophical Perspective"; in *Op. cit.*; *Teleology Revisited*; p. 16.

24. *Op. cit.*; Nagel; *Teleology Revisited*; p. 15.

25. *Ibid.*; pp. 13-14.

26. *Ibid.*; p. 3.

27. *Ibid.*; p. 14.

28. *Ibid.*; p. 16.

29. See: *Ibid.*; p. 10.

30. Indeed, Nagel has told me that this is *just* what he means by "scepticism".

31. See: *Op. cit.*; Nagel; p. 14.

32. *Op. cit.*; Popper; *Objective Knowledge*; p. 21.

33. *Ibid.*; p. 22.

34. See: *Op. cit.*; Nagel; *Teleology Revisited*; p. 12.

35. *Op. cit.*; Popper; *The Logic of Scientific Discovery*; pp. 251-252.

36. *Op. cit.*; Popper; *Objective Knowledge*; p. 18.

37. *Ibid.*; p. 19.

38. *Ibid.*; p. 99.

39. *Op. cit.*; Popper; *The Open Society and Its Enemies*; Volume 2; p. 369.

40. *Op. cit.*; Popper; *Objective Knowledge*; p. 48.

41. *Ibid.*; p. 52.

42. *Op. cit.*; Popper; *The Open Society and Its Enemies*; Volume 2; p. 477.

43. Contrary to *Op. cit.*; *The Encyclopedia of Philosophy*; Volume 3; p. 37.

44. Nagel has told me that he was unaware that Popper uses "psychologism" to refer to the justification of statements by sense perceptions, and that he does not discuss psychologism because he "always thought it meant the Mill question about logic and mathemtics being empirical".

45. *Op. cit.*; Nagel; "The Quest for Uncertainty"; pp. 76-77.

46. See: Nagel, Ernest; "Carnap's Theory of Induction"; in *Op. cit.*; *Teleology Revisited*; p. 164.

47. *Op. cit.*; Popper; *Objective Knowledge*; p. 78.

48. *Ibid.* Isaac Levi, incidentally, has characterized this view as an instance of pernicious wishful thinking. According to Levi (See: Levi, Isaac; *The Enterprise of Knowledge*; The MIT Press (Cambridge, 1980) p. 4.), (3) (above) is based on a confusion between relevant and serious possibility. Levi, moreover, has told me that I have "completely misread Popper" by failing to see that Popper is directing his remarks primarily against a subjectivist interpretation of probability theory. But this, I think, is a pernicious form of wishful thinking. It results, I think, from a failure to appreciate that Popper has more on his mind than simply scoring points on Ramsey. The section at issue is from Popper's "Two Faces of Common Sense" in *Objective Knowledge*, and is subtitled "Analytical Remarks on Certainty" (pp. 78-81). Now it is true that Popper *does* there criticize Ramsey's interpretation of probability, and on similar grounds:

> There exists a subjectivist theory of probability which assumes that we can measure the degree of our belief in a proposition by the odds we should be prepared to accept in betting.
> This theory is incredibly naive. If I like to bet, and if the stakes are not high, I might accept any odds. If the stakes are very high, I might not accept a bet at all. If I cannot escape the bet, say because the life of my best friend is at stake, I may feel the need to reassure myself of the most trivial proposition.

(*Ibid.*; p. 79.)
But this is hardly a developed criticism, and in the context of "Analytical Remarks on Certainty" it has more the tone of an illustration of a point already made. In any event, it is a long jump from this (which, incidentally, is the only reference explicitly made to probability theory in the section) to the claim that Popper's remarks are directed primarily against subjectivist probability theory. On my view, they are primarily analytical remarks on certainty whose upshot is that absolute certainty is a limiting idea, and commonsense certainty is a subjectivist idea and cannot be the aim of objective knowledge. Far from being a *confusion* of relevant and serious possibility, Popper's view here seems to be a simple application of Peirce's social principle: if others think they have good reasons to believe I'm wrong, why should I be cocksure they don't?

9. SUBJECTLESS KNOWLEDGE AND THE THIRD WORLD

Thus far our discussion of Popper's anti-psychologism has focused upon one aspect of his rejection of the justified true belief theory of knowledge, i.e., his denial that justification is a criterion of scientific knowledge. To that extent, we have considered Popper's opposition to epistemological psychologism and, implicit therein, logical psychologism — both of which are primarily concerned with the nature and possibility of justification. But Popper is also critical of linguistic and mathematical psychologism. And in what follows we will focus upon another and perhaps more troublesome aspect of his rejection of the justified true belief theory of knowledge, i.e., his denial that scientific knowledge is a species of belief. This denial, like the rejection of justificationism, is a response to the epistemological paradigm shift from EP_1 to EP_2. But it is, perhaps, the most unintuitive feature of Popper's epistemology. Many philosophers have denied that scientific knowledge can be justified with objective certainty, and others have denied that it can be justified at all. But few, if any, have ever maintained that there can be knowledge without a knowing subject. This, however, is precisely what Popper suggests. Here, Popper's suggestion can best be understood as a consequence of his anti-justificationism and his commitment to objective knowledge. So long as one regards scientific knowledge as a species of belief, the quest for objective knowledge demands that it be distinguished from other species of belief. And so long as one regards scientific knowledge as justified true belief, that distinction will be drawn with reference to the quality of its justification. Popper, as we have seen, has argued that any form of justification short of complete logical demonstration results in a subjectivist epistemology. Moreover, in the absence of complete logical demonstration, the attempt to distinguish knowledge by reference to some other quality of belief also results in subjectivism. Hence, the quest for objective knowledge demands that knowledge itself be characterized as something other than a species of belief. Hence, the introduction of subjectless knowledge, and the third realm.

What is Popper's concept of the third realm, or World 3,[1] and how does it differ from Frege's? We can best approach Popper's notion of World 3 by considering his more intuitive distinction between Worlds 1 and 2. This distinction corresponds to the distinction between physical and mental states. It can, moreover, be drawn independently of any identity thesis one might hold regarding these states. For even if one holds that mental states are, in some sense, reducible to physical states, or vice versa, one must first distinguish these states along *some* lines — if only to make sense of the thesis. Now Popper regards World 1 to be the universe of physical processes, forces, fields of forces, etc.[2] And World 2 is characterized, accordingly, as the world of mental states — including states of consciousness, psychological dispositions, and unconscious states.[3] This distinction between Worlds 1 and 2 corresponds roughly to Frege's distinction between the so-called outer and inner worlds, a distinction which Frege though demanded little philosophical insight:

> A person who is still untouched by philosophy knows first of all things which he can see and touch, in short, perceive with the senses, such as trees, stones, and houses, and he is convinced that another person equally can see and touch the same tree and the same stone which he himself sees and touches. Obviously no thought belongs to these things. Now can he, nevertheless, stand in the same relation to a person as a tree?
>
> Even an unphilosophical person soon finds it necessary to recognize an inner world distinct from the outer world, a world of sense-impressions, of creations of his imagination, of sensations, of feelings and moods, a world of inclinations and decisions.[4]

Frege referred to all of these objects of the inner world, with the exception of decisions, as "ideas".[5] And empiricists like Locke and Hume, as we have seen, regarded such ideas as the contents of statements. But the difficulty with identifying the contents of statements with ideas is just that a person cannot stand in the same relation to another's idea as he can to a tree. While different persons can perceive the same tree, they cannot bear the same idea. For mental states are private to the individual consciousness that bears them. Earlier we saw that Popper characterized Hume's epistemology as irrationalist because it grounded justification on sense perceptions rather than reasons. But one need not go that far to recognize it as subjectivist. For as Frege argued, if ideas are the contents of statements, then it must be ideas, or World 2 entities, that stand in logical relation to one another. Contrary to this, Popper writes:

> One man's thought processes cannot contradict those of another man, or his own thought processes, at some other time; but the *contents* of his thoughts — that is, the statements in themselves — can of course contradict the contents of other thoughts. On the other hand, contents, or statements in themselves, cannot stand in psychological relations; *thoughts in the sense of contents* or statements in themselves and *thoughts in the sense of thought processes* belong to two entirely different "worlds".[6]

So even if we reject the possibility of justification, logical or otherwise, the commitment to a logical methodology of criticism requires that we distinguish between thoughts and thought processes. Just as a sense-impression cannot stand as a premiss in a logical justification of a thesis, no sense-impression can function as a premiss in a logical criticism of a thesis.

Popper's commitment to a logical methodology of criticism led him to the introduction of World 3, a world which includes the objective contents of thoughts,[7] things which can stand in logical relation to one another. Now Popper's World 3 has much in common with Frege's third realm. And Popper goes so far as to characterize his World 3 as resembling "most closely the universe of Frege's objective contents of thought".[8] Insofar as this is concerned, both philosophers are primarily concerned with the objective contents of thoughts. But Frege did not regard the set of objects in the third realm, nor does Popper regard the set of World 3 objects, as co-extensive with the set of objective contents of thoughts. Frege, for example, considered mathematical entities, e.g., numbers, lines, etc., to be third realm objects. And aside from mathematical entities, Popper includes in his World 3 such objects as tools, scientific problems, social institutions, and works of art —[9] none of which can be said to have truth values in the logical sense. Secondly, both philosophers share a common understanding of the "reality" of the objects in these worlds. Just as Frege wrote that "something entirely and in every respect inactive would be unreal and non-existent for us",[10] Popper bases the "reality" of World 3 objects on their ability to causally act upon, or interact with, ordinary real material things.[11] Thirdly, both philosophers agree that whatever interaction exists between objective thoughts and physical objects requires the medium of the inner world, or World 2. Frege, for example, wrote:

> How does a thought act? by being apprehended and taken to be true. This is a process in the inner world of a thinker which can have further consequences in this inner world and which, encroaching on the sphere of the will, can also make itself noticeable in the outer world. If, for example, I grasp the thought which we express by the theorem of Pythagoras, the consequence may be that I apply it, making a decision which brings about the acceleration of masses. Thus our actions are usually prepared by thinking and judgments. And so thought can have an indirect influence on the motion of masses.[12]

And Popper is explicit regarding the necessity of World 2 as a medium for the interaction between Worlds 1 and 3:

> One of the fundamental problems of this pluralistic philosophy concerns the relationship between these three 'worlds'. The three worlds are so related that the first two can interact, and that the last two can interact. Thus the second world, the world of subjective or personal experiences, interacts with each of the other two worlds. The first world and the third world cannot interact, save through the intervention of subjective or personal experiences.[13]

It would be tempting, considering these last two points, to say that both philosophers regard the "reality" of the third realm as, in some way, dependent upon World 2. But this, as we will soon see, would be a mistake. Despite their similarities, there are real and important differences between Popper's World 3 and Frege's third realm.

Now some features of Popper's World 3 which might be thought to distinguish it from Frege's third realm are only apparent. Thus, Frege thought that the objects of the third realm cannot be perceived through the senses,[14] i.e., that they are not spatio-temporal. But Popper often speaks of spatio-temporal objects, e.g., tools, works of art, books, and libraries, as World 3 objects. To that extent, Popper acknowledges that many World 3 objects exist in the form of material bodies, and belong, in a sense, to both World 1 and World 3.[15] But this is misleading. A book is a physical object, and it therefore belongs to World 1.

But what makes a book an object of World 3 is neither its paper nor its binding, but its content: that which remains invariant in the various copies and editions.[16] And the *content* of a book is not a material object, any more than a book, *qua* material object, is its own content. Another feature of World 3 which might be thought to distinguish it from the third realm concerns the so-called "timelessness" of truth. Frege, as we have seen, considered truth to be timeless, and thoughts to be the bearers of truth. But Popper (and this is a real difference) regards the objects of World 3 as creations of the human mind, i.e., of World 2. In this way, it might be thought that for Popper truth is not timeless, but comes into existence with the creation of thoughts. But Popper, for better or worse, thinks that the human genesis of World 3 in no way compromises the timelessness of truth.[17]

Now we've said it would be tempting to say that both Popper and Frege regard the "reality" of the third realm as, in some way, dependent upon World 2. This temptation sprang in part from their theories of the interaction between objective thoughts and physical objects, and in part from Popper's claim that "we accept things as 'real' if they can causally act upon, or interact with, ordinary material things."[18] But Frege's statement was qualified: something entirely and in every respect inactive, would be unreal and non-existent *for us*. Even a tree, if entirely and in every respect inactive, would be unreal and non-existent *for us*. Here, Frege's metaphor is telling: a thought "is not true for the first time when it is discovered, but is like a planet which, already before anyone has seen it, has been in interaction with other planets."[19] More explicitly: when one apprehends or thinks a thought one does not create it but only comes to stand in a certain relation, which is different from seeing a thing or having an idea, to what already existed beforehand.[20] And we should not consider this insignificant. Rather, it cuts to the very heart of Frege's notion of objectivity:

> If we want to emerge from the subjective at all, we must conceive of knowledge as an activity that does not create what is known but grasps what is already there.[21]

Popper, on the other hand, holds that:

> ... it is possible to accept the reality or (as it may be called) the autonomy of the third world, and at the same time to admit that the third world originates as a product of human activity.[22]

Here the difference between World 3 and the third realm can be stated simply: whereas Frege holds that the third realm is completely independent of the human mind for its existence, Popper regards World 3 as an evolutionary creation of man. And while both philosophers hold that objective thoughts can have an effect upon the inner world, Popper, but not Frege, maintains that the inner world can also have an effect upon objective thoughts.[23]

I think this last point should be emphasized. Frege, as we have seen, thought that objective knowledge was a discovery of man. Any suggestion that, e.g., arithmetic is a human creation would have been regarded by Frege as subjectivist — for what is created depends, for its very existence, upon its creator. To that extent, Frege based the objectivity of third realm objects upon their ontological independence from the human mind. But Popper, as we have seen, regards objective thoughts as a by-product of the human mind. Theories, for Popper, are not discovered but invented. And it follows that, for Popper, the objectivity of World 3 objects is not based upon their complete ontological independence from the human mind.

Here it is important to distinguish the objectivity of World 3 objects from their autonomy. Popper considers World 3 objects autonomous in the sense that *once they are created* they may have unforeseen consequences which can, themselves, be *discovered*:

> Let us look at the theory of numbers. I believe (unlike Kronecker) that even the natural numbers are the work of men, the product of human language and of human thought. Yet there is an infinity of such numbers, more than will ever be pronounced by men, or used by computers. And there is an infinite number of true equations between such numbers, and of false equations; more than we can ever pronounce as true, or false.
>
> But what is even more interesting, unexpected new problems arise as an unintended by-product of the sequence of natural numbers; for instance the unsolved problems of the theory of prime numbers (Goldbach's conjecture, say). The problems are clearly *autonomous*. They are in no sense made by us; rather, they are *discovered* by us; and in this sense they exist, undiscovered, before their discovery.[24]

In this way, a large part of World 3 is autonomous. It was discovered or may be discovered as an unintended consequence of theories created by the human mind. But if the autonomy of World 3 objects is related to the possibility of discovery, then it is clear that objectivity and autonomy are, for Popper, distinct concepts. For Popper regards, e.g., natural numbers as World 3 objects and hence objective, despite the fact that he considers them creations of the human mind. What accounts for the objectivity of thoughts, as opposed to their autonomy, is neither their creation nor discovery, but their ability to be formulated and expressed in language.

Popper considers the objectivity which results from the formulation of thoughts in language to be essential to the activity of criticism and, to the extent to which rational knowledge is distinguished by its critical method, the growth of science. While objective thoughts may, in some sense, have their origin in subjective beliefs, such beliefs, as we have seen, can neither stand in logical relations with one another nor be communicated to and criticized by other minds. It is only when a subjective belief is formulated in language and *becomes* a World 3 object that it can be presented as an object for criticism. And it is only when a theory is presented as an object for criticism that it can be considered in Popper's sense, scientific.

Here we can offer a more complete sketch of Popper's notion of objective knowledge. Traditionally, epistemologists construed scientific knowledge to be a form of justified true belief. To that extent, the objectivity of scientific knowledge was assessed with reference to the quality of its justification. Popper, as we have seen, rejected justification as a criterion for objective knowledge — for even the objectivist plea for logical demonstration leads to a form of subjectivism, i.e., an appeal to allegedly infallible sources of knowledge. But Popper also denies that objective knowledge need be believed, or, for that matter, true. To that extent, Popper believes that traditional epistemology is, despite its own intentions, concerned not with scientific or objective knowledge, but with knowledge in a subjective sense, i.e., knowledge in the sense of "I know", or "I believe". And this traditional epistemology, Popper holds, is simply irrelevant to the study of scientific knowledge:

> Traditional epistemology has studied knowledge or thought in a subjective sense — in the sense of the ordinary usage of the word 'I know' or 'I am thinking'. This, I assert, has led students of epistemology into irrelevances: while intending to study scientific knowledge, they studied in fact something which is of no relevance to scientific knowledge. For *scientific knowledge* simply is not knowledge in the sense of the ordinary usage of the word 'I know'. While knowledge in the sense of 'I know' belongs to what I call the 'second world', the world of *subjects*, scientific knowledge belongs to the third world, to the world of objective theories, objective problems, and objective arguments.
>
> Thus my first thesis is that the traditional epistemology, of Locke, Berkeley, Hume, and even of Russell, is irrelevant, in a pretty strict sense of the word. It is a corollary of this thesis that a large part of contemporary epistemology is irrelevant also. This includes modern epistemic logic, *if* we assume that it aims at a theory of scientific knowledge.[25]

So, contrary to traditional epistemology, Popper recognizes two different senses of knowledge: (1) knowledge in the subjective sense, consisting of a state of mind or consciousness, or a disposition to behave or react; and (2) knowledge in an objective sense, consisting of problems, theories, and arguments as such:[26]

> Knowledge in this objective sense is totally independent of anybody's claim to know; it is also independent of anybody's belief, or disposition to assent; or to assert, or to act. Knowledge in the objective sense is *knowledge without a knower*: it is knowledge without a knowing subject.[27]

Scientific knowledge may originate with subjective belief, i.e., it may be causally dependent upon World 2.[28] But what makes subjective belief objective knowledge is its emergence[29] into World 3, i.e., its formulation in language and its presentation as an object for criticism. Such formulation, we might add, is completely independent of anyone's belief in or even awareness of the theory formulated.

Frege, as we have seen, argued that being true is distinct from being thought or believed to be true. But the point of Frege's distinction was directed toward the need for justification. Objective certainty, Frege held, could not be based upon mere belief or even upon a general consensus on the part of the subjects who judge. Rather, it required justification in the form of logical demonstration. But for Popper, the distinction between a belief and the objective content of a statement has nothing to do with justification or truth. This follows directly from the statement that objective knowledge is fallible. Even were Popper to admit that most of what science asserts is true, the fact that what science asserts *may* be false implies that truth is not a criterion for objective knowledge. What impressed Popper as the scientific character of Einstein's theory of gravitation was not that he believed it to be true (which he did not[30]), but that by formulating its consequences in language Einstein presented the theory for criticism and thereby assumed the risk of refutation.[31] But Popper not only holds that there is objective knowledge which no one believes to be true, he also holds that there may be objective knowledge of which no one is even aware:

> ... a book, or even a library, need not even have been written by anybody: a series of books of logarithms, for example, may be produced and printed by a computer. It may be the best series of books of logarithms – it may contain logarithms up to, say, fifty decimal places. It may be sent out to libraries, but it may be found too cumbersome for use; at any rate, years may elapse before anybody uses it; and many figures in it (which represent mathematical theorems) may never be looked at as long as men live on earth. Yet each of these figures contains what I call 'objective knowledge'; and the question of whether or not I am entitled to call it by this name is of no interest.
>
> The example of these books of logarithms may seem far-fetched. But it is not. I should say that aamost every book is like this: it contains objective knowledge, true or false, useful or useless; and whether anybody ever reads it and really grasps its contents is almost accidental.[32]

Hence, Popper is led to speak of knowledge without a knower, and of objective knowledge that is false. Indeed, much of what Popper considers as objective knowledge is, strictly speaking, false. Though Popper, of course, holds that there may be a lot of truth in a false statement. That there is false knowledge is even necessary for Popper's conception of the growth of knowledge – since "all growth of knowledge consists in the improvement of existing knowledge which is changed in the hope of approaching nearer to the truth".[33]

In our discussion of Frege we argued that while the existence of an objective third realm might be a necessary condition for objective knowledge, it is not sufficient. There we assumed that knowledge was a sort of justified true belief, and we argued that what was lacking in Frege's account was a theory of apprehension which explains how the human mind can stand in relation to a third realm object without thereby compromising its objectivity (its mind independence). But since Popper construes objective knowledge to be knowledge without a knowing subject, a theory of apprehension no longer seems necessary for the possibility of objective knowledge. At least, since Popper acknowledges that World 3 is causally dependent upon World 2, the import of any such theory is shifted. Objectivity, in the sense of mind-independence, is here not at stake. There is no need to explain how World 3 objects can be apprehended while *remaining* mind-independent, for World 3 objects were not mind-independent to begin with.

Nevertheless, while Popper maintains that objective knowledge might be contained even in a book that is never read, he does admit that "in order to belong to the third world of objective knowledge, a book should — in principle, or virtually — be capable of being grasped (or deciphered, or understood, or 'known') by somebody".[34] But unlike Frege, Popper does offer a theory of apprehension to explain the mechanics of grasping a World 3 object and the limitations inherent in understanding it. Popper formulates this theory in contra-distinction to Plato's theory of the apprehension of Forms:[35]

> Now Plato described the grasping of the forms or ideas as a kind of vision: our mental eye (*nous*, reason), the "eye of the soul" is endowed with intellectual intuition and can *see* an idea, an essence, an object that belongs to the intelligible world. Once we have managed to see it, to grasp it, we know this essence: we can see it "in the light of truth". This intellectual intuition, once it has been achieved, is infallible.[36]

Contrary to this theory, Popper denies that there is anything like an intellectual sense organ. All that is required for Popper's theory of apprehension is our ability to produce World 3 objects.[37] More importantly, while Popper does appeal to something like intellectual intuition, he denies that such intuition is infallible. Rather, he holds that "it more often errs than not".[38] Popper's theory of apprehension has three main points which can be stated as follows: (1) the apprehension of a World 3 object is an active process of making or recreating that object; (2) while apprehension is a World 2 process, it is one which acts World 3 objects; and (3) this World 2 process is an instance of the model of problem solving which Popper regards as characteristic of most scientific inquiry.

That the apprehension of a World 3 object is an active process is important. It implies that we must *do* something to try to understand a thought, i.e., that we must exercise the will. This distinguishes apprehension from believing. Beliefs are not understood, they are 'had'. And it is not at all clear that believing in-volves an exercise of the will, i.e., that belief is voluntary. While we can choose whether or not to try to understand a thought, belief seems to be something that is forced upon us. If one does not believe that P, *trying* to believe it is of no avail. And it is not at all clear even what one would do to *try* to believe that P. Furrow his brow? But if we don't understand P, there are positive steps we can take to try to understand P — and these often have successful results. Neverthe-less, apprehending, or understanding, is a World 2 process. For it is, after all, the subject who attempts to understand. But despite the fact that the activity of understanding is subjective, or psychological, it "*consists, essentially, in oper-ating with third-world objects*"[39]:

> Admittedly, the activities or processes covered by the umbrella term 'understanding' are subjective or personal or psychological activities. They must be distinguished from the (more or less successful) *outcome* of these activities, from their result: the 'final state' (for the time being) of understanding, the interpretation. Although this *may* be a sub-jective state of understanding, it may also be a third-world object, especially a theory; and the latter case is, in my opinion, the more important one.[40]

The activity of making or recreating a World 3 object can be represented by Popper's general schema for problem-solving by the method of conjecture and refutation stated in its simplest form:

$$P_1 \longrightarrow TT \longrightarrow EE \longrightarrow P_2$$

where "P_1" stands for the problem situation from which we start (here, the problem of understanding a theory); "TT" stands for a tentative theory or imaginative conjectural solution which we first reach (here, our first interpretation); "EE" stands for error elimination by a severe critical examination of the tentative theory (our first interpretation); and "P_2" stands for the revised problem situation (inherent in the confrontation between TT and EE). Here Popper holds that a satisfactory understanding can be reached if the interpretation finds support in the fact that it can throw new light on new problems; or if it finds support in the fact that it explains many sub-problems, some of which were not seen to start with.[41] Now, a more detailed sketch of this procedure, one which takes into account so-called "background knowledge" and revisions made upon such background knowledge, can be given. But what is, perhaps, more interesting for our discussion are the limitations this procedure imposes on any attempt to reach a "final state" of understanding. For this process of understanding, like the quest for objective knowledge, is, at least in principle, never-ending. Rather, our understanding can be said to grow, or deepen from problem situation to problem situation.

Consider the thought expressed by "Popper attempts to conjoin fallibilism with the quest for objective knowledge". Do I understand this thought? Well, can I read English? There is a sense in which I can understand any thought expressed by a grammatical sentence in a language whose terms I am familiar with. The grammar of the sentence may be complex, involving the use of a large number of embedded subordinate clauses. And I may need to reread the sentence several times, even graphing it on paper, to (slowly) reconstruct the relationships between these clauses and the main subject and predicate of the sentence. The sentence may contain terminology with which I am unfamiliar, and I may need to consult a dictionary and even try out several different senses of the unfamiliar terms. I may find the sentence ambiguous and offer more than one initial interpretation. And I may certainly find the sentence (especially at first glance) paradoxical and wonder how anyone in his right mind could assert it. But all this presupposes a basic and rudimentary ability to understand.

A first interpretation (TT) of the grammatically simple sentence, "Popper attempts to conjoin fallibilism with a quest for objective knowledge", might be that Popper somehow considers fallibilism consistent with objective certainty, i.e., statements justified by logical demonstration. And while this might strike me as strange, I might, were motivation lacking, well be satisfied with that interpretation. Further reading, however, leads me naturally to error elimination (EE). I find that Popper denies that objective certainty is possible. So my first interpretation cannot be correct. And this naturally leads me to a new problem situation: how to understand the conjunction of fallibilism with a type of objective knowledge that does not imply objective certainty. A second tentative interpretation presents itself: Popper believes that fallibilism is consistent with justified true belief where justification falls short of logical demonstration. Again, I might feel satisfied with this interpretation and terminate the process of understanding. But further reading provokes still further elimination of errors, new problem situations, and further revisions of interpretations. Popper, I find, denies that knowledge can be or even needs to be justified. So my second interpretation cannot be correct. Popper, it seems must believe that objective knowledge is a sort of unjustified true belief — how strange!

Where does this process end? I read everything Popper has written, and then I reread it fifty times. Will this result in a "final state" of understanding? Perhaps, but *only if I am satisfied with that understanding and terminate the process.* For there is, in addition to what Popper has written, the "background knowledge" of the histories of philosophy and science. And these histories, if I read them, will no doubt have an effect on my understanding of Popper. And there is always the fifty-second reading of the Popperian corpus and the possible error elimination and revision of interpretation which might result from that. To the extent to which "final states" of understanding exist, they are inherently subjective. They depend solely upon a subject's willingness to curb his curiosity and rest content with an interpretation. Just as science, according to Popper, does not aim at settled agreement, understanding does not aim at a final state. For, objectively speaking, one does not exist.[42]

Here we are in a position to better understand the differences between Fregean and Popperian anti-psychologism. It is clear that both Frege and Popper oppose epistemological psychologism in the Humean sense, i.e., the thesis that statements can be justified by sense perceptions. But anti-psychologism, we have argued, has epistemological motivations. And insofar as these motivations are concerned, Fregean and Popperian anti-psychologisms point in different epistemological directions. Frege, as we have seen, thought that there is objective knowledge and that the objectivity of such knowledge is contingent upon the quality of its justification. To that extent, Fregean anti-psychologism argued that psychologistic justification cannot account for the objectivity of knowledge because it grounds justification on something inherently subjective, i.e., sense perceptions and memories of sense perceptions. But Frege did not forsake the need for justification. Epistemologically, Fregean anti-psychologism points back toward the need for purely logical methods of justification and, since Frege thought purely logical justification possible, to the necessity of admitting *a priori* truths. Popper, while agreeing with Frege that there is objective knowledge, does not assess the objectivity of that knowledge with reference to the quality of its justification. Rather, Popper denies both that *a priori* valid statements exist and that justification is possible. To that extent, Popperian anti-psychologism is a lemma in Popper's general argument against justificationism: statements cannot be justified by purely logical demonstration, and they cannot be justified psychologistically either. Not by purely logical demonstration, because this leads to infinite regress or to an appeal to infallible sources of knowledge. Not psychologistically, because sense perceptions are not reasons. Now Fregean anti-psychologism, in stressing the need for justification, results in an appeal to the Intellect or the Reason, as opposed to the senses, as an infallible source of knowledge. But Popper, as we have seen, regards any appeal to sources of knowledge, *a priori* or otherwise, as subjectivist. Popperian anti-psychologism, on the other hand, results in a general denial of the need for justification. But since Frege held justification to be a criterion of knowledge, he would regard Popperian anti-psychologism as leading to the very sort of scepticism he (Frege) was anti-psychologistic in order to avoid. So while both philosophers agree that statements cannot be justified by sense perceptions, neither would rest content with the import of the other's thesis.

Now Frege's introduction of the third realm was primarily an attempt to provide the means necessary for purely logical demonstration. If the objectivity of knowledge requires that statements be justified only by other statements, then a statement in itself, i.e., a thought, or the sense of an indicative sentence, cannot be a mental entity — for mental entities are not objective, but private to the individual consciousness which bears them. Moreover, if the objectivity of knowledge requires justification by purely logical methods, then the laws of logic cannot themselves be based upon empirical observation (sense perceptions) — for this would render them subject to revision and undercut the objectivity of the very means of justification. But Popper's introduction of World 3 clearly has nothing to do with providing the means for purely logical justification. If purely logical justification is impossible, then there is no need to provide means for it. Rather, Popper's introduction of World 3 is intended to provide the means for *purely logical criticism*. Just as a sense perception cannot stand as a premiss in a logical argument which justifies a statement, no sense perception can stand as a premiss in a logical argument which criticizes a statement. So while both the Fregean and Popperian introductions of objective thoughts are made to satisfy the requirements of logical arguments, their intended uses of logical arguments differ. But the introduction of World 3 has yet another function in Popperian epistemology. It provides the basis for Popper's concept of subjectless knowledge, a concept which, as far as I can see, does not appear in Frege's writings.

Now Popper's concept of subjectless knowledge is a legitimate use of the word "knowledge". It corresponds to the sense of "knowledge" as information, or a branch of learning. And Popper's claim that it is objective knowledge in this sense which is the proper subject matter for epistemology is, no doubt, an attempt to rid epistemology of all psychologistic tendencies. But this radical extension of his anti-psychologism is independent of, and seemingly at odds with, Popper's notion of conjectural knowledge and science's adherence to the methodology of conjecture and refutation. Whether we like it or not, it is the conscious subject who conjectures theories, and the conscious subject who attempts to refute them. Despite Popper's claim that it was the failure to recognize subjectless knowledge which led traditional epistemology to focus on irrelevances, the growth of knowledge (which Popper considers the fundamental problem of epistemology[43]) depends at least in part upon scientists proposing (psychologically *a priori*) theories as solutions to problems, and then coming to see the unforeseen consequences of those theories. We can, indeed, *talk* of these problems, theories, and consequences as World 3 entities. And gazing at the growth of knowledge from the perspective of World 3 might even shed some light on World 2. But we cannot avoid the knowing subject simply by refusing to speak of him. For better or worse, a scientist can only criticize that of which he is aware. If the growth of knowledge occurs through criticism, then it is the unforeseen consequences of a theory which remain forever unseen which are, practically speaking, irrelevant to epistemology. Popper's fear of the knowing subject is, I think, a consequence of his attempt to avoid scepticism by appealing to critical methodology to provide a non-arbitrary, or rational, choice between competing theories. If an appeal to a decision on the part of a knowing subject is necessary to make critical methodology operative, then Popper's epistemology might itself be in danger of psychologism. In what follows we will suggest that this is precisely the case.

NOTES AND REFERENCES

1.   Henceforth, we will adopt Popper's revised terminology and speak of "World 3" to distinguish it, at least terminologically, from Frege's "third realm".

2.   See: Popper, Karl R., and Eccles, John C.; *The Self and Its Brain*; Springer (New York, 1977) pp. 36-38.

3.   *Ibid.*; p. 28.

4.   *Op. cit.*; Frege; "The Thought: A Logical Inquiry"; p. 26.

5.   *Ibid.*

6.   *Op. cit.*; Schilpp; *The Philosophy of Karl Popper*; Volume 1; p. 144.

7.   Popper quotes Frege in this regard, "I understand by a *thought* not the subjective act of thinking but its objective content..." (See: *Op. cit.*; Popper; *Objective Knowledge*; p. 109.)

8.   Popper, Karl; "Epistemology Without a Knowing Subject"; in *Op. cit.*; *Objective Knowledge*; p. 106. See also: pp. 109, 126-127; and Popper, Karl; "On the Theory of the Objective Mind"; in *Op. cit.*; *Objective Knowledge*; pp. 153, 156, 162. It is, of course, Popper who characterizes his World 3 as Fregean. And while there are numerous similarities, we will argue that Popper's notion of World 3 differs significantly from Frege's.

9.   *Op. cit.*; Popper; *The Self and Its Brain*; p. 38.

10.   *Op. cit.*; Frege; "The Thought: A Logical Inquiry"; p. 37.

11. *Op. cit.*; Popper; *The Self and Its Brain*; p. 10.

12. *Op. cit.*; Frege; "The Thought: A Logical Inquiry"; p. 38.

13. *Op. cit.*; Popper; *Objective Knowledge*; p. 155.

14. *Op. cit.*; Frege; "The Thought: A Logical Inquiry"; p. 29.

15. *Op. cit.*; Popper; *The Self and Its Brain*; p. 38.

16. *Ibid.*; pp. 38-39.

17. *Op. cit.*; Schilpp; *The Philosophy of Karl Popper*; p. 148. Popper, we should note, does not say *how* the timelessness of truth is compatible with the human genesis of World 3.

18. *Op. cit.*; Popper; *The Self and Its Brain*; p. 10.

19. *Op. cit.*; Frege; "The Thought: A Logical Inquiry"; p. 29.

20. *Ibid.*; pp. 29-30.

21. *Op. cit.*; Frege; *The Basic Laws of Arithmetic*; p. 23.

22. *Op. cit.*; Popper; *Objective Knowledge*; p. 159.

23. This, I think, is what Frege had in mind when he wrote that the interaction between objective thoughts and the inner world lacks "reciprocal action". (See: *Op. cit.*; Frege; "The Thought: A Logical Inquiry"; p. 38.)

24. *Op. cit.*; Popper; *Objective Knowledge*; pp. 160-161.

25. *Ibid.*; p. 108.

26. *Ibid.*; pp. 108-109.

27. *Ibid.*; p. 109.

28. For the causal dependence of World 3 on World 2 see: *Ibid.*; p. 114.

29. For the emergence of World 3 from World 2 see: *Ibid.*; pp. 46-49.

30. *Op. cit.*; Popper; *Conjectures and Refutations*; p. 34.

31. *Ibid.*; p. 36.

32. *Op. cit.*; Popper; *Objective Knowledge*; p. 115.

33. *Ibid.*; p. 71.

34. *Ibid.*; p. 116.

35. I will not here consider the question whether or to what extent Popper's reconstructions of Plato's theories are accurate. It is, nevertheless, interesting to consider the contrasts

Popper draws between his World 3 and Plato's world of intelligible Forms:

> Though Plato's world of intelligible objects corresponds in some ways to our World 3, it is in many respects very different. It consists of what he called "forms" or "ideas" or "essences" – the objects to which general concepts or notions refer. The most important essences in his world of intelligible forms or ideas are the Good, the Beautiful, and the Just. These ideas are conceived of as immutable, as timeless or eternal, and as of divine origin. By contrast, our World 3 is man-made in its origin (man-made in spite of its partial autonomy...); a suggestion which would have shocked Plato. Moreover, while I stress the existence of World 3 objects, I do not think that essences exist; that is, I do not attribute any status to the objects or referents of our concepts or notions. Speculations as to the true nature or true definition of the good, or of justice, lead in my opinion to verbal quibbles and are to be avoided. I am an opponent of what I have called "essentialism". Thus in my opinion, Plato's ideal essences play no significant role in World 3. (That is, Plato's World 3, though clearly in some sense an anticipation of my World 3, seems to me a mistaken construction.) On the other hand, Plato would never have admitted such entities as problems or conjectures – especially false conjectures – into his world of intelligible objects...

(*Op. cit.*; Popper; *The Self and Its Brain*; pp. 43-44.)

36. *Ibid.*; p. 44.

37. *Ibid.*; p. 45.

38. *Ibid.*; p. 44.

39. *Op. cit.*; Popper; *Objective Knowledge*; p. 164.

40. *Ibid.*; pp. 162-163. Popper contrasts this view with comments on the interpretation of Husserl's anti-psychologism. These comments are marred by Popper's suggestion that Husserl is, in some sense, to blame for the psychologism prevalent in contemporary hermeneutics. They are, nonetheless, of interest to our discussion:

> In spite of the vogue of anti-psychologism which started with Husserl's *Logische Untersuchungen*, 1900-1..., psychologism – that is, neglect or even denial of the third world – is still powerful, especially among those interested in the theory of understanding ('hermeneutics'). Husserl's anti-psychologism was without doubt the result of Frege's criticism of Husserl's psychologistic *Philosophie der Arithmetik. Psychologische und Logische Untersuchungen*, 1891. In his *Logische Untersuchungen* (in which he refers to Bolzano), Husserl states with marvellous clarity (vol. i, p. 178): 'In all ... sciences we have to insist upon the fundamental distinction between three kinds of interrelations: (a) The interrelations of our *cognitive experiences*...;' (this is, what I here call the *second world*) '(b) The interrelations of the objects under investigation...;' (especially my *first world* – but it can be any of the others) 'and (c) The logical interrelations...'. (These belong to my third world.) It may well be, however, that it is just this most important passage which is to be blamed for the still so prevalent confusion. For in the place after (a) indicated by the dots, Husserl refers to the psychological interrelations of 'judgments, insights, conjectures, questions', and especially also acts of intuitive *understanding* 'in which a long discovered theory is thought out with insight'. The reference to 'judgments', 'conjectures' and 'questions' (on a level with 'insights') might have led to confusion, especially as Husserl speaks under (c) *only* of truths, apparently to the exclusion of false propositions, conjectures, questions, or problems; he mentions 'the *truths* of a scientific discipline, more especially of a scientific theory, of a proof or a conclusion'. (It should be remembered that Husserl and many even more recent thinkers looked upon a scientific theory as a scientific hypothesis which has been *proved true*: the thesis of

the conjectural character of scientific theories was still widely decried as absurd when I tried to propagate it in the nineteen thirties.) The way in which Husserl refers in this passage to *understanding* (cp. also vol. ii, pp. 62ff.) may also be responsible for some of the still prevailing psychologistic tendencies.

(*Ibid.*; p. 162; footnote 12.) Whether or not Husserl's anti-psychologism was due to Frege's critique is, however, a subtle and controversial issue, and it should not be thought without question. But what Popper fails to appreciate here is that his introduction of the thesis of the conjectural character of scientific theories changes the entire character of the problem of psychologism. Prior to Popper, falsehoods would be of no interest to the anti-psychologist, because the anti-psychologist was interested in *knowledge*, i.e., justified true belief. And no *conjecture*, true or false, could possibly provide anti-psychologistic grounds for justification.

41. *Ibid.*; pp. 164-165.

42. It follows as a corollary to this thesis that a book cannot be criticized for failure to provide a final understanding — unless, of course, it pretends to.

43. See, e.g.; *Op. cit.*; Popper; *Objective Knowledge*; p. 142.

10. OBSERVATION AND CRITICISM

Popper's notion of subjectless knowledge is intriguing, but susceptible to exaggeration. It serves as a heuristic toward understanding his epistemology to the extent to which it exposes certain psychological states, e.g., the conviction or sincerity of a subject, as irrelevant to the logical evaluation of scientific theories. But overemphasis on the alleged *subjectlessness* of scientific knowledge might all too easily be taken to imply that the growth of knowledge can and, in order to avoid subjectivism, must be explained without any reference at all to individuals or social groups. And this interpretation all too easily results in the witch-hunt of exposing each Popperian reference to individuals or social groups as an instance of psychologism. This, I think, would be a mistake. On the one hand, it invites a sort of scholasticism which attempts to replace so-called "psychological predicates" with "objectivist" terminology. On the other hand, it misses the point of Popper's denial that scientific knowledge is a species of belief, which is not verbal but philosophical. Nevertheless, engaging (briefly) in just this sort of which-hunt might serve to sharpen our focus on what may be a real locus of psychologism in Popper's philosophy.

Let's begin with two illustrations. In, e.g., his criticism of subjectivism in logic[1] Popper says that epistemic logic deals with such formulae as '*a* knows *p*' or '*a* knows that *p*' and '*a* believes *p*' or '*a* believes that *p*', where '*a*' stands for the knowing or believing subject and '*p*' stands for the known or believed proposition. This formulation makes it clear that Popper's criticism is not simply that beliefs are World 2 states. For the contents of beliefs can be formulated in propositions (World 3 objects) and believing, like understanding, can be expressed as a relation between a subject and a proposition. Nevertheless, Popper's thesis is that this sort of approach is subjectivist and has nothing to do with scientific knowledge:

> ... the scientist, I will call him '*S*', does neither know nor believe. What does he do? I
> will give a very brief list:
>> '*S* tries to understand *p*.'
>> '*S* tries to think of alternatives to *p*.'
>> '*S* tries to think of criticisms of *p*.'...[2]

Exaggeration of the alleged subjectlessness of scientific knowledge might here lead one to think that Popper's reformulation of a scientist's activities is itself psychologistic. Calling the knowing or believing subject a scientist does not alter the fact that he is a subject. And trying to understand, think of alternatives to and criticisms of a proposition are activities which involve that subject as essentially as believing and knowing.

In a different vein, Popper's thesis that the degree of corroboration of a hypothesis depends, in part, upon the severity of the tests to which it has been subjected has been criticized as psychologistic.[3] The problem here is in explaining what constitutes a *severe* test. Popper's initial attempt at such an explanation linked the severity of the test to the sincerity of the tester:

> ... I must insist that *C(h,e)* (the corroboration C of a hypothesis h by evidence e) can be interpreted as degree of corroboration only if *e* is *a report on the severest tests we have been able to design*. It is this point that marks the difference between the attitude of the inductivist, or verificationist, and my own attitude. The inductivist or verificationist wants *affirmation* for his hypothesis. He hopes to make it *firmer* by his evidence *e* and looks out for '*firmness*' — for '*confirmation*'. At best, he may realize that we must not be biased in our selection of *e*: that we must not ignore unfavourable cases; and the *e* must comprise reports on our *total* observational knowledge, whether favourable or unfavourable. ...
>
> In opposition to this inductivist attitude, I assert that *C(h,e)* must not be interpreted as the degree of corroboration of *h* by *e*, unless *e* reports the results of *our sincere efforts to overthrow h*. The requirement of sincerity cannot be formalized — no more than the inductivist requirement that *e* must represent our total observational knowledge. Yet if *e* is *not* a report about the results of our sincere attempts to overthrow *h*, then we shall simply deceive ourselves if we think we can interpret *C(h,e)* as degree of corroboration, or anything like it.[4]

Alan Musgrave claims that this explanation of severity is psychologistic in that it makes the severity of a test depend in part upon the psyche of the tester. "For the *sincerity* with which a test is devised and performed seems to be distinctively psychological, to depend upon the state of mind of him who performs it."[5] Now psychologism in the assessment of a hypothesis' degree of corroboration would indeed be troublesome. Popper, as we have seen, attempts to avoid the charge of scepticism by appealing to corroboration reports to provide an objective decision procedure for rationally determining the choice between competing theories. If this procedure is operative only contingent upon some psychological state of an individual, then Popper would be open to the charge that his epistemology renders the choice between competing scientific theories relativistic or arbitrary after all.

I do not wish to consider here whether the assessment of a hypothesis' degree of corroboration involves an appeal to psychologism. (Later we will argue, but on different grounds, that it might well involve such an appeal.) What is more interesting for the present discussion is the form which Popper's and Musgrave's attempts to eliminate psychologism from the assessment of a hypothesis' degree of corroboration take. Musgrave, confident that the psychologism is only apparent, writes:

> Fortunately a remedy is at hand: Popper also gives an *objective* analysis of the severity of tests, an analysis which needs no recourse to the sincerity of testers.
>
> The intuitive idea behind this objective analysis is that the more unlikely or unexpected (in the light of what we already know, of our 'background knowledge' b) is a

prediction p from a hypothesis h, then the more severe will be the test of h provided by testing p. Thus, for example, if we can predict from h a 'new effect' (that is, something completely unexpected in the light of b), then to test this prediction will constitute a severe test of h.[6]

Again, if we exaggerate the subjectlessness of scientific knowledge, this might be seen as a jump from the psychologistic pan to the psychologistic fire. In lieu of assessing the sincerity of a tester, we are now asked to assess his expectations, i.e., what seems more or less "likely". But facts about the expectations of a tester seem every bit as psychological as facts about his sincerity.

Now this line of criticism may be tempting. It is, however, too simple. The point of Popper's epistemology without a knowing subject is not that epistemology can do without a subject, but that it can do without that subject's *knowing*. Popper nowhere denies the existence or importance of World 2, the world of subjects. All to the contrary, without World 2 it is World 3 that would not exist. Rather, Popper simply claims that insofar as science is concerned, questions about World 2 states are subordinate to questions about their World 3 products. But this is not simply a suggestion that we speak in World 3 vocabulary. Popper, as we have already seen, thinks that Carnap's insistence that we speak in the so-called "formal mode of speech' simply masks his psychologism. Rather, Popper's point is philosophical and concerns what he considers essential to scientific activity. Scientific activity, according to Popper, is essentially *critical* activity. And it is only when a subject presents his beliefs for criticism by formulating their contents in language (and thereby producing World 3 objects) that they become of interest to science.

We may well liken believing to understanding by characterizing it as a relation between a subject and a World 3 object (a proposition). But it is the relationship of believing, rather than the necessity of a subject, to which Popper objects. For Popper, criticism is essential to scientific activity; believing is not. A scientist *may* indeed believe or claim to know a proposition. But the conviction with which a scientist holds a proposition to be true has nothing essential to do with his formulation of its content in language and his subsequent criticism of it. Indeed, such believing may well be an obstacle to criticism. Understanding and trying to criticize a theory essentially involve a subject who understands and tries to criticize. But these relations do not essentially involve that subject's belief or conviction in the theory understood or criticized. The important point, for Popper, is that we may doubt without criticizing and criticize without doubting.[7] Similarly, the severity of a test of a hypothesis has nothing to do with whether its tester actually expects or believes that one of its predictions is true or false. What is important is whether or not the consequences of that hypothesis in some way conflict with the consequences of a competing theory. And this is something which Popper holds can be assessed on purely logical grounds.

We could develop this thought at length, but I think the point has been made. The point is that the justified true belief theory of knowledge regarded the fact that a proposition is believed (by someone) to be as essential to its status as an article of knowledge as the facts that it is true and justified. Contrary to this, Popper considers the question whether or not a proposition is believed to be irrelevant to its status as scientific knowledge. Moreover, Popper holds that belief can actually be an obstacle to the growth of knowledge. If a scientist believes a theory then he has reached a position, justified or not, concerning its truth. This position may, of course, be subject to revision. But the strength of his conviction might well discourage him from making any further attempt to criticize it. If his belief is strong, then he might even feel confident in ignoring the efforts of others to criticize it. Time is precious, why waste it on rehashing old issues? And if his belief is *very* strong, he might even consider such efforts to be indicative of a disrespect for science. But Popper considers the activity of criticism to be essential to the growth of knowledge. Without criticism, scientific knowledge does not grow, but remains static.

Let's return, for a moment, to the problem of Fries' trilemma. This trilemma — dogmatism vs infinite regress vs psychologism — was a consequence of the objectivist plea for justification by rational argument. Popper, as we have seen, resolved it not by accepting one of its horns, but by rejecting the demand for justification. But Popper admits that his rejection of justificationism does not altogether eliminate psychologism from epistemology, it simply renders it innocuous:

> What is our position now in regard to Fries' trilemma, the choice between dogmatism, infinite regress, and psychologism? The basic statements at which we stop, which we decide to accept as satisfactory, and as sufficiently tested, have admittedly the character of *dogmas*, but only in so far as we may desist from justifying them by further arguments (or by further tests). But this kind of dogmatism is innocuous since, should the need arise, these statements can easily be tested further. I admit that this too makes the chain of deduction in principle infinite. But this kind of '*infinite regress*' is also innocuous since in our theory there is no question of trying to prove any statement by means of it. And finally, as to psychologism: I admit, again, that the decision to accept a basic statement, and to be satisfied with it, is causally connected with our experiences — especially our *perceptual experiences*. But we do not attempt to *justify* basic statements by these experiences. Experiences can *motivate* a decision, and hence an acceptance or a rejection of a statement, but a basic statement cannot be *justified* by them — no more than by thumping the table.[8]

Now this passage seems to admit that psychologism plays a role in the acceptance of basic statements, though *not* the role of justification. But Popper, we should note, seems to vacillate on the question whether the causal connection between observation and the acceptance of a basic statement is psychologistic. In demanding observability as a material requirement for basic statements, Popper writes:

No doubt it will now seem as though in demanding observability, I have, after all, allowed psychologism to slip back quietly into my theory. But this is not so. Admittedly, it is possible to interpret the concept of an *observable event* in a psychologistic sense. But I am using it in such a sense that it might just as well be replaced by 'an event involving position and movement of macroscopic physical bodies'. Or we might lay it down, more precisely, that every basic statement must either be itself a statement about relative positions of physical bodies, or that it must be equivalent to some basic statement of this 'mechanistic' or 'materialistic' kind. (That this stipulation is practicable is connected with the fact that a theory which is intersubjectively testable will also be inter-sensually testable. This is to say that tests involving the perception of one of our senses can, in principle, be replaced by tests involving other senses.) Thus the charge that, in appealing to observability, I have stealthily readmitted psychologism would have no more force than the charge that I have admitted mechanism or materialism. This shows that my theory is really quite neutral and that neither of these labels should be pinned to it. I say all this only so as to save the term 'observable', as I use it, from the stigma of psychologism.[9]

Perhaps Popper simply intends this passage to underscore the fact that the requirement of observability does not *imply* that basic statements are *justified* by observation. Nevertheless, I find this passage strange. On the one hand, I fail to see how the fact that we can, in principle, replace tests involving the perception of one of our senses with tests involving the perception of other senses in any way alters or makes less problematic the fact that these are tests involving the perception of our senses. And the major premiss of the anti-psychologistic attack has usually been the denial that tests involving the perception of our senses are inter-subjective. On the other hand, Popper's appeal to physicalism in response to this charge of psychologism seems reminiscent of Carnap's insistence that we speak in the formal mode of speech — a move Popper has himself criticized as a mere camouflage of psychologism. Indeed, Popper himself has noted the similarity between psychologism and physicalism:

> Most people would see that any attempt to base logical statements on protocol sentences is a case of psychologism. But curiously enough, when it comes to empirical statements, the same kind of thing goes by the name of 'physicalism'.[10]

Perhaps what Popper really means is that the appeal to observation in the testing of empirical statements is unavoidable — regardless of whether we call it psychologism or physicalism — and that so long as we do not regard observation as *justifying* statements this will cause no harm. Here we will consider the question whether psychologism in its critical form is really so innocuous.

What I wish to suggest here is that Popper's admission of dogmatism, infinite regress, and psychologism in the *criticism* of a theory *may* be innocuous, but it is so only to the extent to which criticism completely foregoes attempts at justification. To avoid complication, I want to take Popper's comments on corroboration at face value: theories which have a high degree of corroboration are not, for that reason, justified or confirmed. So I agree that the testing of strictly universal theories by basic statements is in no way an attempt to justify

164

or confirm those theories *as true*. Nevertheless, it is not obvious that such test-ing *completely* forgoes attempts at justification. Criticism, one might say, is just the other side of the justificationist coin. This can, perhaps, be most clearly seen by consideration of Popper's generalization of the logical problem of in-duction: Can the claim that an explanatory universal theory is true *or that it is false be justified* by 'empirical reasons'?[11] Popper's answer to this question is affirmative: *"the assumption of the truth of test statements sometimes allows us to justify the claim that an explanatory universal theory is false"*.[12] It was this logical asymmetry that led Popper to propose adherence to conjecture and refutation as the proper methodology of scientific inquiry. And this adherence to the methodology of conjecture and refutation is what allegedly saves Popper's epistemology from the charge of irrationalism: *Modus Tollens* is, after all, a deductively valid inference form. Moreover, it is this possibility of *justifying* the claim that a universal theory is false (through *Modus Tollens*) which is supposed to save Popper's epistemology from the charge of scepticism. If the choice between competing theories is not arbitrary but rational, it is because *Modus Tollens* provides a rational (logically valid) method for the elimination of the-ories. We rationally "prefer the theory T_2 which has passed certain severe tests to the theory T_1 which has failed these tests, because a false theory is certainly worse than one which, for all we know, may be true".[13] Now there are problems with this last statement stated thus simply, but I do not wish to quarrel with the claim that a theory which may be true is rationally preferable to one shown false. The point to be made, however, is that corroboration reports can provide a rational decision procedure for determining the choice between competing theories only to the extent to which the "justification" of the claim that a uni-versal theory is false is itself rational. And if Fries' trilemma poses a challenge to the rationality of *any* justification of a theory as true, then I fail to see how it is any less a threat to the rationality of the justification of a theory as false.

Why is Fries' trilemma a challenge to the rationality of justification? Pop-per's appeal to *Modus Tollens* was admittedly an attempt to save the rationality of science by substituting deductive inference forms for inductive ones. But Fries' trilemma is not essentially a polemic against induction, or even against inference, but a problem for *any* attempt at *justification* by rational or reasoned argument. The reason why psychologistic justification cannot be considered rational is simply that sense perceptions are not reasons, i.e., they are not state-ments. This criticism, if taken seriously, undermines any attempt to argue that inductive inference provides rational justification. For even if we consider the inference from singular statements to universal statements rational, the demand for justification leaves the problem of justifying the singular statements which serve as the premises of an inductive argument. Again, if we demand justification of these singular statements by rational or reasoned argument we are left with infinite regress or dogmatism. If we demand justification, but not by *reasoned* argument, we are left with psychologism. I rehash this point here in order to emphasize that while Popper regards the logical validity of an argument as a necessary condition for rational justification, he does not consider it a sufficient one. An argument may well be logically valid, but if its premises are accepted dogmatically then the "justification" provided by that argument cannot be considered rational.

The methodology of conjecture and refutation is essentially the method of criticizing universal theories by counter-examples. The statements which are the potential counter-examples (potential "falsifiers") of a theory are called "basic statements". These statements are *potential* counter-examples to a theory because a basic statement may well be consistent with a theory. Popper places three requirements on basic statements — two formal and one material. The formal requirements are: (a) from a universal statement without initial conditions, no basic statement can be deduced; and (b) a universal statement and a basic statement can contradict each other.[14] It follows from (a) and (b) that a basic statement must have a logical form such that its negation is not itself a basic statement. And it follows from this that basic statements have the logical form of singular existential statements. The material requirement Popper places on basic statements is: (c) basic statements must be testable, inter-subjectively, by "observation".[15] In other words, the event which a basic statement describes must be an "observable"event. The relationship between observation and basic statements traditionally held to obtain is that observation can show a basic statement to be true, but observation (or better, the failure to observe) cannot show a basic statement to be false. As for "observable", Popper insists that it need not be interpreted psychologistically, but he otherwise declines to offer an explicit definition, preferring instead to regard it as primitive.

Now what is the epistemic basis of scientific theories, and how are they tested? Simply put, scientific theories, according to Popper, have no basis. Rather, they are free creations of the human mind. They originate psychologically *a priori*, but they are not for that reason to be considered *a priori* valid (or objectively certain). But once a theory has been formulated in language (and has become a World 3 object), any number of, perhaps unforeseen, consequences can be derived from it. These consequences are not themselves basic statements. They are the *negations* of basic statements, or as Popper calls them, "instantial statements". These "instantial statements" are considered predictions derived from the theory. They are the "assertions which may clash with observations".[16] Finally, the testing of a theory is simply the attempt to see whether or not one of these instantial statements does, in fact, clash with observation, i.e., it is the attempt to show that at least one of these predictions is false.

Consider the familiar theory (T): All swans are white. From this theory an instantial statement, or prediction, (P), is deduced: If there is a swan at the place k, then there is a white swan at the place k (or, more simply, at k, there is either no swan or a white swan). Clearly, there is a potentially infinite number of such instantial statements $(P_1, P_2...P_n)$ that can be derived from T. Now the testing of T is simply the attempt to see whether or not one of these instantial statements clashes with observation. So we look and see (or sniff and smell). For

166

the test to be operative we must accept a basic statement. Here there are two possibilities: (a) there is a white swan at the place k; (b) there is a non-white swan at the place k. (a) clearly does not refute T. If (a) is accepted, then it is said to corroborate T, i.e., it is consistent with T. (b), however, is inconsistent with T. If accepted, (b) is said to falsify T. (A third possibility, (c) there is no swan at the place k, is also consistent with T. (c), however, does not fulfill Popper's requirements for basic statements, and hence cannot be said to provide corroboration of T.)

Now all this seems simple enough. But the question we must now consider is "What is the epistemic status of basic statements?" Here Popper's answer is explicit, but it betrays a deep tension in his thought. In a section of *The Logic of Scientific Discovery* which is, interestingly enough, entitled "The Relativity of Basic Statements. Resolution of Fries' Trilemma" Popper writes:

> Every test of a theory, whether resulting in its corroboration or falsification, must stop at some basic statements which we *decide to accept*. If we do not come to any decision, and do not accept some basic statement or other, then the test will have led nowhere. But considered from a logical point of view, the situation is never such that it compels us to stop at this particular basic statement rather than at that, or else give up the test altogether. For any basic statement can again in its turn be subjected to tests, using as a touchstone any of the basic statements which can be deduced from it with the help of some theory, either the one under test, or another. This procedure has no natural end. Thus if the test is to lead us anywhere, nothing remains but to stop at some point or other and say that we are satisfied, for the time being.[17]

From a logical point of view, basic statements have the status of decisions,[18] or conventions, or dogmas. But what about the requirement of observability? Again, perceptual experiences may *motivate* the decision to accept a basic statement, but they cannot compel us to accept that statement. Popper emphasizes this point in contradistinction to positivism — a passage which is, perhaps, more interesting for its parenthetical remark:

> ... I differ from the positivist in holding that basic statements are not justifiable by our immediate experiences, but are, from the logical point of view, accepted by an act, by a free decision. (From the psychological point of view this may perhaps be a purposeful and well-adapted reaction.)[19]

But what about the requirement of observability?

Basic statements are statements about physical bodies, about their position and movement. Unlike protocol sentences, they are not statements about personal experiences.[20] Basic statements are inter-subjectively testable. And Popper recommends that we adopt a procedure according to which we stop only at those basic statements which are especially easy to test, i.e., those statements about whose acceptance or rejection the various investigators are likely to reach agreement.[21] Popper admits that we do make records or protocols, such as certificates of tests issued by a department of scientific or industrial research.[22] And, if the need arises, these protocols can be reexamined. Such protocols may or may not be necessary. But testing, according to Popper, stops at basic statements and not protocol sentences "because the inter-subjective testing of statements about perceptions ... is relatively complicated and difficult".[23] But if basic statements are really accepted as *free* decisions, then why the requirement that they be inter-subjectively *testable* at all? And what sort of test does Popper have in mind? Is this simply a test to see whether or not we can reach a consensus of agreement among scientific investigators? Or is it a test to see whether or not a scientific theory clashes with observation? And what sort of "clash" would this be? Is it a clash with *observation*, or with the basic *statements* which report or describe observable events? If it is really a clash with observation, then can it be considered a *logical* (or rational) clash? And if it is a clash with the basic statements which report or describe observable events — statements which are accepted or rejected by allegedly free decisions —, then what about the requirement of observability?

Perceptual experiences, admittedly, can motivate the decision to accept or reject a basic statement. But so might stomach-aches or a desire to get home and watch the Yankees. Stomach-aches, Popper might complain, are not inter-subjectively observable. They are certainly not perceivable through the senses. But a rainy day is as inter-subjectively observable as any other event. And rainy days, as we all know, can motivate decisions. This is tempting, but it may seem unsportsmanlike. Popper's appeal to *Modus Tollens* implies that it is not observations in the raw, but basic statements that may logically clash with theories. But our problem here does not concern the relationship between a basic statement and a theory (which is a relatively straight-forward and simple matter), but that between a basic statement and the perceptual experiences which may motivate its acceptance or rejection.

Perhaps Popper's point is that the acceptance or rejection of a basic statement is not a *personal* decision, but a *social* convention. So we need not fear that a scientist might accept "There is a non-white swan at the place k" on account of a rainy day, for we can always count upon other members of the scientific group to check his decisions. But here there is the problem of circumscribing the parameters of the scientific group. Who is to be included? All those who feel they have something to say on the matter? Or just those who accept or reject the officially accepted or rejected basic statement? Need one have a University or research position? Or just a degree? (Do degrees in Psychology count?) In any event, if the rationality of science depends upon our ability to "rationally" decide between competing theories, and our "rational" decision procedure depends upon our ability to falsify theories, and falsification depends upon the acceptance or rejection of basic statements, then — induction or not — this sounds dangerously close to saying that the difference between the rational scientist and the lunatic is that the latter is in the minority.[24]

Now Popper does say that decisions to accept or reject basic statements are reached in accordance with a procedure governed by rules:

> Of special interest among these is a rule which tells us that we should not accept *stray basic statements* – i.e. logically disconnected ones – but that we should accept basic statements in the course of testing *theories*; of raising searching questions about these theories, to be answered by the acceptance of basic statements.[25]

Still, this rule tells us nothing about the relationship between observation and the acceptance or rejection of a basic statement.

Now Popper seems to have in mind some sort of distinction between observation and perceptual experiences. And such a distinction is, indeed, well-entrenched. Here one need not appeal to Kant. As every student of Sherlock Holmes can attest, one might easily perceive without thereby observing. (Even Dr. Watson knew this, though he was not too adept at observation.) And it seems to be the case, as Popper insists,[26] that observation presupposes a theory. In order to observe, we must first know *what* to observe. But while we may well perceive without observing, is it possible to observe (empirically) without perceiving? This seems a far more difficult matter. In fact, it seems impossible.

All this has been said without a mention of the problem of recognizing a counter-example *as* a counter-example. If, with Popper, we decline the appeal to essentialism, this becomes a difficult and perplexing problem. Consider the aforementioned theory (T): All swans are white. Once T has been conjectured we deduce the familiar instantial statement (P): at k, there is either no swan or a white swan. With T and P in hand we now set out to investigate k in order to determine whether observation corroborates or clashes with T. Now suppose that in the area k we observe but one bird, and this bird resembles a swan in all respects except its conjectured color. How do we proceed? Observation presupposes a theory. And our theory here tells us that all swans are white. But this theory is merely a conjecture. Indeed, it is a conjecture which we are here trying to falsify. Perhaps we should appeal to another theory, one which, say, distinguishes swans from non-swans by structural characteristics. But this theory is a conjecture too, and one that is not to be relied upon. Let's make the problem simple. Suppose that here there is no difficulty concerning the relevance of perceptual experiences: all the scientific investigators agree that it is the perceptual experience of this non-white bird, and not, say, that of a rainy day, which is the motivating factor in their decision. Now does this non-white bird falsify T? Well, it is neither the non-white bird nor our observation of it which can falsify T. And once we have formulated and accepted or rejected a basic statement, the matter really *is* quite simple. For we will either say that at k there is no swan, or that at k there is a non-white swan. The former will not corroborate T since it lacks the form of a basic statement. But the latter will certainly refute T. But this simply evades the issue. The problem is in deciding which statement to accept. It is the problem of deciding whether we are observing a non-white swan or a non-swan bird. Careful reading of Popper here suggests an answer. We should accept the basic statement: at k there is a non-white swan. Our decisions are, in part, determined by considerations of utility.[27] And here we are, after all, trying to refute T. But I somehow doubt that this will do.

I do not want to be misunderstood here. Popper would be the last to suggest that either the decision to accept or reject a basic statement as true or the related decision to consider some phenomenon as a counter-example to a universal theory is or can be dictated to us by logic or observation alone. And I would certainly be the last to say that we are ever in any way logically compelled to decide one way or the other. To that extent, I fully agree that basic statements have the logical character of free decisions, conventions, or dogmas. My problem is not with this. Rather, it is that in the face of Fries' trilemma — which I do take seriously — I fail to see how the *assumption* of the truth of a test statement sometimes allows us to justify the claim that an explanatory universal theory is false. The *assumption* of the truth of a basic statement cannot *justify* any statement as true or false — no more than the *assumption* that all swans are white justifies "All swans are white". And we cannot get around this simply by formulating the assumption in language. The appeal to dogmatism in criticism is every bit as problematic as the appeal to dogmatism in justification. And if it is possible to criticize a theory only relative to the acceptance or rejection of statements which have the logical character of free decisions, then I see no way to avoid the problem of scepticism, even as understood by Popper. The relativity of the basic statements which test theories implies a relativism with regard to our rational preference of theories. And this relativism, in Popperian vernacular, is nothing else but scepticism.

None of this, however, is to demean Popper's claim that scientific knowledge is objective. But such scientific objectivity must be understood in a reconstructed sense. As Sidney Morgenbesser writes:

> ... it is in accord with common usage to assert that scientific sentences, such as Newton's laws, are objective in the sense that they concern phenomena independent of the judger or of any human being. But there is a second sense of the word 'objective' to which we now turn. In this second usage a sentence is considered objective if it is supported by evidence gathered in certain standard ways, and is one which can be agreed to by almost anyone willing to review the evidence in appropriate manner.[28]

The first sense of "objective" Morgenbesser cites might be called the "absolutist" sense. It is the sense of "objective" used by Frege. The second sense of "objective" is more akin to that used by Popper, so long as we do not consider what evidence that supports a sentence as justifying it. And this sense of "objective" is one that is consistent with relativity. As Morgenbesser goes on to say:

> These standard conditions will vary from domain of inquiry to domain of inquiry and cannot be specified once and for all.[29]

Nevertheless, I find Popper's insistence that basic statements fulfill a material requirement of "observability" confusing. The requirement is, no doubt, intended to insure the empirical character of science. Science may not be empirical with regard to the genesis or justification of theories, but it is so with regard to their testing. And the requirement of observability is, moreover, clearly what is intended to insure scientific objectivity in the second of Morgenbesser's senses. Scientific testing can be objective only to the extent to which basic statements are inter-subjectively testable. But if the acceptance or rejection of basic statements is really the result of free decisions, then it is not at all clear what role observation plays or what force it has. To say that perceptual experiences motivate our decisions seems to answer the question half-way. Surely Popper wants a stronger relationship than this. And in practice, a stronger relationship is undoubtedly assumed. To deny that such experiences *justify* basic statements may well avoid the charge of psychologism. But it seems to result, nevertheless, in the very sort of relativism which provoked Popper's anti-psychologism to begin with.

Perhaps Popper's point is one of taxonomy. The decision to accept or reject a basic statement due to perceptual experiences may well be, from the psychological point of view, a purposeful and well-adapted reaction. Nevertheless, it cannot be analyzed by logical techniques. This, no doubt, is the case. And to that extent, the analysis of the acceptance or rejection of basic statements is simply of no interest to the *logic* of science. But here we should recall that Popper considers the growth of knowledge to be the fundamental problem of epistemology. Since it is the acceptance or rejection of basic statements which ultimately makes the growth of knowledge possible, one might here expect that Popper would agree with Kuhn: *so much the worse for the logic of science.* Understanding the logic of scientific inquiry is, no doubt, a first and necessary condition for understanding the growth of knowledge. And it is an important insight to see that basic statements have the logical character of free decisions, and that the analysis of such decisions falls outside the domain of logic. But the Kuhnian point is that it is just this insight which makes it necessary for epistemology to supplement the logic of discovery with a psychology of research. Supplementing the logic of discovery with a psychology of research will in no way alter the relativistic character of the preference of scientific theories. But understanding why certain perceptual experiences motivate certain decisions rather than others cannot but help us better understand the growth of knowledge. In any event, since the exclusion of a psychology of research in no way avoids, but only obscures relativism, there seems to be no real reason to legislate against it. If Popper's primary concern is to rid his theory of the stigma of psychologism, then better we rid psychologism of its stigma.

Popper's thought seems to be caught in a sort of triangular tension. At one vertex is his deep distrust of authority of any kind. This distrust of authority is what leads to his characterization of any epistemology which appeals to allegedly infallible sources as subjectivist. And it is this distrust of cognitive sources which results in Popper's anti-justificationism — an anti-justificationism which does not stop with the recognition of fallibilism but extends to a refusal to accept a high degree of corroboration as in any way confirming a theory or establishing it as reliable. For Popper, any suggestion that a theory is, in any way, justified, even by the most aware and best-intentioned of investigators, leads to authoritarianism. For it encourages the tendency to regard the highly corroborated theory as beyond reproach. At a second vertex is Popper's profound respect for science, and his deep faith that knowledge can grow and society can progress by adhering to the scientific method of conjecture and refutation. This respect and faith is what motivates Popper's rejection of traditional empiricism, a movement which shared Popper's distrust of authority but which was criticized as leading to irrationalism, relativism, and scepticism — positions which have traditionally been associated with a cavalier and disrespectful attitude concerning the integrity of science. At a third vertex is Popper's strong commitment to empiricism which is expressed in a criterion of demarcation which regards a theory as scientific only to the extent to which it can provide a clash with observation.

In a like tension, but on a different plane, is Popper's opposition to psychologism, a position which tugs against all three of these vertices. The commitment to empiricism and the requirement that basic statements be "observable" suggests psychologism — if only the psychologistic justification that a universal theory is false. But the respect for science demands anti-psychologism — if only to avoid the stigma of irrationalism, relativism and scepticism. Finally, psychologism cuts both ways against anti-justificationism. For observation proves to be both a challenge to and a candidate for authority.

Still, I am deeply disturbed by my own characterization of Popper's epistemology as relativistic. For Popper is fully aware of each of these criticisms that I've brought to bear. He is explicit that the acceptance of a basic statement in no way implies that it is justified. And he emphasizes that the impossibility of justifying basic statements is the very reason why theories are not subject to conclusive falsification. Still, Popper continues to regard his epistemology as the best defense against relativism. And this leads me to believe that my own analysis has somehow missed the point. If I am correct, then this point is subtle and, ironically, has less to do with the mechanics of theory acceptance than with the psychological attitudes that Popper believes should govern the enterprise of science. Specifically, it concerns the value Popper holds for the critical attitude of rationalism and the importance of truth as the regulative ideal of rational inquiry. And in the next chapter I will attempt to explain this point through a consideration of the basic issues that separate Popper's epistemology from that of Thomas S. Kuhn.

NOTES AND REFERENCES

1.   See: *Op. cit.*; Popper; *Objective Knowledge*; p. 140.

2.   *Ibid.*

3.   See: Musgrave, Alan E.; "The Objectivism of Popper's Epistemology"; in *Op. cit.*; Schilpp; *The Philosophy of Karl Popper*; pp. 576-581.

4.   *Op. cit.*; Popper; *The Logic of Scientific Discovery*; p. 418.

5.   *Op. cit.*; Musgrave; "The Objectivism of Popper's Epistemology"; p. 577.

6.   *Ibid.*; p. 577.

7.   *Op. cit.*; Popper; *Objective Knowledge*; p. 141.

8.   *Op. cit.*; Popper; *The Logic of Scientific Discovery*; p. 105.

9.   *Ibid.*; p. 103.

10. *Ibid.*; pp. 98-99.

11. *Op. cit.*; Popper; *Objective Knowledge*; p. 7. My emphasis.

12. *Ibid.*

13. *Op. cit.*; Popper; *Conjectures and Refutations*; p. 235.

14. *Op. cit.*; Popper; *The Logic of Scientific Discovery*; pp. 100-101.

15. *Ibid.*; p. 102.

16. *Op. cit.*; Popper; *Conjectures of Refutations*; p. 256.

17. *Op. cit.*; Popper; *The Logic of Scientific Discovery*; p. 104.

18. Frege, it is interesting to recall, regarded decisions as events in the inner world, and hence psychological (though not ideas).

19. *Op. cit.*; Popper; *The Logic of Scientific Discovery*; p. 109.

20. *Ibid.*; p. 105.

21. *Ibid.*; p. 104.

22. *Ibid.*; p. 105.

23. *Ibid.*

24. The allusion here is to Russell as quoted by Popper. (See: *Op. cit.*; Popper; *Objective Knowledge*; p. 5.)

25. *Op. cit.*; *The Logic of Scientific Discovery*; p. 106.

26. *Op. cit.*; *Conjectures and Refutations*; p. 46.

27. *Op. cit.*; Popper; *The Logic of Scientific Discovery*; p. 108.

28. Morgenbesser, Sidney; "Approaches to Ethical Objectivity"; in *Moral Education*; ed. by Barry I. Chazan and Jonas F. Soltis; Teachers College Press (New York, 1973) p. 76.

29. *Ibid.*

11. TRUTH AND THE DENIGRATION OF INQUIRY:
TWO FACES OF RELATIVISM

Justification is a concept as fundamental to western philosophy as any other. Whether we speak of beliefs, desires, theories, or actions, the fundamental philosophical presupposition is that their propriety can be rationally affirmed only to the extent to which they can be rationally justified. Indeed, even to speak of *propriety* in such contexts is already to make implicit reference to justification. That justification is and has been considered a prerequisite for rational knowledge is underscored by the priority of epistemology in modern philosophy. For while "epistemology" literally translates as "theory of knowledge", it has in fact been practiced almost exclusively as the science of justification. And this is simply part and parcel of the prevalent characterization of anti-psychologism as an attitude which distinguishes epistemology from psychology as justification is distinguished from discovery. In chapter one, we distinguished EP_1 from EP_2 by saying that the former, but not the latter, construes rational knowledge as entailing objective certainty. There I claimed that the twentieth century has witnessed an epistemological paradigm shift away from EP_1 toward EP_2, and that the conceptual slack accompanying this shift has been a primary cause for confusion in twentieth century analytic philosophy. Specifically, I emphasized that from the perspective of EP_1, any EP_2 epistemology, i.e., any epistemology that construes of knowledge as fallible, would, for that reason, be regarded as sceptical or relativistic. To that extent, I argued that Frege's EP_1 anti-psychologism, i.e., the epistemological defense of *a priori* valid knowledge coupled with the metaphysical defense of a third realm of eternal and immutable truths, was designed to provide for the sort of *justification* that would make such objective certainty possible. But later, in chapter seven, I argued that Popper has effected something of the magnitude of a second epistemological paradigm shift by introducing into the EP_2 framework a wholesale denial of the possibility and necessity of justification. And in chapters eight and nine I suggested that the failure to take Popper's anti-justificationism seriously is a primary cause of the prevalent misinterpretation of Popper's epistemology. Hence, some EP_2 philosophers who embrace fallibilism nonetheless complain that it is nonsense to speak of knowledge without justification, just as introspectionists complained that it is nonsense to call a science of human behaviour a "psychology". This justificationist attitude runs deep, so deep that its very critics are sometimes unconsciously influenced by it themselves. Among Popperians, this influence has given rise to the so-called "problem of the empirical basis", a problem which, as we have seen, concerns Popper's account of the relationship between basic statements and perceptual experiences. And here, what many Popperians think turns on this issue is the rationality of science itself. In my view, the problem of the empirical basis results from a failure to take Popper's anti-justificationism seriously. To the extent to which Popperians completely forego justification, the problem does not arise. And to the extent to which the problem does arise, Popperians do not completely forego justification. But even philosophers impressed with Popper's arguments against the possibility and necessity of justification nonetheless find it difficult to abstract themselves completely from the justificationist framework. And in chapter ten I illustrated this difficulty by characterizing criticism as just the other side of the justificationist coin. From the justificationist's perspective, it is difficult to conceive of criticism as anything but criticism of the claim that a statement is justified. To the extent to which such criticism is rational, the justificationist construes criticism as an attempt to *justify* that claim *as false*. Thus, as we noted in chapter eight, there is a strong tendency among EP_2 epistemologists to regard Popper's anti-justificationism as a difference more in the expression than in the pragmatics of the situation. Still, I am dissatisfied with this analysis. In my view, there is a real, albeit subtle, difference between Popper's epistemology and EP_2 justificationism. But this difference concerns not so much the mechanics of theory acceptance as our *attitudes* toward theories accepted. While Popper's argument against justificationism is logically based, his realignment of rationality with criticism is not. Nor is it a merely technical or puzzle-solving move. Rather, it indicates a deep and fundamentally different attitude concerning the goals of inquiry and the nature of scientific knowledge. And in this chapter, I will attempt to develop this difference through a consideration of the issues that separate Popper's critical rationalism of conjecture and refutation from the epistemology of paradigm commitment proposed by Thomas S. Kuhn.

In 1962 Thomas S. Kuhn introduced the phrase "scientific paradigm" into the epistemological discussion. In *The Structure of Scientific Revolutions*, Kuhn characterized scientific paradigms as "universally recognized scientific achievements that for a long time provide model problems and solutions to a community of practitioners".[1] And with the help of this concept, Kuhn bifurcated scientific activity into two major and complementary phases: normal science and extraordinary or revolutionary science. According to Kuhn, most scientific inquiry occurs under the rubric of research programmes defined for the most part by a specific scientific paradigm. Hence, the term "normal science". Within normal science, fundamental presuppositions plus a delineation of the scope and methodology of inquiry are set by the over-arching and universally recognized paradigm. Thus, the work of the normal scientist consists primarily in explaining unexplained phenomena in terms of that particular theoretical framework. To that extent, Kuhn characterized the bulk of scientific inquiry not as the work of conjecture and refutation, but as exercises in puzzle-solving, as attempts to fit the pieces of nature into the patterns defined by the paradigm. For Kuhn, whatever "testing" occurs within normal science is not so much a test of the paradigm, but of a particular researcher's skill in providing an adequate fit.

But Kuhn's major point is that while such normal puzzle-solving activity is characteristic of most scientific inquiry, it is not characteristic of all. For Kuhn recognized that not all puzzles are solved. And as recalcitrant puzzles, or *anomalies*, accumulate, as the scientific community encounters more and more phenomena that cannot be fitted neatly into the set patterns defined by a specific paradigm, science gradually enters into a period of crisis. Here, progress demands the revolutionary creation of a new paradigm that can account for all of what the old theory explained, plus the anomalous phenomena as well. And as the term "revolutionary" suggests, the creation and acceptance of such a new paradigm is also characterized as non-rational. While normal science is a rule-governed activity contained well within the bounds of most accepted canons of rationality, revolutionary science is not. Here, Kuhn emphatically denied that paradigms are or can be conclusively falsified. For even when the test of a paradigm yields a universally acknowledged counterexample, the wealth of background knowledge not included in the paradigm but implicit in its test is too rich to conclusively determine the theory as false. More important, debates concerning competing paradigms are debates concerning the foundations of rational inquiry. As such, they leave little common ground for a non-question begging comparison of theories. So-called "paradigm shifts" occur not as the result of reasoned argument, but by a bandwagon process of ideological and political conversion somewhat akin to a religious experience. Such paradigm shifts usually involve a revision of ontological commitments. In the course of such ontological revision, new terms are introduced into the semantic structure to denote entities not recognized by the old theory, and familiar terms are redefined and acquire a different meaning peculiar to the new conceptual framework. As a result, it is often difficult to express the propositions of the new theory in the language of the old paradigm. Hence, Kuhn's celebrated thesis that competing scientific paradigms are incommensurable.

Now there are many and glaring similarities between the epistemologies of Popper and Kuhn — so many and so glaring that one might well feel that whatever differences exist must be minor and of small import. Both Popper and Kuhn oppose the commonsense inductivist picture of scientific progress that was sketched by Bacon, handed down to the British Empiricists, and finally completed by the Logical Positivists. To that extent, both deny that science progresses through the accumulation and generalization of facts. Instead, each emphasizes the logical and psychological priority of theory to observation. For both Popper and Kuhn, the sharp distinction between observation and theory is logically and psychologically untenable. All observation is and necessarily theory-laden. Hence, both Popper and Kuhn have abandoned the polemic surrounding inductive inference, a polemic traditionally thought central to and definitive of the philosophy of science. Instead, each focuses upon the revolutionary and psychologically *a priori* character of theory change. In so doing,

178

each emphasizes that scientific knowledge does not grow in a test tube, that new theories are generated primarily in response to recalcitrant problems that confront older theories when they are applied in new and unfamiliar contexts. And to that extent, both agree that scientific progress cannot be understood via logical analysis alone, that one must also be sensitive to the human values and goals that govern the social institution or tradition in which scientific problems arise. Finally, but perhaps most basic, both Popper and Kuhn are fallibilists and have repudiated the view that science aims at or can achieve absolute or justified certainty.

These agreements mark broad strokes in the history of philosophy, and I emphasize them here primarily because I do not wish in what follows to be misinterpreted as denying or trivializing the very strong affinities between Popper and Kuhn. Again, they are many and glaring. Writ large on the history of philosophy, Popper and Kuhn have fought many the same battles against many the same enemies. Nevertheless, there are differences. And that there are differences has, of course, been recognized. But the attempt to specify exactly what these differences are in a way that does not reduce them to mere differences in emphasis has proved difficult. As Kuhn himself writes:

> Sir Karl and I do appeal to the same data; to an uncommon extent we are seeing the same lines on the same paper; asked about those line and those data, we often give virtually identical responses.... Nevertheless, [I am convinced] that our intentions are often quite different when we say the same things. Though the lines are the same, the figures which emerge from them are not.[2]

Kuhn goes on to characterize these differences as the result of a gestalt shift rather than a disagreement. And consistent with his emphasis on the role of psychology in epistemology, Kuhn specifies the possibility of falsification, the incommensurability of theories, and the existence of normal science as the lines upon which he and Popper place different emphasis.

Now these alleged differences cited by Kuhn are the very issues on which the debate between Popper and Kuhn has centered. As such, this debate has been thought to have important methodological implications for psychologism in particular and scientific inquiry in general. On the one hand, Kuhn's insistence that epistemology be construed as a psychology of research has struck many researchers as a liberating alternative to Popper's anti-psychologistic logic of discovery. Here, Kuhn's suggestion is that the findings of social psychology may yield positive consequences for the evaluation of scientific theories. On the other hand, Kuhn's claim that normal scientific inquiry occurs under the rubric of a scientific paradigm has given fresh hope to social scientists still concerned with establishing their disciplines as empirical sciences. Here, the hope is that such researchers might yet reach consensus on paradigms for inquiry, and that such consensus would silence all questions concerning the scientific status of their respective disciplines. Such considerations, conjoined with an awareness of Popper's sharp denunciations of psychologism and specific psychological theories, have led many social scientists to align themselves with Kuhn's epistemology and against Popper's. But this, of course, presupposes that the differences cited by Kuhn are substantive and show Kuhn's epistemology to have positive consequences for the social sciences. In my view, these presuppositions are ill-founded. On the one hand, careful analysis of the major issues on which Popper and Kuhn have been thought to differ reveals that, insofar as these issues are concerned, there is no appreciable difference at all. On the other hand, consideration of the subtle but important issue on which Popper and Kuhn do differ suggests that Popper's epistemology is the more attractive for both scientific inquiry and unification of science.

Here I do not wish to be misunderstood. I agree with Kuhn that he and Popper place different emphasis on the role of normal science, the incommensurability of theories, and the possibility of falsification. And I agree that these differences in *emphasis* are both real and important. Still, I feel that Kuhn's analysis fails to cut to the heart of the matter. The fact that the Popper/Kuhn debate remains unresolved after twenty years suggests that it is not merely emphasis that is here at issue. Specifically, it is my view that these differences in emphasis are symptomatic of a more fundamental and less clearly recognized disagreement concerning the aim of science, the nature of rationality, and the role of truth in scientific inquiry. As such, this disagreement gives rise to what I shall call "the two faces of relativism". That this disagreement and the two faces of relativism have not been clearly recognized is, in my view, the result of a rampant misinterpretation that is part and parcel of the conceptual slack that has accompanied the epistemological paradigm shifts mentioned earlier. And in what follows, I will try to make these intuitions explicit.

In *The Structure of Scientific Revolutions*, Kuhn characterized Popper as emphasizing "the importance of falsification, i.e., of the test that, because its outcome is negative, necessitates the rejection of an established theory".[3] Kuhn goes on to acknowledge that the role which Popper attributes to falsification is similar to that which he (Kuhn) assigns to anomalous experiences as paving the way for paradigm change. But he also cautions that anomalous experiences should not be identified with falsifying ones, since not all anomalies lead necessarily to the rejection of an established paradigm. More important, Kuhn there explicitly doubts that conclusive falsifying experiences exist. Now it might, at first glance, seem that Kuhn vacillates on this point. For on the very next page he writes:

> Popper's anomalous experience is important to science because it evokes competitors for an existing paradigm. But falsification, though it surely occurs, does not happen with, or simply because of, the emergence of an anomaly or falsifying instance. Instead, it is a subsequent and separate process that might equally well be called verification since it consists in the triumph of a new paradigm over the old one.[4]

So while falsification surely occurs, falsifying experiences do not. But this, perhaps, is not as ironic as it may first appear. For it is, in fact, intrinsic to Popper's anti-psychologism that observations and experiences can play no role in a logical argument. Explicitly, it is the statements that *report* observations, and not the observations themselves, that can falsify theories.

But the idea that falsification is a variant of verification points to the locus of Kuhn's criticism. And in his "Logic of Discovery or Psychology of Research?", Kuhn clarifies the issue by asking "What is falsification if it is not conclusive disproof?"[5] There, Kuhn claims that both "falsification" and "refutation" are antonyms of "proof". As such, they are drawn principally from the vocabularies of logic and formal mathematics and imply the ability to compel rational assent from any member of the relevant professional community. Now these remarks seem to signal a sharp criticism of Popper's position. But the issue is subtle, and it is important to clarify exactly what Kuhn's criticism is. Specifically, Kuhn's criticism is *not* that Popper maintains the possibility of conclusive falsification. On the contrary, Kuhn quotes Popper that:

> In point of fact, no conclusive disproof of a theory can ever be produced; for it is always possible to say that the experimental results are not reliable or that the discrepancies which are asserted to exist between the experimental results and the theory are only apparent and that they will disappear with the advance of our understanding.[6]

Rather, Kuhn's criticism is that "having barred conclusive disproof" Popper "has provided no substitute for it, and the relation he does employ remains that of logical falsification".[7] As such, Kuhn views Popper's denial of the possibility of conclusive falsification as "an essential qualification which threatens the integrity of his basic position".[8] Hence, Kuhn concludes that "Though he is not a naive falsificationist, Sir Karl may, I suggest, legitimately be treated as one".[9]

Popper, however, rightly regards this conclusion as "really astonishing".[10] And in his *Realism and the Aim of Science*, he replies that "It is exactly like saying: 'Although Popper is not a murderer, he may, I suggest, legitimately be treated as one' ".[11]

What's going on here and why?

Kuhn clearly sees Popper's "basic position" as the allegiance to logical analysis. But this is a distortion. And that it is a distortion is something that Kuhn should know. For in what immediately precedes and follows the passage cited by Kuhn, Popper writes:

> I am quite ready to admit that there is a need for a purely logical analysis of theories, for an analysis which takes no account of how they change and develop. But this kind of analysis does not elucidate those aspects of the empirical sciences which I, for one, so highly prize. A system such as classical mechanics may be 'scientific' to any degree you like; but those who uphold it dogmatically — believing, perhaps, that it is their business to defend such a successful system against criticism as long as it is not *conclusively disproved* — are adopting the very reverse of that critical attitude which in my view is the proper one for the scientist....
>
> If you insist on strict proof (or strict disproof) in the empirical sciences, you will never benefit from experience, and never learn from it how wrong you are.[12]

Now it is true and well-known that Popper distinguished science from metaphysics by the empirical falsifiability of its theories. But here it is important, following Popper,[13] to distinguish between two senses of "empirical falsifiability". Popper explicitly draws this distinction in *Realism and the Aim of Science*. But as the passage last cited indicates, it is implicit in *The Logic of Scientific Discovery*. According to one sense of "empirical falsifiability" (henceforth "falsifiability$_1$") a statement or theory is falsifiable$_1$ if and only if there exists at least one basic statement that conflicts with it logically, i.e., that contradicts it. It is, of course, not necessary that this potential falsifier actually be true. Otherwise, every scientific theory would, in fact, be false. Rather, the point of falsifiability$_1$ is to emphasize the importance of critical testing in science. And in order for the test of a theory to be effective *as a test*, it is necessary that some possibly true empirical statement, if actually true, suffices to show that theory false. An example of a simple theory that is falsifiable$_1$ is the proverbial "All swans are white". So long as one does not maintain that whiteness is an essential property of swans, there always exists the possibility that the statement "there exists a non-white swan" might be observed to be true. An example of a theory that is not falsifiable$_1$ is, according to Popper, "All human actions are egotistic, motivated by self-interest".[14] Popper does not consider this theory to be falsifiable$_1$ because "no example of an altruistic action can refute the view that there was an egotistic motive hidden behind it".[15] This, presumably, because motives are not intersubjectively observable. But it is an entirely different question whether an alleged falsification is ever so compelling that one is forced to regard the theory in question as falsified. Confusion regarding this point, and regarding Popper's position concerning it, has led Popper to speak of a second sense of "empirical falsifiability" (henceforth "falsifiability$_2$"). According to Popper, a theory is falsifiable$_2$ if and only if "the theory in question can *definitively* or *conclusively* or *demonstrably* be falsified".[16] Here, the point to be made is that the fact that a theory is falsifiable$_1$ in no way entails that it is falsifiable$_2$. Insofar as this is concerned, Popper distinguished science from metaphysics by the falsifiability$_1$ of its theories, and consistently maintained that even when a theory is falsifiable$_1$, it is never falsifiable$_2$.[17]

Kuhn's notions of conclusive proof and refutation are an integral part of the conceptual slack that has accompanied the shift from EP$_1$ to EP$_2$. They are residues from the traditional quest for certainty which both Popper and Kuhn reject. Within EP$_1$, allegiance to conclusive logical argument functioned as a criterion of rationality because EP$_1$ epistemology sought justified certainty, and it is only the valid deductive argument form that necessarily preserves truth from premises to conclusion. Now it is true that Popper regards classical logic, in particular the *Modus Tollens*, as the organon of rational criticism. And to deny the possibility of conclusive verification only to insist upon conclusive falsification *would* be a callow mistake. But to interpret Popper as doing so, or to suggest that he is committed to do so in order to make sense of rational criticism would be to miss his point. And to say that Popper does not maintain the possibility of

conclusive falsification but can be legitimately treated as doing so is simply unfair. Contrary to Kuhn, Popper's "basic position" is not an allegiance to logical
analysis, but to fallibilism and the critical *attitude*. And this critical attitude, far
from being an element of formal logic, is or should be an essential component of
the individual and group scientific psyche.

This point is often missed and should be emphasized. Again, it is well
known that Popper distinguished science from metaphysics by the falsifiability$_1$
of its theories. But whatever else it might be, falsifiability$_1$ is not *simply* a logical
demarcation. *Any* universal generalization might be regarded as falsifiable$_1$, *so
long as its proponents are willing to admit possible contrary evidence as falsification.*[18] What Popper criticized was not simply the logical form of metaphysical
statements, but the unwillingness of metaphysicians to adopt the critical attitude
he regards as essential to rational discourse. This, perhaps, is best illustrated
by Popper's critique of Freudian psychology.[19] So long as Freudians are willing
to "explain away" possible counterexamples to their theory via theoretical
entities (e.g., repressed or unconscious desires) that are held to be in principle
unobservable, Freudian psychology cannot, according to Popper, be regarded as
properly scientific. Again, Popper regards classical logic as the appropriate
organon of criticism. But this is not to suggest that logical argument can or
should *compel* rational assent. Insofar as this is concerned, Popper emphasized
time and again that the acceptance of the basic statements that might provide
contrary evidence to a universal theory is neither logically nor psychologically
compelled. Such statements are in no way justified, but have the *logical* character of conventions or dogmas. They are accepted or rejected as the result of free
decisions which may be reevaluated and revised at any point. Finally, the acceptance of such basic statements is a necessary prerequisite for the process of scientific testing and rational criticism.

Now this can be argued at length, but I think the point has been made. The
point is that this apparent difference between Popper and Kuhn regarding the
possibility of conclusive falsification is merely apparent. It results less from a
difference in emphasis than from Kuhn's misinterpretation of Popper's "basic
position". That basic position is not an allegiance to logical analysis, but to
fallibilism and the critical attitude. As such, Popper's commitment to criticism
extends not only to strictly universal theories, but to the basic statements that
purport to falsify them as well. While Popper does appeal to classical logic as
the organon of criticism, he would be the last to suggest that logic alone suffices
to compel assent. Indeed, the very idea that assent must or should be compelled
seems to be the very antithesis to what Popper regards as the rational enterprise.

The second issue I want to discuss concerns the so-called "incommensurability
of theories". And here, misinterpretations abound on both sides of the debate.
Initially, it is important to recognize that most of the interest and controversy
generated by Kuhn's thesis that competing paradigms are incommensurable

results from an exaggeration of the claim. This exaggeration is widespread, and Popper's account is representative. According to Popper, Kuhn's incommensurability thesis is tantamount to what Popper calls "The Myth of the Framework", i.e., the view that different theories are like mutually untranslatable languages.[20] Were competing paradigms like untranslatable languages, then they would not admit of the critical comparison that Popper regards as essential to rational discourse. Popper, of course, claims that such frameworks are translatable and, ironically, accuses Kuhn of exaggerating a difficulty into an impossibility. Now this, if true, would again signal an important difference in epistemology. But in fact, Popper's account falls wide of the mark. While Kuhn accepts the analogy between paradigms and linguistic frameworks, he is explicit that no one (well, at least not Kuhn) ever believed competing paradigms to be untranslatable.[21] Rather, Kuhn's claim is that when paradigms compete:

> ... the parties to such debates inevitably see differently certain of the experimental or observational situations to which both have recourse. Since the vocabularies in which they discuss such situations consist, however, predominantly of the same terms, they must be attaching some of those terms to nature differently, and their communication is inevitably only partial. As a result, the superiority of one theory to another is something that cannot be proved in debate. Instead ... each party must try, by persuasion, to convert the other.[22]

So Kuhn does not deny the translatability of paradigms. The vulgar introspectionist may regard the mind as a stream of consciousness consisting of immaterial mental entities — ideas, sensations, and the like. And the sophisticated neuropsychiatrist may identify the mind simply with the brain and central nervous system. Still, the introspectionist and the neuropsychiatrist can communicate — despite the fact that the introspectionist's mind, according to the neuropsychiatrist, does not exist!

But what Kuhn does deny, and what he seems to think Popper is committed to, is the existence of a theory-neutral observation language to provide a basis for *non-question begging* comparison of theories.[23] But here it is Kuhn who falls wide of the mark. For Popper was one of the first to challenge the positivist belief in a primitive observation language with the claim that observation is and must be theory-laden.

Now to admit the translatability of paradigms but deny the existence of a theory-neutral basis for comparison might, at first glance, seem paradoxical. But the idea that communication, and hence rational argument, requires the existence of a theory-neutral observation language is yet another residue from the traditional quest for certainty. It is a corollary to what I earlier called "The Clothesline Theory of Communication".[24] As we have seen, the Clothesline Theory holds that a necessary condition for communication is that the persons communicating grasp or apprehend the same object of meaning. The material signs, e.g., sound waves, ink blots, raised dots, etc., that are words are not themselves meanings. Rather, they are the clothing, or "material garments", of meanings. In order to communicate, a person takes a meaning, dresses it in its material garments, hooks it to the clothesline, and sends it over to the person with whom he wishes to communicate. That person takes the clothed meaning off the line, undresses it, and apprehends the meaning. Since this theory holds that communication can occur only to the extent to which the meanings of the signs which occur in it are fixed, it was only this exactness of communication that made justification via logical demonstration possible. But as Quine[25] has shown, there is, in radical translation, always an essential indeterminacy of meaning. And as should be obvious, radical translation is simply a dramatization of the problems inherent in *any* communication situation. Simply put, communication is rarely, if ever, exact. More precisely, even if communication is exact, it is impossible to conclusively determine it as such. All communication may require the assumption of a similarity of meaning. But this assumption is always subject to revision. Finally, while Kuhn acknowledges that competing paradigms admit of mutual translation, he also stresses that such translation is always partial and never perfect.

Here, we are in a position to defuse the debate concerning the incommensurability of theories. Again, Kuhn's claim is *not* the claim that competing paradigms are mutually untranslatable, but simply the denial of a theory-neutral observation language. Now Kuhn's claim that Popper is committed to the existence of such a language may be the result of an unsympathetic reading. But it is also a direct consequence of his view that Popper is committed to conclusive falsification. And this, as I've already argued, is a mistake resulting from a distortion of Popper's basic position. Once we abandon EP_1, there is no longer any reason to think that falsification must be conclusive. In fact, Popper sees communication simply as a special instance of his general schema for critical problem solving. When posed with a problem of interpretation, we construct a tentative hypothesis. From this, we attempt to eliminate errors through a critical test of the consistency of our hypothesis. And the elimination of errors engenders a new tentative hypothesis which is itself subject to a reiteration of the process. For Popper, the myth of a complete, exact, or final understanding is just that – a myth. Hence, the denial of a theory-neutral observation language does not entail that competing paradigms are untranslatable – this, because neither translation nor communication is perfect. And so long as no one pretends that conclusive falsification is possible, incommensurability poses no essential threat to the critical evaluation of theories. Finally, since Popper and Kuhn agree that both conclusive falsification and perfect communication are impossible, there would here seem to be no real basis for debate.

Still, where Popper speaks of "rational argument", Kuhn insists on "conversion" and "persuasion". And traditionally, these terms have marked opposite poles of the rhetorical spectrum. According to the traditional view, a rational belief is a belief in a proposition justified by valid deductive argument from premises themselves derived from an infallible cognitive source. Any belief in a proposition not so justified was thus attributed to persuasion. But here, Kuhn's use of "persuasion" is not as radical as it might first appear. As Kuhn himself writes:

> The point I have been trying to make is a simple one, long familiar in philosophy of science. Debates over theory-choice cannot be cast in a form that fully resembles logical or mathematical proof. In the latter, premises and rules of inference are stipulated from the start. If there is a disagreement about conclusions, the parties to the ensuing debate can retrace their steps one by one, checking each against prior stipulation. At the end of that process one or the other must concede that he has made a mistake, violated a previously accepted rule. After that concession he has no recourse, and his opponent's proof is then compelling. Only if the two discover instead that they differ about the meaning or application of stipulated rules, that their prior agreement provides no sufficient basis for proof, does the debate continue in the form it inevitably takes during scientific revolutions. That debate is about premises, and its recourse is to persuasion as a prelude to the possibility of proof.[26]

Kuhn, of course, is right. The point is both simple and familiar. It can, in fact, be traced to Aristotle who wrote that "all instruction given or received by way of argument proceeds from pre-existent knowledge".[27] But EP$_1$ justificationists insisted that this pre-existent knowledge is not the product of persuasion, but based either upon *a priori* valid cognition or incorrigible sense perception. These philosophers argued that it is only through the recognition of the authority of at least one of these alleged infallible cognitive sources that rational assent could be compelled. But neither Popper nor Kuhn recognizes either of these sources as infallible. And, ironically, Kuhn's point is simply a variant of the argument that Popper used to reject justificationism. Not all statements can be justified by other statements; otherwise there would result an infinite regress. But nor can statements be *rationally* justified by appeal to infallible cognitive sources. For cognitive sources, whatever else they might be, are not *reasons*. More important, history has shown that no cognitive source should be regarded as infallible. Hence, for Popper, the acceptance of a statement by a free decision is a necessary prerequisite for the very possibility of rational argument. It is, as Kuhn puts it, a prelude to the possibility of proof. So, for both Popper and Kuhn, agreement concerning initial premises cannot be rationally compelled. And this is simply a corollary to their mutual denial of the possibility of conclusive proof and refutation. Here, the point to be made is that once we abandon justificationism, the traditional distinction between rational belief and persuasion is no longer tenable. One might still argue whether what remains should be called "reason" or "persuasion". But having abandoned the conceptual framework that gave rise to that distinction, the debate seems to have lost its initial force.

The third issue I want to address concerns the role of normal science. Here I think there is a real disagreement between Popper and Kuhn, though it is not the one most commonly cited. In "Logic of Discovery or Psychology of Research?" Kuhn writes that:

186

> ... Sir Karl has characterized the entire scientific enterprise in terms that apply only to its occasional revolutionary parts. His emphasis is natural and common: the exploits of a Copernicus or Einstein make better reading than those of a Brahe or Lorentz; Sir Karl would not be the first if he mistook what I call normal science for an intrinsically uninteresting enterprise.[28]

Kuhn's criticism is that Popper has completely ignored the *existence* of normal puzzle-solving research. But this seems unfair. While it is clear that normal science is not the focus of Popper's inquiry, *The Logic of Scientific Discovery* begins with the words:

> A scientist engaged in a piece of research, say in physics, can attack his problem straight away. He can go at once to the heart of the matter: that is, to the heart of an organized structure. For a structure of scientific doctrines is already in existence; and with it, a generally accepted problem-situation. This is why he may leave it to others to fit his contribution into the framework of scientific knowledge.[29]

Far from ignoring the existence of normal science, *The Logic of Scientific Discovery* begins with its recognition. Nevertheless, Popper has acknowledged Kuhn's criticism by conceding that the distinction between normal and revolutionary science is something of which he has "at best been only dimly aware".[30] Popper, of course, does not think that the distinction is as sharp as Kuhn maintains. So there are a number of minor skirmishes concerning the historical accuracy of Kuhn's account. Still, these skirmishes concern the details of the distinction and reflect no disagreement concering the *existence* of normal science.

But while Popper concedes the existence of normal science, he sharply rejects the view that normal science is or should be considered the distinctive or essential component of the scientific enterprise. On the contrary, Popper goes so far as to characterize normal puzzle-solving research and the attitude which it represents as "a danger to science".[31] According to Popper:

> 'Normal' science, in Kuhn's sense, exists. It is the activity of the non-revolutionary, or more precisely, the not-too-critical professional: of the science student who accepts the ruling dogma of the day; who does not wish to challenge it; and who accepts a revolutionary theory only if almost everybody else is ready to accept it – if it becomes fashionable by a kind of bandwagon effect.[32]

Again, and more telling:

> ... the 'normal' scientist, as Kuhn describes him, is a person one ought to be sorry for. ... The 'normal' scientist, in my view, has been taught badly. I believe, and so do many others, that all teaching on the University level (and if possible below) should be training and encouragement in critical thinking. The 'normal' scientist, as described by Kuhn, has been badly taught. He has been taught in a dogmatic spirit: he is a victim of indoctrination. He has learned a technique which can be applied without asking for the reason why.... As a consequence, he has become what may be called an *applied scientist*, in

contradistinction to what I should call a *pure scientist*. He is, as Kuhn puts it, content to solve 'puzzles'.[33]

Here, I hope it is clear that what separates Popper and Kuhn is not the question whether normal science *exists*. Both agree that the existence of normal science is an historical fact that cannot be denied. So contrary to what some have suggested, the debate cannot be resolved by historical evidence alone. Rather, the disagreement is *normative*, and concerns the value that should be ascribed to the critical attitude. Viewed somewhat differently, the disagreement concerns the nature of the bond that unites scientists into a social institution. To regard normal puzzle-solving research as the essence of science is to denigrate the critical attitude. It is to characterize the bond that unites scientists in terms of shared *beliefs*. What emerges from this view is a picture of the scientific community as an essentially closed society, a community that does and should acknowledge inquiry only to the extent to which it falls within the parameters of a generally accepted theoretical framework. To regard criticism as the essence of science is, on the other hand, to characterize that bond in terms of a shared *attitude*. And what emerges from this view is Popper's picture of the scientific community as an essentially open society, as a community that ideally strives to avoid all dogma and to be receptive to any and all inquiry so long as inquirers are ready and willing to submit their results to critical review.

Now it is sometimes thought that this disagreement concerning the value of normal science can be traced to a difference between Popper's and Kuhn's respective methodologies of inquiry. According to this view, Popper's epistemology is primarily prescriptive in nature. While Popper acknowledges the importance of historical research, his methodological prescriptions are in no way based upon its results. For Popper, a statement concerning the essence of science is a statement concerning how scientific research *should* proceed in order to achieve its goals, and not, necessarily, how it in fact does. Kuhn's methodology, on the other hand, is characterized in this view as primarily historical in nature. As such, it aims at providing an accurate descriptive generalization of the scientific enterprise as a social institution. And as such, it naturally focuses upon the shared beliefs that have historically provided the factual and methodological framework of that institution. To the extent to which Kuhn's epistemology has a prescriptive content, the norms expressed are based primarily upon his descriptive account of how scientific progress has actually occurred.[34] Thus, it is thought entirely natural that Kuhn should regard normal puzzle-solving research as essential to the scientific enterprise. For in fact, it is this puzzle-solving activity, performed under the rubric of a generally accepted paradigm, that has historically been most characteristic of scientific research as performed in Universities, scientific associations, journals, and laboratories.

It may be true that Kuhn's is primarily an historical thesis. But in my view, it is a history writ large and not too concerned with fine details. Perhaps it would be more apt to say that what Kuhn has provided is a conceptual framework, or paradigm from which to view the history of science. Simply put, the statement that scientific change occurs through a series of non-rational paradigm shifts itself becomes a paradigm for interpreting the history of science. Just as the social historian must learn the concepts of institution, nation, etc. in order to make sense of social history, the historian of science, in Kuhn's view, must learn the concepts of normal science and paradigm shift in order to properly interpret the history of science. In effect, Kuhn is less concerned with making claims about specific events in the history of science than he is in telling us what to look for in interpreting it. "Don't look for conclusive experiments, justifications, or falsifications. Look for ideological and political affiliations. Look for revolutionary and non-rational paradigm shifts!" But if this is correct, then much of the historical criticism levelled against Kuhn is, strictly speaking, irrelevant. Kuhn's picture of the history of science will not be refuted by a single counterexample, or even by a cluster of counterexamples. For there is no suggestion of strict universality in his claim. But nor is Kuhn making a statistical generalization. Rather, his is like the claim that people are greedy or unreflective, given to explain certain types of action. It's the sort of generalization that directs our attention to certain aspects of human nature.

Popper's epistemology, on the other hand, is neither descriptive nor prescriptive *in the methodological sense*. Whether or not the history of scientific change lives up to Popper's sketch *is* quite irrelevant. But to say that the methodology of science should be that of conjecture and refutation is, in a way, to say that science should have no methodology, i.e., no method peculiar to science over and above rational discourse in general. Popper is explicit that his is a *methodological* relativism.[35] The scientist can and should use whatever method he chooses, so long as he uses it critically and in an effort to discover truth. But if this is correct, then much of the criticism aimed at showing that Popper's epistemology is historically false or methodologically inadequate is also irrelevant. This, because Popper makes no pretense to offer history or methodology. So what, then, is Popper up to? In my view, Popper is up to giving a prescription concerning scientific *attitudes* that will foster scientific theory change without being justificationist on the one hand or non-rationalist on the other.

Still, it might be thought that this goes a long way toward defusing the debate concerning normal science. But in my view, it simply casts it in sharper relief. Both Popper and Kuhn reject the positivist view that there is a sharp distinction between statements of values and statements of fact. So-called "facts" are not only theory-laden, they are value-laden as well. But while Kuhn adopts a naturalistic approach to questions of value, Popper does not. Simply put, Kuhn employs the denial of the value/fact distinction as a rationale for deriving the values that scientists should hold from those which they in fact do. Popper, on the other hand, rejects the sharp distinction between value and fact to liberate himself from positivist strictures against acknowledging the basic values of his epistemology.

Here, Kuhn may be right. At least, Morrell and Thackray, in their history of the early years of the British Association for the Advancement of Science, emphasize the importance of ideological and political affiliations in the structure and function of the society[36] :

> The British Association sought to unite differing, even opposing, interests in the pursuit of a transcendent end. That end was truth-knowledge-*scientia*. However, it was truth according to a particular construction; not simply *scientia*, but the Advancement of Science. Defining, demarcating, and delimiting science in ways satisfactory to its audiences, its patrons, its performers, supporters, and hangers-on was essential if the BAAS was to succeed.[37]

According to Morrell and Thackray, "careers were promoted and constituencies shaped; knowledge was advanced and research programmes upheld; funds were raised and lobbies managed; and specific interests were served"[38] through the politics of science. And despite the Association's nominal allegiance to democracy, the "politics of science" had its elitest consequences. The dissemination of the power of the British Association into the hands of a small group who defined its interests, dispensed its funds, appointed its officers, and articulated its politics soon resulted in the dissemination of the Association's economic resources into the hands of an equally small group of researchers:

> Though the membership ran into thousands, just over half the money drawn landed in the pockets of only ten men. Six savants controlled no less than 39 per cent of all the research money actually spent. The Committee of Recommendations chose to direct the largest sums of money towards London, Edinburgh, and Cambridge men, while making an infrequent gesture to provincial philosophers. The occasional grant to a foreigner was an undemanding reminder of the internationality of science. The list of favoured benificiaries, mainly established metropolitan stars plus a few rising younger men, shows patronage strongly at work.[39]

Historically speaking, the basic value of scientists might well be just that of establishing their careers and reputations within the scientific community. It might well be that of achieving the status, authority, and economic advantages characteristic of the elite of any social institution. Nevertheless, Popper remains unabashed in saying that the basic value of scientists *should* be the commitment to the tradition of critical rationalism, i.e., to the search for truth via the critical discussion and testing of theories. And to my mind, the possibility that Kuhn *is* right provides Popper with ample cause for saying so.

Finally, we have arrived at the heart of the issue between Popper and Kuhn. But this is neither the possibility of conclusive falsification, nor the incommensurability of theories, nor even the existence of normal science. Rather, it is the role of truth in inquiry, or, as sometimes expressed, the limits of rationality. Initially, it is important to recognize what this disagreement is *not* about. It is not about the ability of reason to infallibly discover the truth. Both Popper and Kuhn are fallibilists. But nor does their disagreement concern whether the fallibilistic determination of truth is relative or absolute. Neither Popper nor Kuhn envisions the determination of truth as theory-independent. It is true that Popper often claims to believe in "absolute" or "objective" truth. But this is always qualified as "absolute" or "objective" truth *in Tarski's sense*. And in Tarski's sense, a statement can be *determined* to be true only within the framework of a given language.[40] But nor should this conjunction — the belief in absolute truth, but the denial that truth can be determined independent of theory — be regarded as paradoxical. As Gödel has shown, provability is an inherently weaker notion than truth.[41] Now the belief that the truth of a statement can be determined independently of its theoretical context is an intrinsic component of the traditional quest for certainty. It is one of the supporting planks of the EP_1 platform. And to argue that the determination of truth is theory-dependent is to argue against that traditionally revered epistemological paradigm. But again, there is no disagreement here. Rather, the disagreement concerns the *role* of truth in theory-choice. Both Popper and Kuhn agree that truth, in its theory-neutral sense, can no longer be considered as a criterion of knowledge. But while Popper upholds the role of truth as a regulative ideal of scientific inquiry, truth, quite literally, drops out of the Kuhnian picture.

By a "regulative ideal" I mean a standard or goal that governs the structure of behaviour within a certain social institution. Examples of regulative ideals might be justice in the judicial system, maximization of profit in capitalism, or winning in Lombardian football. To say that truth is the regulative ideal of science is, in part, to say that the discovery of truth is the primary aim of scientific inquiry. More important, it is to say that the choice between competing theories is to be made with reference to that ideal. Put thus simply, Popper's claim might appear both trivial and uncontroversial. But this is far from the case. Since Popper is a fallibilist, he denies the existence of a *criterion* of truth, i.e., a decision procedure for determining truth. Hence, his insistence that truth is the regulative ideal of rational inquiry is generally thought to be, at best, paradoxical. If it is impossible to determine the truth or falsity of a theory, then what sense does it make to uphold truth as the standard for theory-choice? In my view, this paradox is *merely* apparent. It too results from the conceptual slack that has accompanied the shift from EP_1 to EP_2 and Popper's subsequent rejection of justificationism. Both EP_1 and EP_2 generally equated the rationality of a belief with its degree of logical justification. In EP_1 absolute truth clearly functioned as the regulative ideal for rational inquiry. But this was because truth there was construed as a criterion of knowledge. As such, the denial of the possibility of determining truth was, for EP_1 philosophers, tantamount to scepticism. But the great scientific revolutions of the twentieth century, in particular the decline of Euclidean Geometry and Newtonian Mechanics, have left philosophers generally sceptical of criterions of truth. If Kant's best candidates for apodeictic certainty, if the theories which everyone regarded as infallibly true are subject to revision, then what hope remains for determining the truth of any theory? Here, what gradually emerged was the EP_2 view that one cannot speak of truth per se, but only as relativized to the conceptual framework of a particular theory or language. This view is, perhaps, best illustrated by Carnap's famous distinction between internal questions, i.e., questions which can be raised within a given linguistic framework, and external questions, i.e., questions concerning the framework itself. According to Carnap, answers to internal questions "may be found either by purely logical methods or by empirical methods, depending upon whether the framework is a logical or a factual one".[42] External questions, on the other hand, cannot be answered by appealing to the methods prescribed by the framework, for these are questions concerning the framework itself. Nor can they be answered by appealing to a higher order framework, for this would lead immediately to infinite regress. Rather, external questions are answered only through a *decision* to adopt or not to adopt the framework in question. As such, theories (or linguistic frameworks) were construed as being themselves neither true nor false, but as setting the criteria by which other statements *within the theory* could be determined to be true or false. But here, the determination of a statement as *true* amounted to nothing more than the determination of that statement as *consistent* — consistent either with the theory itself, or with the world as defined by the theory. Still, the most interesting and important questions concern the mechanics of theory-choice. And here, truth was thought to be simply inoperative. Instead, EP$_2$ philosophers generally focused upon such concepts as practicality, fertility, simplicity, and convenience as the standards that govern theory-choice.

I think that it is undeniable that EP$_1$ and EP$_2$ each conflates the concept of truth with a criterion of truth. In other words, each considers it nonsense to speak of truth in lieu of a specified decision procedure for determining whether or not a given statement is true. This, of course, is not to say that EP$_1$ and EP$_2$ conflate the concept of truth with the *same* criterion of truth. On the contrary, criterions of truth have been notoriously plentiful, ranging from divine revelation at one pole of the spectrum to mere consistency at the other. Still, this conflation is an essential ingredient of justificationism. If knowledge is equated with statements justified as true, then to speak of statements *as* true, but not *justified as true*, is to engage in flights of rhetoric persuasion antithetical to rational discussion. Truth, as the regulative ideal of rational inquiry, follows simply from the commitment to justificationism. And for EP$_2$ philosophers, the denial of the existence of an objective criterion of truth simply illustrates the limits of rationality. But the rejection of justificationism does not entail the rejection of truth as a regulative ideal. And that it does not is something that I hope to make obvious. But first, it is important to recognize that the conflation of the concept of truth with a criterion of truth is responsible for what I perceive to be a prevalent denigration of inquiry. Within EP$_1$, this conflation gave rise to a species of dogmatism which, in the name of rational science, denigrated all inquiry directed toward questioning whatever theories had already been accepted as scientific knowledge. Since such theories were regarded as infallibly true, further inquiry was considered both unnecessary and pernicious. It was unnecessary, because a final decision had already been made and was not subject to revision. It was pernicious, because such inquiry could only be interpreted as an attempt to undermine science. Now the shift from EP_1 to EP_2[43] was obviously a liberalization of this view. Nevertheless, EP_2 justificationism also evokes a species of dogmatism which results in a denigration of inquiry. If the concept of truth is conflated with a criterion of truth, but the truth of a statement can only be determined within the conceptual framework of a given theory, then it is impossible to determine the truth of *competing* theories. Hence, rational inquiry concerning foundational problems is denigrated because it is thought possible only by begging the very questions at issue. Simply put, all rational knowledge is, at base, non-rational. As such, one instance of non-rationality is as good as any other. What results from this view has often been called "foundational relativism". But so long as one remains within a justificationist framework, this is little more than scepticism without tears.

Now Popper's anti-justificationism escapes foundational relativism by denying that there are foundations to be relativistic about. But even Popperians who fully accept the fallibilist methodology of conjecture and refutation nonetheless complain that there is more that a whiff of inductivism, and hence, justificationism, in Popper's epistemology. Inductive inference was introduced into epistemology as an attempt to salvage the justificationist platform – the move toward inductive justification being an essential weakening of the EP_1 concept of justification as logical proof. But justificationists who recognize only inductive justification have, for the most part, also abandoned EP_1. So why the hullabaloo? As far as I can see, the hullabaloo is caused by Popper's belief[44] that "justification craves finality. Criticism does not". The distinction is subtle, and perhaps psychological. But it is not *merely* psychological. For our World 2 mental states may indeed affect their World 3 theoretical products. In sum, to focus on justification is to focus on finality, but to focus on criticism is to invite revision. And so long as we regard a theory's survival of tests as indicative of its confirmation, or reliability, or justification, it will be difficult to avoid the admittedly psychological tendency to regard its high degree of corroboration as attesting to its finality. But this, of course, is what Popper regards as the greatest obstacle to the growth of knowledge.

Still, many would object. For *really*, isn't criticism just the other side of the justificationist coin? And isn't Popper really committed to some form of justificationism? For if theories are refuted by basic statements, and the difference between being refuted and being unrefuted is not arbitrary, then must there not be something like rational justification of basic statements? This, of course, is just the argument I raised toward the end of chapter ten. Popper is explicitly opposed to relativism – the view that the choice between competing theories is rationally arbitrary – and introduced his theory of corroboration to bolster that opposition. But if the choice between competing theories is not rationally arbitrary because some theories can be provisionally eliminated through *Modus Tollens*, and *Modus Tollens* depends upon the acceptance of a basic statement by a "free decision", then why isn't the choice between competing theories *based* upon that free decision, and in that sense arbitrary? But this, I'm now inclined to believe, misses Popper's point. And here, the point turns on the meaning of "arbitrary". Popper, first of all, is explicit that from the *logical* perspective, the choice between competing theories *is* arbitrary.[45] But the logical perspective is very narrow. In the logical sense, a statement is arbitrary if it is not logically justified. And Popper's point is that basic statements, and hence theories, cannot be justified by either deductive or inductive inference. But Popper emphasizes that the decision to accept or reject a basic statement is not arbitrary *in any other sense.*[46] Specifically, it is not *rationally* arbitrary because it is motivated by the search for truth. The claim that truth is the regulative ideal of rational inquiry thus saves Popper from relativism in Feyerabend's sense: that literally *anything* goes![47] But this sort of non-arbitrariness is, of course, fully consistent with the fact that different investigators, each motivated by the critical search for truth, might differ in their choice. But this, Popper never denied.

So long as we accept the equation of rationality with logical justification (be it deductive or inductive justification), Popper's point will remain opaque. But the justificationist theory, as we have seen, was able to salvage rationality only by acknowledging its limits. By conflating the concept of truth with a criterion of truth, justificationists concluded that fully rational knowledge is, according to their own theory of rationality, impossible. But Popper's *critical* rationalism equates the rationality of a theory not with its justification, but with its susceptibility to criticism. Not all statements can be justified, but each can be criticized. And so long as each can be criticized with reference to its truth, the rationality of science remains fully intact. Here, we are in a better position to see the difference between Frege's and Popper's anti-psychologisms. While Frege was opposed to *psychological* justification, Popper is opposed to psychological *justification.* And this formulation also provides us with a better perspective from which to view the differences between Popper and Nagel. What Popper opposes is not the use of sense perceptions in theory-choice, but the use of sense perceptions to *justify* basic statements. But still, the question remains. Is is really possible to speak meaningfully of truth in lieu of a criterion of truth?

Earlier I said that it is possible to maintain truth as a regulative ideal of science even in the absence of a criterion for determining whether or not truth has been achieved. That this is possible should really be obvious. Consider the case of capitalism. To say that the regulative ideal of capitalism is the maximization of profit is simply to say that capitalists aim at maximizing their profits. Confronted with competing strategies for maximizing profits, a decision will be based upon a judgment concerning which strategy will best achieve that goal. And despite the best efforts of marketing analysts, such a judgment ultimately requires a decision on the part of an executive. This, I suggest, is uncontroversial. Still, no one would ever suggest that all such decisions are successful. Despite the best laid plans of capitalists, businesses do go bankrupt, executives lose their jobs, and the world goes on! But what is more interesting is that capitalists can aim at maximizing their profits, they can base their practical decisions on that goal, without ever being in a position to determine whether or when profits have been maximized. Even were it possible to determine that one strategy for maximizing profits is better than another — which in general it is not since we are here dealing with counterfactuals — that would still not suffice to determine whether that strategy was the *best* strategy for maximizing profits, and hence, whether profits had in fact been maximized. In the face of a possibly infinite number of such strategies, capitalists are committed to risk, to bold guesses concerning which policy will prove most successful. Nevertheless, the commitment to maximization of profit is meaningful and has real and important consequences. For in practice, it might well result in a decision to sacrifice the quality of goods in order to maximize profits — a decision that would be unthinkable were the maintenance of the quality of goods regarded as the regulative ideal.

This, I suggest, provides a heuristic for understanding Popper's commitment to truth as the regulative ideal of science. Simply put, this is the commitment to regard truth as the standard for criticism. Again, one might be committed to this ideal without ever being able to determine whether or when it has been achieved. Insofar as this is concerned, Popper is simply committed to basing his criticism and decisions concerning theory-choice on what *appears* to be the truth, not necessarily on what is. Appearances, of course, may be deceptive. But this is Popper's primary reason for insisting that all theories be regarded as fallible. Mistakes are possible, but they should be mistakes regarding *truth*, and not regarding simplicity or practicality. Finally, the decision to adopt a regulative ideal other than truth has clear implications for the nature of scientific inquiry, just as the decision to adopt quality as the regulative ideal of business has clear implications for capitalism.

Still, the claim that Popper thus escapes relativism might appear to be a jest. From the perspective of EP_1 and much of EP_2, anti-justificationism is less of an escape that a confession. Now it is an historical fact that few philosophers have ever been content to characterize themselves or to be characterized as relativists. And this, perhaps, is understandable. For relativism, in each of its various forms, has traditionally been associated with a cavalier attitude regarding knowledge in general and science in particular. Simply put, "relativism", like "psychologism", is a term of philosophical ill-repute. But here we should remember that from the perspective of EP_1, *all* EP_2 philosophy is relativistic. And the fact that most EP_2 philosophers do not call themselves "relativists" is simply another illustration of the sort of linguistic tact discussed in chapter two. Here, neither Popper nor Kuhn are exceptions to the historical rule. Neither is content with the accusation of relativism, and Popper goes so far as to characterize relativism as "the main intellectual malady of our time".[48] But despite their allegiances to different senses of "justification", both EP_1 and EP_2 philosophers concurred that relativism is a consequence of the denial that foundational principles can be rationally justified. And in this sense of "relativism", both Popper and Kuhn are relativists. Still, there are two faces of relativism, and the face that Popper shows is decidedly different from Kuhn's.

Earlier I suggested that justificationism, in each of its forms, results in a species of dogmatism that leads to a denigration of inquiry concerning foundational problems. Here, I hope that it is obvious that justificationism should have been abandoned upon the denial of an objective criterion of truth. That EP_2 philosophers instead weakened their concept of justification was undoubtedly a result of their fear of relativism. Insofar as this is concerned, both Popper and Kuhn should be applauded for unmasking EP_2 justificationism as a mere camouflage of relativism. Still, Kuhn's suggestion that foundational problems cannot be rationally discussed reveals a deep commitment to the justificationist *theory* of rationality and, in particular, to the view that scientific knowledge is a species of belief that differs from other species by its degree of justification. According to Kuhn, foundational problems cannot be rationally discussed because foundational beliefs cannot be rationally justified. But Popper, as we have seen, rejects the equation between rationality and justification. Science, according to Popper, consists not of beliefs, but of theories. And for Popper, foundational problems can be rationally discussed because foundational theories can be logically criticized. It is this difference, I suggest, that reveals the two faces of relativism.

Traditionally, philosophers opposed relativism because they feared it would ultimately lead to a general breakdown of community and social institutions. This fear, however, presupposed that social bonds could be forged only by a community of belief. So long as it was held that such belief could be justified by reason, the rational tradition was thought to be the best defense against relativism. But when logical analysis revealed that all logical inference depends upon statements that cannot themselves be justified, this defense was shown to be inadequate. Both Popper and Kuhn recognize the inadequacy of rational justification in forging solidarity of belief concerning foundational principles, but there part company. For Popper, the inadequacy of rational justification points toward a reinterpretation of the rational tradition as one committed to the critical evaluation of theories. Rational man, on the Popperian view, emerges neither as the Cartesian perceptor of clear and distinct ideas, nor as the Carnapian embodiment of a probabilistic decision theory. Rather, he can best be described as a sort of epistemological Buddhist — one deeply committed to the quest for truth, ready to entertain competing theories, and even willing to apply them in practice, but always wary of forming deep attachments to any specific claim to truth. Such a man may be characterized as having beliefs. But what the epistemological Buddhist lacks is the *commitment* to belief. More precisely, his theories are viewed as epistemological tools that may be discarded without pathos when they cease to be effective toward meeting his ends. Kuhn, on the other hand, sees the inadequacy of rational justification as pointing toward the need for rational man to commit himself non-rationally to the belief structure of a particular paradigm. Insofar as this is concerned, Kuhn's relativism

196

frowns on inquiry concerning foundational problems by labelling it "non-rational". While relativism is thus acknowledged, it gives rise to a sort of conservative defense of whatever belief system is construed as rational according to the established scientific community. Revolutionary science is also acknowledged, and in a sense glorified — for periodic paradigm shifts allow troubled communities to reunite themselves in faith. But the critical attitude is discouraged. Instead, normal science is regarded as the essence of the scientific enterprise, and dogmatic commitment to a paradigm is upheld as a necessary prerequisite for rational knowledge and social harmony. Popper's relativism, on the other hand, smiles on foundational inquiry as the very essence of rationality. According to Popper, it is the willingness of scientists to engage in foundational inquiry, and not their commitment to a particular belief structure, that makes scientific community, in the full sense, possible. For in the face of a plurality of belief concerning foundational principles and when faced with the impossibility of rational justification, it is only the rationalist's critical attitude that can prevent the segmentation of scientists into heterogeneous sub-communities isolated from communication by their commitments to different paradigms. Whatever social harmony is thus achieved is, in Popper's view, illusory and pernicious. For in the final analysis, it is the breakdown of communication, and not the plurality of belief, that poses the worst threat to society. And here, it is the critical attitude that emerges as the best hope for keeping rational discussion alive.

In the beginning of this chapter, I suggested that our analysis would reveal Popperian epistemology as the more attractive for scientific inquiry and the unification of science. At this point in our discussion, I would hope that the reasons for my suggestion are obvious. It might, however, be best to illustrate these reasons via a consideration of the situation in psychology. In the one hundred or so years since psychology set itself the task of evolving into an empirical science, psychologists have displayed an almost philosophical acumen at disagreeing over foundational issues. The major divisions between introspectionism, psychoanalysis, behaviourism, and neuropsychology only serve to mark the tip of the iceberg when it comes to disagreement in psychology. For each of these major divisions itself branches to include a plethora of competing views: Freudian, Adlerian, Jungian, Watsonian, Skinnerian, etc., etc., etc. Even today, psychologists of different schools proceed from such opposing perspectives and use methods and techniques that are so different that it often seems impossible for them to communicate with one another. In my view, this situation results less from an essential incommensurability of paradigms than from an almost smug unwillingness on the part of normal researchers to investigate the conceptual foundations of competing schools. If nothing else, this provides corroboration for Kuhn's description of science. What is worse, however, is that Kuhn's description of science is sometimes appealed to as a justification for ignorance. Today, education in psychology is a Kuhnian delight. It usually begins with a biased survey of competing schools that serves as an indoctrination into one of the various psychological theories. More important, the institutional demands for success set upon researchers in any one of these competing schools function, with rare exception, as a practical discouragement from investigating opposing views. Today, the Kuhnian hope for psychology is that one of these competing theories, or perhaps one as yet unarticulated, will finally emerge as the unchallenged and universally accepted paradigm of psychology, and thereby insure the scientific status of the discipline. But even should this hope be realized, it will, *pace* Kuhn, most probably be due more to the fertility of that paradigm's ideological and political affiliations than to its success in surviving severe criticism. In my view, any such unification of psychology predicated upon the non-rational silencing of opposing views would be a unification sorely bought. What is, to my mind, more attractive is the sort of unification that results from the critical examination of foundational principles. While this sort of unification may not yield unification in belief, it will at least provide unification in rational discussion. And this sort of unification, in my view, is the best hope for understanding in psychology, and in science and philosophy at large.

NOTES AND REFERENCES

1. Kuhn, Thomas S.; *The Structure of Scientific Revolutions*; University of Chicago Press (Chicago, 1962) p. viii.

2. Kuhn, Thomas S.; "Logic of Discovery or Psychology of Research?"; in *Criticism and the Growth of Knowledge*; ed. by I. Lakatos and A. Musgrave; Cambridge University Press (Cambridge, 1970) p. 3.

3. *Op. cit.*; *The Structure of Scientific Revolutions*; p. 146.

4. *Ibid.*; p. 147.

5. *Op. cit.*; "Logic of Discovery or Psychology of Research"; p. 15.

6. *Ibid.*

7. *Ibid.*; p. 14.

8. *Ibid.*

9. *Ibid.*

10. Popper, Karl R.; *Realism and the Aim of Science*; Rowman and Littlefield (Totowa, 1983) p. xxxiv.

11. *Ibid.*

12. Popper, Karl R.; *The Logic of Scientific Discovery*; Hutchinson (London, 1959) p. 50.

13. *Op. cit.*; *Realism and the Aim of Science*; pp. xix-xxv.

198

14. *Ibid.*; p. xx.

15. *Ibid.*

16. *Ibid.*; p. xxii.

17. This is contrary to Lakatos (see: Lakatos, Imre; "Falsification and the Methodology of Scientific Research Programmes"; in *Criticism and the Growth of Knowledge*; pp. 91-195), who discerns an evolution in Popper's thought from the belief that scientific theories are $falsifiable_2$ to the belief that they are not. Lakatos calls the former position "naive falsificationism", and the latter position "sophisticated falsificationism". He thus distinguishes between $Popper_1$, the naive falsificationist, and $Popper_2$, the sophisticated falsificationist. Ironically, Lakatos also distinguishes $Popper_1$ and $Popper_2$ from a third Popper, $Popper_0$, a dogmatic falsificationist who never existed, but was invented and criticized by the Logical Positivists. I say that this is ironic because, in my view, Lakatos' $Popper_1$ is also an invention.

18. I am not sure whether or not Popper would agree with this statement, but I do think it captures the spirit of his remarks concerning $falsifiability_1$. Consider Popper's example of a theory that is not $falsifiable_1$: (T) "All human actions are egotistic, motivated by self-interest". Surely the statement (S) "There is an altruistic human action, an action not motivated by self-interest" logically contradicts (T). Still, (T) might not be considered $falsifiable_1$ since (S) might not be considered a basic statement. Here, the argument would be that (S) is not intersubjectively testable. Now I do not wish to deny this. Nevertheless, the point to be made is that (S) could be considered intersubjectively testable, if, for example, the concept of motivation were defined in behaviourist terms and "altruistic motives" and "egotistic motives" were defined behaviouristically as antonyms. Popper, in any event, offers a similar argument concerning the verifiability of "God exists" in "The Demarcation between Science and Metaphysics" (See: Popper, Karl R.; "The Demarcation between Science and Metaphysics"; in *Conjectures and Refutations: The Growth of Scientific Knowledge*; Routledge & Kegan Paul (London, 1962) pp. 275-276.

19. See: Popper, Karl R.; "Science: Conjectures and Refutations"; in *Conjectures and Refutations: The Growth of Scientific Knowledge*; p. 34f.

20. See: Popper, Karl R.; "Normal Science and Its Dangers"; in *Criticism and the Growth of Knowledge*; p. 56.

21. Kuhn, Thomas S.; "Reflections on my Critics"; in *Criticism and the Growth of Knowledge*; p. 267.

22. Kuhn, Thomas S.; "Postscript-1969"; in *The Structure of Scientific Revolutions*; ed. by T.S. Kuhn; University of Chicago Press (Chicago, 1969) p. 198.

23. I say that Kuhn *seems* to think that Popper is committed to the existence of a theory-neutral observation language, because Kuhn seems to vacillate on the point. On the one hand, Kuhn writes in "Logic of Discovery or Psychology of Research?" that Popper and he are "correspondingly sceptical of efforts to produce any neutral observation language". (*Op. cit.*; "Logic of Discovery or Psychology of Research?"; p. 2.) On the other hand, Kuhn writes in "Reflections on my Critics" that many philosophers "continue to assume that theories can be compared by recourse to a basic vocabulary consisting entirely of words which are attached to nature in ways that are unproblematic and, to the extent necessary, independent of theory. That is the vocabulary in which Sir Karl's basic statements are

framed". (*Op. cit.*; "Reflections on my Critics"; p. 266.) Perhaps what Kuhn means is that while Popper is explicitly sceptical of a theory-neutral observation language, his epistemology nonetheless commits him to one.

24. See chapter five, above.

25. See: Quine, Willard van Orman; *Word and Object*; MIT Press (Cambridge, Mass., 1960).

26. *Op. cit.*; "Postscript-1969"; p. 199.

27. Aristotle; *Analytica Posteriora*; in *The Basic Works of Aristotle*; ed. by R. McKeon; Random House (New York, 1941) p. 110.

28. *Op. cit.*; "Logic of Discovery or Psychology of Research?"; p. 6.

29. *Op. cit.*; *The Logic of Scientific Discovery*; p. 13.

30. *Op. cit.*; "Normal Science and Its Dangers"; p. 52.

31. *Ibid.*

32. *Ibid.*

33. *Ibid.*; pp. 52-53.

34. Feyerabend claims that Kuhn's epistemology is ambiguous as to whether it offers historical description or methodological prescription. Feyerabend writes that Kuhn wants to give "historical support to value judgments which he just as many other people seem to regard as arbitrary and subjective. On the other side he wants to leave himself a safe second line of retreat: those who dislike the implied derivation of values from facts can always be told that no such derivation is made and that the prescription is purely descriptive". (Feyerabend, Paul; "Consolations for the Specialist"; in *Criticism and the Growth of Knowledge*; p. 199.)

35. *Op. cit.*; *The Logic of Scientific Discovery*; pp. 15-23.

36. I do not place too much weight on this historical account, though this has nothing to do with any doubts concerning the scholarship of Morrell and Thackray. Rather, the point is that countless historical accounts can be cited that pay no attention to the political and ideological affiliations of the scientific institution. It is a commonplace that history is rewritten in each generation. And this generation seems to be one peculiarly interested in the political and ideological influences of almost everything. Insofar as this is concerned, I have been unable to ascertain whether and to what extent Morrell and Thackray have been influenced by Kuhn.

37. Morrell, J. & Thackray, A.; *Gentlemen of Science*; Oxford University Press (London, 1981) p. 224.

38. *Ibid.*; p. 298.

39. *Ibid.*; pp. 318-319.

40. See: Tarski, A.; "The Semantic Conception of Truth and the Foundations of Semantics"; in *Philosophy and Phenomenological Research*, Volume 4, pp. 341-376.

41. See: Gödel, Kurt; "Über Formal Unentscheidbare Satze der *Principia Mathematica und Verwandter Systeme, I*"; *Monatshefte für Mathematik und Physik*, Volume 38, pp. 173-198.

42. Carnap, Rudolf; "Empiricism, Semantics, and Ontology"; in *The Linguistic Turn*; ed. by Richard Rorty; The University of Chicago Press (Chicago, 1967) p. 173.

43. EP_1 epistemology seems to bear an obvious relationship to the infallibilist claims made by the Roman Catholic Church for their religious doctrines. And the shift to EP_2 epistemology seems to bear a corresponding relationship to the Reformation. Of course, the historical dates for these shifts do not overlap. Still, it might be an interesting study to ascertain whether or not these relationships are anything more than conceptual.

44. Popper, Karl R.; (personal communication).

45. Popper, Karl R.; "Replies to my Critics"; in *The Philosophy of Karl Popper*; ed. by P.A. Schilpp; Open Court (La Salle, 1974) p. 1111.

46. *Ibid.*

47. See: Feyerabend, Paul; *Against Method*; Verso (London, 1975).

48. Popper, Karl R.; "Facts, Standards, and Truth: A Further Criticism of Relativism"; in *The Open Society and Its Enemies*; by Karl R. Popper; Princeton University Press (Princeton, 1961) p. 369.

12. PSYCHOLOGISM WITHOUT TEARS

In our discussion of Frege, we associated psychologism with the denial of *a priori* knowledge, i.e., *a priori* valid statements. There we showed that Frege thought such statements necessary for objective justification in the EP₁ sense. And insofar as *a priori* validity is associated with apodeictic certainty, we argued that anti-psychologism is maintained to oppose fallibilism – in Frege's case, fallibilism with regard to logic and mathematics; but more generally, fallibilism with regard to whatever domain for which anti-psychologism is maintained. But our discussion of Popper's fallibilistic anti-psychologism gave pause for thought. There we found that one can consistently maintain anti-psychologism within a fallibilistic epistemology. But we also found that the price for doing so is the complete abandonment of the quest for justification. Indeed, we found that Popperian anti-psychologism is simply a lemma in Popper's general argument against the possibility of justification and the need for maintaining justification as a criterion of objective knowledge. To that extent, our analogy between philosophy and chess holds sound. In tight philosophical *Weltanschauungen*, as in tight chess games, one must sacrifice in order to move.

Our discussion has been initially, but not merely or even primarily, historical. This point deserves emphasis. Were it our only concern to get clear on what Frege and Popper meant by "psychologism", then our findings would be of cursory interest only. Rather, our point in delving into history has been to determine the grounds of psychologism in order to see whether and to what extent contemporary anti-psychologism links up with traditional concerns. Insofar as this is concerned, my impression is that many twentieth century epistemologists have, either consciously or unconsciously, embraced psychologism. by maintaining the need for justification but denying the possibility of *a priori* knowledge, i.e., *a priori* valid statements. In so doing, they have made the shift from EP₁ to EP₂. This move, as we have already shown, has usually been accommodated by a weakening of the criteria for justification. Nevertheless, even when the commitment to psychologism has been conscious, few philosophers have recognized or accepted its consequences. If I am correct, then the epistemological consequence of psychologism, at least for justificationists, is just what Frege always thought it to be: epistemological relativism with regard to foundational principles. When confronted with disagreements concerning foundational principles, be it in logic or ethics, the psychologistic justificationist can only acknowledge the fact and say simply: those laws hold for them, these laws hold for us. Given our discussions of Frege and Popper, the relationship between psychologism and epistemological relativism should come as no great surprise. As we have noted time and again, it was the fear of epistemological relativism which was the motivation for anti-psychologism in the first place. But if I am correct, then the shift to EP_2 has a further social consequence for the enterprise of philosophy. In short, it entails a revision of the very concept of philosophical investigation.

Much of western philosophy has been devoted to providing answers to the questions, "How much can we know?" and "How can we know it?" As such, much of what has occurred in the history of western philosophy can be viewed as a sort of contest between the cognitivist and the sceptic. In the EP_1 version of this game, the cognitivist defends the position that objectively certain knowledge is possible (in this or that domain), while the sceptic presents arguments to show that it's not. And as such, philosophical investigation in the western world naturally divides itself into the construction and justification of theories on the one hand, and the criticism of theories constructed on the other. While cognitivists and sceptics have traditionally been at odds concerning the possibility and scope of certainty, they have at least shared this common ground: both have agreed that whatever justification or criticism is offered must be framed in rational argument, and that the laws of classical logic serve as the organon of justification and criticism. Indeed, it is just this agreement concerning the organon of criticism and justification that makes western philosophy possible. If the cognitivist and the sceptic disagreed as to what counts as a justification and what counts as a criticism, then there would remain no common ground at all upon which to adjudicate their various claims. As Frege realized, unless there are common standards for judgment, there is little hope for a common science.

But if philosophy is a game played out through the moves of criticism and justification, then the hope of all philosophers is that this game is not intramural. In other words, philosophers ideally intend their arguments to convince not simply those who already agree (however implicitly) with their conclusions, but those who do not yet agree as well. And insofar as this involves the instillation of belief, philosophers have, since Plato, been adamant that such belief should not be instilled simply by rhetorical persuasion, but through the force of rational argument. For the philosophical mind, intellectual solidarity is not enough. Such solidarity must be wrought on the pain of irrationality.

Were there never disagreement in belief, philosophical investigation would have no cause. But philosophical disagreement can occur on many different levels. Philosophers may, for example, agree as to the truth of the premises of an argument, but differ as to the validity of an inference. More interestingly, philosophers may differ as to the truth of the premises themselves. Following Popper, we can call any criticism or justification which concerns itself with the validity of an argument "immanent", and any criticism or justification which concerns itself with the truth of the premises of an argument "transcendental". Frege, as we have already shown,[1] considered the aim of a proof to be twofold: (1) to place the truth of a proposition beyond all doubt; (2) to afford us with insight into the dependence of truths upon one another. But Frege must have been thinking primarily of immanent justification. In immanent justification (1) and (2) are accomplished simultaneously. If there is no dispute concerning the truth of premises, making the logical relationships between premises and conclusion explicit itself functions to remove all doubt concerning the truth of the conclusion. On the transcendental level the case is very different. Here a rigorous proof will also make the logical relationships between statements explicit. But if one has doubt concerning the truth of premises, even the most rigorous of proofs will not suffice to place the truth of the conclusion beyond all doubt. Indeed, to speak of a "proof" on the transcendental level is almost to jest. It is not exactly a case of the blind leading the blind. But it is somewhat analogous to supporting a broken leg with a broken crutch. On the transcendental level, whatever cause one might have to doubt a statement might itself be sufficient cause to doubt the statements which purport to prove it.

As we have already seen, Mill expressed this point in his doctrine that every syllogism, *considered as an argument to prove the conclusion*, contains a *petitio principii*.[2] And it has also been expressed, perhaps metaphorically, in the doctrine that the content of the conclusion of a valid argument is contained in the conjunction of its premises. To that extent, the conclusion of a valid argument does not add content to, but subtracts content from its premises. At best, it alters the form in which such content is expressed. Now Mill is not alone in this judgment. And the point should really come as no great surprise. Aristotle noted early on that:

> All instruction given or received by way of argument proceeds from pre-existent knowledge. This becomes evident upon a survey of all the species of such instruction. The mathematical sciences and all other speculative disciplines are acquired in this way, and so are the two forms of dialectical reasoning, syllogistic and inductive; for each of these latter makes use of old knowledge to impart new, the syllogism assuming an audience that accepts its premises, induction exhibiting the universal as implicit in the clearly known particular.[3]

Aristotle goes on to say that the pre-existent knowledge required is of two kinds. "In some cases admission of the fact must be assumed, in others comprehension of the meaning of the term used, and sometimes both assumptions are essential."[4] In the twentieth century, the distinction between agreement as to meaning and agreement as to fact has become blurred. But the point to be made is that on the transcendental level, it is this very required pre-existent knowledge that is the point of dispute.

Now if Mill is correct and every deductively valid argument contains a *petitio principii*, then it might seem that the critical methodology of analytic philosophy sets forth paradoxical criteria for the evaluation of arguments. On the one hand, critical methodology deplores circularity. *Petitio principii*, we are told, is a logical fallacy. Simply put, good arguments do not beg the question. Circular arguments have little worth as justifications – this, because they are dialectically ineffective. If an argument assumes that P, it is neither feat nor surprise if it concludes that P. Critical methodology tells us that the demonstration that an argument is circular is always a good argument against that argument. On the other hand, critical methodology demands deductive validity. Good arguments are valid arguments, though not all valid arguments, of course, are good. And the first step toward proving a statement is to express it as the conclusion of an argument whose form is such that the falsity of its conclusion is inconsistent with the truth of its premises. If the conclusion of an argument may be false despite the truth of its premises, then that argument has no *logical* force and cannot serve as a proof of its conclusion. Finally, as every initiate to philosophy knows, the demonstration that an argument is invalid is a sufficient condition for its dismissal.

But what is interesting is that it is not the case that all valid arguments are dismissed as circular. Some philosophers have suggested that while all deductively valid arguments are indeed circular, such circularity is not vicious so long as the content of the conclusion is distributed among a large enough number of premises. Nevertheless, circles are not defined by the length of their periphery. And any argument can be expressed via conjunction as having exactly one premise. Now it might be thought that judgments of circularity are based upon the apparent obviousness of the transition from premises to conclusion. All valid arguments may be circular, but such arguments should be *rejected* as circular only when the transition from premises to conclusion appears too obvious for words. This, of course, would not be a formal definition of circularity. For whether or not a transition appears obvious is, in Dewey's phrase, a matter most personal and psychological. To the philosopher well-trained in logic, the proof for the completeness of the predicate calculus may seem so obvious as to render all explanation otiose. But such is not the case for the beginner. Who, in studying elementary logic, has not felt the frustration of asking for an explanation of a proof only to be told with hands held high, "It's obvious!"? And who, in teaching elementary logic, has had the ingenuity to respond to such a request other than by simply retracing the steps of the argument – slowly?

The fact that all valid arguments involve a *petitio principii* simply underscores Aristotle's point that all instruction given by way of argument proceeds from pre-existent knowledge. But the fact that valid arguments are not always dismissed as circular cannot be due simply to the fact that the logical relations between propositions are not always clear. For if Frege is correct about the twofold aim of proof, then it is the clarification of the logical relations between propositions which functions to place the truth of a proposition beyond doubt. It is not so much the obviousness of the transition which results in the judgment of circularity, but the obviousness of the premise. Simply put, justifications are requested only when the truth of a statement is dubious. And justifications are rejected as circular when the truth of the premises seems as dubious as the truth of the statements they "prove".

The possibility of transcendental disagreement indicates that the acceptance of the laws of classical logic as the organon for philosophical justification and criticism does not, for extra-logical disputes, suffice to compel intellectual solidarity. And transcendental disagreement concerning the laws of logic themselves is simply disagreement as to whether or not classical logic should be accepted as the organon for philosophical justification and criticism. It is a credit to the logical acumen of philosophers that recognition of this point has resulted in a concentration on foundational questions. But this concentration on foundational questions, more than anything else, displays the limits of rational justification. Fries' trilemma taught us that it is fruitless to require that all our knowledge be rationally justified. What follows upon such a demand is infinite regress. Justification, unless we regress infinitely, must end somewhere. The issue that separates the psychologistic philosopher from the anti-psychologist is "Where?" But regardless of whether we rest content with sense perception or make claims to *a priori* validity, it would seem that psychologism and anti-psychologism are, in this respect, in the same boat. Whatever justifications are presented, their effectiveness as tools of rational persuasion presupposes the acceptance of their premises. What Fries' trilemma has taught is that in the case of transcendental disagreement concerning foundational questions, rational justification is impotent. Any such justification must itself appeal to pre-existent knowledge. And were that the case, the dispute would not be foundational after all.

Foundational philosophy considers the question "Is there a class of propositions – the foundations – that are self-evident or immediately justified?" and "If so, how is that class defined?" Since foundational propositions are held to be self-evident or *immediately* justified, they cannot be based upon other *statements*. Traditionally, what has been held as accounting for the self-evidence of such propositions is their derivation not from other propositions, but from cognitive *sources*. Ironically enough, it was the disagreement concerning such sources that gave rise to the two great epistemological *Weltanschauungen*, classical rationalism and empiricism. The latter, as we have seen, recognized sense perception as the only valid source of knowledge, while the former acknowledged the possibility of *a priori* intuition. We have already seen that Fregean anti-psychologism is simply a development of the rationalist position. But the point to be made is that for all the anti-psychologistic claims made for the distinction between the context of discovery and the context of justification, Fregean anti-psychologism was never disinterested in the question of cognitive sources. Rather, by construing psychology as an empirical science, it simply maintained that there exist cognitive sources that are free of all psychology.

But if the dispute between psychologism and anti-psychologism concerns the question of cognitive sources, what is epistemologically significant in that dispute concerns the cognitive authority that can be ascribed to scientific systems built upon such sources. Systematic science, as we have seen, requires strictly universal statements. And regardless of how we construe the status of the justification that sense perception provides (or fails to provide) for singular statements, it has, since Hume, been a commonplace that neither sense perception nor the singular statements derived from sense perception can provide rational justification for strictly universal statements. Frege noted this point in writing that "induction itself depends on the general proposition that the inductive method can establish the truth of a law, or at least some probability for it."[5] If systematic science is to have a measure of rational cognitive authority, then its strictly universal statements cannot be based on sense perception alone. If we deny the possibility of *a priori* apprehension of such general propositions, then "induction becomes nothing more than a psychological phenomenon, a procedure which induces men to believe in the truth of a proposition, without affording the slightest justification for so believing."[6] But if such general propositions are to be regarded as absolutely true, true independently of anyone's recognition of their truth, then thoughts must be objects of a third realm.

In chapter three we saw that Frege argued for the existence of the third realm primarily from considerations for the possibility of communication and objective knowledge. But we soon came to see these arguments as problematic. In chapter five we saw that Frege's arguments from communication presupposed what we called "the clothes line theory of communication" – a theory which we suggested seems less than plausible. And in chapter six we saw that even were thoughts third realm objects and even were there no difficulty in apprehending such objects, that alone would not suffice to explain how thoughts can be recognized as true. But even were there no problems with Frege's theories of communication, apprehension, and recognition, the possibility of objective knowledge (as understood by Frege) would still be problematic. Frege thought that if we want to emerge from the subjective at all, we must conceive of knowledge as an activity that does not create what is known but grasps what is already there.[7] In chapter six we expressed this by saying that what really argues for the existence of the third realm is Frege's doctrine that truth is absolute. For even if thoughts are third realm objects, that alone does not entail that thoughts are *completely* independent of the human mind. As Popper has shown,[8] the objects of the third realm might be *products* of the human mind and still maintain a sufficient measure of objectivity and autonomy. But if thoughts are objects of the third realm and the objects of the third realm are products of the human mind, then it follows that there are at least some thoughts that are created and not discovered. And if these created thoughts are foundational ones, then it would seem that Frege's vision of objective knowledge is an impossible dream.

The issue whether or not thoughts are products of the human mind is the issue whether and to what extent cognitive theories are human creations. What Popper has shown is that one might well maintain the existence of a third realm and still regard cognitive theories as human creations. Now it would, to my mind, be very difficult, if not impossible, to determine whether a thought is created or discovered. To what standards would we appeal? And would these standards themselves be created or discovered? Nevertheless, many philosophers have regarded this issue, and the position one adopts regarding it, as having important implications for the nature of cognitive authority. We have already considered the difficulties in apprehending a thought and recognizing it as true. But were theories objects to be discovered, then it might seem that once a theory is apprehended and recognized as true, it should not be held as conditional in any sense. Popper has criticized this view as the doctrine that truth is manifest. But even were thoughts objects to be discovered and even were truth manifest upon their discovery, would it follow that truth is absolute?

Frege characterized the objects of the third realm as being neither physical nor mental, neither temporal nor mutable. But this all too obviously falls short of a positive description. Suppose we were to construe the third realm as a sort of logical space in which thoughts are systematically positioned with reference to their truth according to logical laws. Would it then be necessary to construe this logical space as completely uniform? Might it not be the case that the third realm consists of various regions and that the truths which exist in these regions are governed by different logical laws? And were this the case, would there be any reason to suppose that the existence of such different regions is itself obvious? Some regions of the third realm might be well hidden. In order to discover the truths which exist in these regions, one might need to journey down dangerous pathways and surmount arduous obstacles. The most difficult and arduous of these obstacles might well be laws of logic themselves. Were one to think that the laws which govern one region define the limit of logical space rather than a mere region, he would naturally conclude that the thoughts which exist in that region and the laws which govern them are the only ones. But this would be slightly analogous to a primitive man living on an island who construed the surrounding waters as the limit of the world and the objects on the island as the extent of reality. And were there another more adventurous man who crossed these waters and returned with wondrous tales of life on the other side, he might well be dismissed as a liar or a lunatic. For this, after all, is the way thinks are with primitive men. But if this is the way things are with the third realm, then would it be so surprising to find that the laws which govern one region of logical space contradict those which govern another? No more than it is surprising to find that the laws of one country contradict those of another. Would such a discovery mean that thoughts are physical or mental, temporal and mutable? Not at all. But it would mean that truth is not absolute.

I've presented this vision of the third realm as a logical space consisting of various regions governed by different laws neither to argue for the existence of such a realm nor to suggest an accurate description of it. I simply want to underscore the significance of *a priori* intuition for philosophical justification. If philosophy is a game played out through the moves of justification and criticism, and if the aim of philosophy is to compel intellectual solidarity on pain of irrationality, then Fries' trilemma teaches that rational argument (alone) cannot achieve this goal. Philosophers must ultimately appeal to the intuition of foundational principles. But unless man is compelled by reason to accept certain foundational principles rather than others, the inevitable circularity of deductive reasoning places the goal of philosophy beyond reach. Insofar as this is concerned, the claim to *a priori* intuition, and the association of a prioricity with strict universality, necessity, and apodeictic certainty, is a claim as to what must be accepted intuitively on pain of irrationality.

We've said that much of what has occurred in the history of philosophy can be viewed as a contest between the cognitivist and the sceptic. By construing knowledge as apodeictically certain, EP_1 philosophers set the standards for justification (artificially?) high. While few EP_1 philosophers have actually embraced scepticism, they have always been more acute at recognizing *a priori* truth than in explaining *how* such truth is recognized. Kant asked the question, "How are synthetic propositions *a priori* possible?" But *that* they are was thought obvious. One need only to point to arithmetic and geometry.

By the eighteenth century empiricism had established itself as the dominant epistemological *Weltanschauung*. There is no doubt that a good measure of the rise of empiricism can be attributed to the success of the experimental method and the prevailing political climate of the times. But in assessing the rise of empiricism, one cannot exaggerate the influence of anthropological discovery. As philosophers became more aware of societies whose most basic beliefs differed from their own, claims that their foundational principles are strictly universal and necessary — that they set the criteria for rationality — became less and less plausible. But while psychologistic accounts were given for ethics, aesthetics, metaphysics and the natural sciences, even the radical empiricism of David Hume acknowledged the necessity of mathematical truths. The empiricist movement reached its apex in the nineteenth century when John Stuart Mill, in *A System of Logic*, offered an inductivist account of arithmetic and geometry. There Mill explicitly states that introspection is the only basis or justification for the principles of mathematics and logic. And later, in *An Examination of Sir William Hamilton's Philosophy*, Mill classified logic under psychology, distinguishing the former from the latter as the part from the whole. All this followed from Mill's general epistemological principles, according to which:

> ... all knowledge consists of generalizations from experience. ... There is no knowledge *a priori*; no truths cognizable by the mind's inward light, and grounded on intuitive evidence. Sensation, and the mind's consciousness of its own acts, are not only the exclusive sources, but the sole materials of our knowledge.[9]

On my view, anti-psychologism in logic and mathematics was Frege's attempt to preserve one last rationalist stronghold from this empiricist onslaught. At base, it was an attempt to carve out some final ground for apodeictic certainty of strictly universal truths. Since Frege fully recognized the fallible character of sensation, this attempt required the introduction of a third realm of immutable and eternal truths — a world of absolute truth that could be apprehended by the light of pure reason. And even the failure of Frege's logicist programme did not shake this attempt. For in the end, Frege thought that arithmetic certainty could be based on the laws of "fundamental logic" and the geometrical source of knowledge — a source Frege held to be free of all psychology.

But despite Frege's efforts, empiricism continued its advance into the twentieth century. The decline of Newtonian Mechanics and Euclidean Geometry was a shocking blow to rationalism. While it did not, in itself, refute the possibility of *a priori* synthetic knowledge, it did render the best held candidates for that status suspect. Philosophers, as a matter of course, took to denying the possibility of *a priori* synthetic knowledge. And the Logical Positivists, in an amazing *tour de force*, doctrinized this tendency into a theory of cognitive significance — the verifiability criterion of meaning.

But even here, Fregean anti-psychologism continued to exert its influence over rationalists and empiricists alike. The effect of the verifiability criterion of meaning was to redefine philosophy as investigation into the analytic. Philosophers from the early Wittgenstein through Carnap and the Logical Positivists argued against the genetic and psychologistic "fallacies" and sought to eliminate all psychological (or subjective, or arbitrary) elements from philosophical analysis — even to the point of eliminating philosophy itself. The Vienna Circle capitalized on the distinction between the context of discovery and the context of justification. Justification was construed as logical proof, logic as *a priori* analytic, and epistemology as concerned only with the context of justification. It is in this context alone, Carnap assured us, that philosophy can attain objectivity. But this redefinition of philosophy also had its disturbing side-effects. Foundational principles came to be regarded as either analytically decidable or neither true nor false at all, but conventions to be accepted or rejected on the basis of pragmatic considerations. And with the dissemination of Poincare's philosophy, the choice between Euclidean and non-Euclidean geometries, a choice which Frege had regarded as one between truth and untruth, was construed as a choice between equivalent alternatives to be decided on the basis of mathematical simplicity.

Now the facts concerning the development and acceptance of non-Euclidean geometries are well-known. We will not rehearse them here except to note one point of, perhaps, psychological interest. The conceptions of the geometries of Lobatschewsky and Bolyai were, genetically speaking, the results of failed attempts at *reductio ad absurdum*. But these *reductios* were neither attempts to prove Euclidean geometry false nor attempts to establish alternative theories. It is true that these *reductios* substituted contraries for Euclid's parallel postulate. But while the parallel postulate may have seemed more complicated than Euclid's other postulates, nobody seems to have seriously doubted its truth. Carnap is explicit on this point:

This axiom seemed so obvious that, until the beginning of the last century, no one doubted its truth. The debate that centered about it was not over its truth, but over whether it was necessary as an *axiom*. It seemed to be less simple than the other axioms of Euclid. Many mathematicians believed that it might be a *theorem* that could be derived from the other axioms.[1]

In other words, non-Euclidean geometries were born of failed attempts to sim-
plify Euclidean geometry, to demonstrate that the science could be based on
four rather than five postulates.

But if this is true, then it is psychologically interesting that the mere *construction* of a self-consistent non-Euclidean geometry should pose such a threat
to the Kantian doctrine that Euclidean geometry is *a priori* synthetic. The point
is elementary: the fact that a set of axioms is self-consistent does not imply that
its members are true. Indeed, consistency tests for a set of axioms do not even
address the question of truth. And the fact that the parallel postulate can be
denied without contradiction shows only that it is synthetic. But this is exactly
what the Kantian doctrine had asserted in the first place. So given the then
prevalent assumption of the truth of the parallel postulate, one might suppose
that the failure at *reductio ad absurdum* would have been taken to indicate that
it *is* necessary to state the parallel postulate *as an axiom*.

Nevertheless, Gauss seems to have suggested early on that the "true" geometry could be determined by practical measurements in space on the interior
angles of triangles. And Reichenbach thought that the resulting plurality of self-
consistent geometries rendered the question of truth empirical:

> If several kinds of geometries were regarded as mathematically equivalent, the question
> arose which of these geometries was applicable to physical reality; there is no necessity
> to single out Euclidean geometry for this purpose. Mathematics shows a variety of
> possible forms of relations among which physics selects the real one by means of obser-
> vations and experiment. ... Mathematics reveals the possible spaces; physics decides
> which among them corresponds to physical space. In contrast to all earlier conceptions,
> in particular to the philosophy of Kant, it becomes now a task of physics to determine
> the geometry of physical space.[11]

But what is interesting from our perspective is that Reichenbach goes on to
attribute the view that Euclidean geometry is *a priori* to the absence of alternative theories:

> With respect to geometry there had been a difference; only *one* kind of geometry had
> been developed and the problem of choice among geometries had not existed.[12]

The moral of this story is admittedly a psychological claim. So I do not pretend
that it is infallible, strictly universal, or necessary. Nevertheless, it *is* plausible.
The moral is that it is easy to claim apodeictic certainty for a theory when there
are no alternatives. And if this psychological claim is true, then it naturally
engenders a practical moral for philosophy. To develop a metaphor attributed
to Neurath: when rebuilding a ship at sea, one should never place too much
weight on any one plank.

Now is the situation really so different with regard to logic? We have challenged Dummett's contrast of the Cartesian and Fregean approaches to philosophy.[13] But there is little doubt that Frege forced us all to focus more sharply

on logic and language. Ironically, the fruit of this focus has tended toward an extension of fallibilism to logic, as manifested in the pragmatist denial of the analytic/synthetic distinction.[14] In "Two Dogmas of Empiricism" Quine suggests that a thoroughgoing corrigiblism (or fallibilism), even with regard to logical laws, is part and parcel of the rejection of the two empiricist dogmas, i.e., the analytic/synthetic distinction and the verificationist approach to science:

> The totality of our so-called knowledge or beliefs, from the most casual matters of geography and history to the profoundest laws of atomic physics or even of pure mathematics and logic, is a man-made fabric which impinges on experience only along the edges. Or, to change the figure, total science is like a field of force whose boundary conditions are experience. A conflict with experience at the periphery occasions readjustments in the interior of the field. Truth values have to be redistributed over some of our statements. Reevaluation of some statements entails reevaluation of others, because of their logical interconnections – the logical laws being in turn simply certain further statements of the system, certain further elements of the field. Having reevaluated one statement we must reevaluate some others, which may be statements logically connected with the first or may be the statements of logical connections themselves. But the total field is so underdetermined by its boundary conditions, experience, that there is much latitude of choice as to what statements to reevaluate in the light of any single contrary experience. No particular experiences are linked with any particular statements in the interior of the field, except indirectly through considerations of equilibrium affecting the field as a whole.
>   If this view is right, it is misleading to speak of the empirical content of an individual statement – especially if it is a statement at all remote from the experiential periphery of the field. Furthermore, it becomes folly to seek a boundary between synthetic statements, which hold contingently on experience, and analytic statements, which hold come what may. Any statement can be held true come what may, if we make drastic enough adjustments elsewhere in the system. Even a statement very close to the periphery can be held true in the face of recalcitrant experience by pleading hallucination or by amending certain statements of the kind called logical laws. Conversely, by the same token, no statement is immune to revision. Revision even of the logical law of the excluded middle has been proposed as a means of simplifying quantum mechanics; and what difference is there in principle between such a shift and the shift whereby Kepler superseded Ptolemy, or Einstein Newton, or Darwin Aristotle?[15]

And much to the same effect, Putnam, in rejecting "the traditional philosophical distinction between statements necessary in some eternal sense and statements contingent in some eternal sense", writes:

> ... could some of the 'necessary truths' of logic ever turn out to be false *for empirical reasons*? I shall argue that the answer to this question is in the affirmative.[16]

And again:

> I am inclined to think that the situation is not substantially different in logic and mathematics. I believe that if I had the time I could describe for you a case in which we would have a choice between accepting a physical theory based upon a non-standard logic, on

the one hand, and retaining standard logic and postulating hidden variables on the other. In this case, too, the decision to retain the old logic is not merely the decision to keep the meaning of certain words unchanged, for it has physical and perhaps metaphysical consequences. In quantum mechanics, for example, the customary interpretation says that an electron does not have a definite position prior to position measurement; the position measurement causes the electron to take on suddenly the property that we call its 'position' (this is the so-called 'quantum jump'). Attempts to work out a theory of quantum jumps and of measurement in quantum mechanics have been notoriously unsuccessful to date. It has been pointed out that it is entirely unnecessary to postulate the absence of sharp values prior to measurement and the occurrence of quantum jumps, if we are willing to regard quantum mechanics as a theory formalized within a certain non-standard logic, the modular logic proposed in 1935 by Birkhoff and von Neumann, for precisely the purpose of formalizing quantum mechanics.[17]

It is interesting that in rejecting the analytic/synthetic distinction both Putnam and Quine cite the example of quantum logics. If today we are more prepared to deny the *a priori* validity of the laws of logic, it is because we live in an historical context which has witnessed the revision of some of our most basic extra-logical beliefs, and the construction of alternatives to classical logic as well.

Now what we have quoted from "Two Dogmas of Empiricism" is, admittedly, one of Quine's more radical moments. More recently, Quine seems to have taken a more conservative stance. Haack, for example, writes:

> The attack in 'Two Dogmas' on synonymy etc. *would* threaten an account of logical truths as analytic because *true in virtue of the meaning of logical constants*. Now in *Word and Object* Quine renews his attack on meaning notions, but makes an exception in the case of logical connectives, which, he claims, do have determinate meaning (*Word and Object*, ch. 2); and this paves the way for his acceptance (*Philosophy of Logic*, ch. 6) of a meaning-variance argument to the effect that the theorems of deviant and classical logics are, alike, true in virtue of the meaning of the (deviant or classical) connectives; which in turn, seems to lead him to compromise his earlier insistence that fallibilism extends even to logic.[18]

This last remark, that Quine's later conservatism regarding the laws of logic is compromising to his earlier statements regarding fallibilism in logic is significant. It suggests that the denial of fallibilism in logic is itself inconsistent with the denial of the analytic/synthetic distinction. Haack, herself, seems to draw this conclusion in *Deviant Logic*:

> It is worth observing at the outset that this argument of Quine's (the argument from translation), which, if it were sound, would show that there can be no genuine rivals to classical logic, is incompatible with another thesis, propounded in e.g. the last section of 'Two Dogmas of Empiricism' ... to the effect that none of our beliefs, beliefs about the laws of logic included, is immune from revision in the light of experience. According to this view it is at least theoretically possible that we should revise our logic. In practice, as Quine observes in 'Two Dogmas', he is inclined to be conservative about his logic, for the ramifying adjustments necessitated by a change of logic are liable to be excessively widespread. But, in principle at least, the possibility of revising logic is left open. However, the *Philosophy of Logic* thesis is that there can be no such thing

as a real, but only an apparent, change of logic. It is worth stressing, also, how important a change is made in Quine's philosophy by his acceptance of this thesis. For it commits him to admitting a distinction between linguistic change and factual change which it was one of the crucial points of ("Two Dogmas of Empiricism") to deny.[19]

Of course, our acceptance of fallibilism in logic is not to be predicated on Quine's. Nevertheless, it is not clear to me that Quine actually rules out the possibility of logical revision in *Word and Object*. There, his thesis may be intended solely as a prescription for translation. In other words, our logic *is* revisable in light of experience, but it is bad practice to assume a deviant logic in the translation of others. This would be fully in line with Quine's practical conservatism regarding logic. But in *Philosophy of Logic* Quine does seem to suggest that the question of deviant logics is, at base, a question of deviant meanings.

Early on, Quine seems to have used the thesis that no statement is immune to revision as a premise in his argument against the analytic/synthetic distinction. But one may reverse this strategy by denying the analytic/synthetic distinction on separate grounds and using that rejection as a premise for fallibilism in logic. This, moreover, is the strategy Haack recommends.[20] But the point to be made is that to say that there are no real but only apparent deviances in logic seems tantamount to saying that there are, after all, some statements which are to be held "come what may". And *that* seems dangerously close to reaffirming the analytic/synthetic distinction. Now it has been suggested that Quine's use of meaning-variance arguments does not commit him to an affirmation of *a priori* valid statements. Rather, Quine's maxims about translation are motivated by the idea of perceiving the obvious. Now I do not wish to deny this. But if there is one thing that Quine's work on radical translation has taught, it is that what is obvious in perception is, perhaps, not so obvious.

But regardless of whether or not we accept the analytic/synthetic distinction, it seems strange to me that so many philosophers regard this response — that deviance in theory is, at base, deviance in meaning — as putting the issue to rest. Putnam, in speaking of non-Euclidean geometries, cautions against the "fallacy" of explaining away deviant theories as *merely* meaning variants:

> The distinction between statements necessary relative to a body of knowledge and statements contingent relative to that body of knowledge is an important methodological distinction and should not be jettisoned. But the traditional philosophical distinction between statements necessary in some eternal sense and statements contingent in some eternal sense is not workable. The rescuing move which consists in saying that if a statement which appears to be necessary relative to a body of knowledge at one time is not necessary relative to the body of knowledge at a later time, then it is not really the same statement that is involved, that words have changed their meaning, and that the old statement would still be a necessary truth if the meanings of the words had been kept unchanged, is unsuccessful.[21]

And Parsons, in "Ontology and Mathematics", writes:

214

... it would be too naive to take (the dispute about the law of the excluded middle) as a straight disagreement about a single statement whose meaning is clearly the same. On the other hand, it would not do either to take the difference as 'verbal' in the sense that each one can formulate what the other means in such a way that the disagreement will disappear.[22]

Now I do not want to deny that there are often deviances in meaning. Nor do I want to deny that philosophical disagreements often *involve* deviances in meaning. Nevertheless, I do think that insofar as recalcitrant philosophical disagreements are concerned, deviance in theory is rarely *merely* deviance in meaning. And when it comes to recalcitrant philosophical disagreements concerning foundational principles, the difference between deviance in theory and deviance in meaning is simply too close to call.

Now how does all this affect our discussion of psychologism? So long as one maintains the possibility of intuiting *a priori* valid statements (either analytic or synthetic), not one bit. So long as one acknowledges such *a priori* intuition, the anti-psychologist can continue to claim that logic, and the other sciences as well, are grounded on infallible foundational principles, and construe the recognition and acceptance of such principles as criteria for rationality. But once one has denied the possibility of such *a priori* intuition, then it seems that the consequence, at least for the justificationist, is epistemological relativism. Here one might think that such relativism is unmotivated. Rather, it might be thought that if psychologism is true, then the worst that follows is fallibilism. I hope it is clear that even were fallibilism the worst consequence of psychologism, it would be sufficient to motivate Frege's concern. Nevertheless, the transition from a thoroughgoing fallibilism to epistemological relativism is really not so great. Here, one need only to consider that insofar as justification is concerned the issue is ultimately one of foundations. Unless philosophers can provide firm and secure foundational principles, principles which we are compelled to accept on pain of irrationality, then it seems that the whole procedure of attempting to compel belief through rigorous rational argument is a charade. Let me be clear about this. Such attempts to compel belief may be fruitful once philosophers have reached agreement concerning foundational principles. But to my mind, issues concerning the consistency of a position are, in Morgenbesser's phrase, dessert questions. They may, indeed, be delicious. But they are served only after the main course. Insofar as transcendental justification and criticism are concerned, it would seem that no one theory could ever be rationally preferable to another. This is what I mean by "epistemological relativism". It does not mean that it could not be the case that one theory is true and the others false. Rather, the relativism is epistemological. What this relativism means is not that truth and falsity are in the same boat, but that, ultimately, all attempts to justify theories as true or false are.

Does the acceptance of psychologism imply that we are never in a position to assess the rationality of beliefs or actions? Not at all. But it does mean that such assessments of rationality are also relative. In chapter eight we saw that Nagel thinks that the rationality of a behaviour should be assessed by its ability to achieve the goals for which it was designed. With this I fully agree. But this simply underscores the point. Rational judgments of rationality are one and all immanent. They are possible only given the acceptance of foundational principles (goals, values, etc.), and are made only with reference to the foundational principles accepted.

Were the relationship between psychologism and the denial of *a priori* intuition obvious to contemporary philosophers, then this discussion would have little motivation. But this, unfortunately (or should I say fortunately?) is not the case. The causes of this unclarity are many. One, ironically, is an offshoot of anti-psychologism itself. It is the widespread disregard among analytic philosophers for the history of philosophy. Another, perhaps doubly ironic, is the fact that analytic philosophers like to consider their work as somehow cumulative. We like to think that we do not work in conceptual isolation, but build on the successes and failures of our predecessors. To that extent, philosophical education is sometimes thought to involve the accumulation of philosophical "facts". That Frege put the ghost of psychologism to rest, thereby making the world safe for objectivity, is one such "fact". That Quine (or Wittgenstein, or somebody) showed the Kantian distinction between analytic and synthetic truths untenable is another. And so, many contemporary philosophers continue to espouse anti-psychologism, in the name of objectivity, while denying the existence of *a priori* valid statements.

On my view, anti-psychologism, in a justificationist programme, is simply the view that there are *a priori* valid statements which provide philosophers with objectively certain grounds for justification, and objectively certain standards for criticism. If this is correct, then what I suggest is that once one has denied the existence of *a priori* valid statements, anti-psychologism, at least in a justificationist programme, is completely without grounds. Here, too, our analogy between philosophy and chess holds sound. The shift from EP_1 to EP_2 has cast something like a fog over the chessboard of philosophy. And just as chess players leave pieces dangling unprotected and unprotecting long past the time that they ceased to provide strategic force, philosophers too sometimes maintain positions through a period of conceptual change that erodes their grounds. In my opinion, something like this has occurred with regard to psychologism. Within an EP_2 justificationist programme, anti-psychologism dangles with, ironically enough, only a psychological force.

Now some philosophers seem to recognize the tension between anti-psychologism and the denial of *a priori* validity, and argue for a return to psychologism. Gilbert Harman, for one, has proposed and defended a thesis he describes as "psychologistic":

What is being suggested here is a kind of psychologism: the valid principles of inference are those principles in accordance with which the mind works.[23]

Harman, however, is here speaking of the valid principles of *inductive* inference. And this confuses matters, since validity is a concept usually associated with deduction. Nevertheless, Harman seems to be unaware of the consequences of his move. And it seems to me that he no soon as announces his psychologism than he betrays it:

> Of course, a simple statement like this is an idealization. Things can go wrong, we may fail to consider all the evidence; we can be biased; we commit fallacies. Still, the test of good inference is not whether it corresponds with rules that have been discovered *a priori*. The test can only be whether the inference seems right to someone who does his best to exclude things that can lead him astray.
>
> Some philosophers criticize psychologism in logic on the grounds that it detracts from the certainty of logical truths and even makes them false, since some people reason invalidly. Some of this charge is answered by pointing out that the relevant rules concern the working of the mind when nothing goes wrong: how it works ideally. The rest of the complaint, that psychologism detracts from the certainty of logical truths, holds only for principles of deduction. [24]

But how are we to determine when nothing goes wrong, when the mind is working ideally? Harman seems to recognize much of what we have urged as the grounds of psychologism. He seems, for example, to associate psychologism with the denial of the *a priori*. And he recognizes that philosophers have opposed psychologism because they feared it would detract from the certainty of logical laws. Nevertheless, he seems to be taking back with his left hand what he gave with his right. Frege thought that when confronted with deviant reasoners, the psychologistic logician could only say: those laws hold for them; these laws hold for us. Nevertheless, Harman feels that the psychologistic logician is equipped with rules concerning how the mind works "ideally". But on what are such rules to be based? Judgments concerning how the mind "ideally" works are obviously not to be equated with judgments concerning how it in fact works. For otherwise, there would be no need to speak of how it works "ideally". Perhaps Harman intends such rules to be based on inductive evidence. But in that case, Harman would be caught in a circle. Worse, it would then seem that the rules of valid inference are based on consensus. And this seems to undermine the very point for introducing them — for might not most people reason fallaciously? But if Harman does not intend the rules of "ideal" reasoning to be based on inductive evidence, then what are they based on? I am not clear whether or not Harman intends such rules to be gleaned from *a priori* intuition. But the very reference to "ideal" rules seems to be the very antithesis of psychologism.

More recently, some philosophers have tried to explode the psychologism/anti-psychologism dichotomy itself. Isaac Levi, for example, has concluded his book *The Enterprise of Knowledge* with a chapter entitled "The Curse of Frege". According to Levi, the curse of Frege is neither psychologism nor anti-psychologism, but a conceptual framework which polarizes the dichotomy and compels philosophers to regard the choice between psychologism and anti-psychologism as mutually exclusive:

> ... I regard anyone to be suffering from the curse of Frege who submits to the polarization and chooses either in favor of method and against psychologism, sociologism, and historicism or chooses against method and in favor of psychologism, sociologism, and historicism.[25]

According to Levi, there is a third option, namely objective albeit context-dependent rules. Now I do not wish to deny the importance of context-dependent rules. And I fully agree with Levi that even within a context oriented epistemology there is "objectivity enough". Nevertheless, the question remains whether this is really a "third option". Here, the point to be made is that for Frege, and for anyone who views epistemology from the EP_1 perspective, the polarization of psychologism and anti-psychologism *is* mutually exclusive – and rightly so. Either there are *a priori* valid grounds for justification and standards for criticism, or there are not. For Frege, the very admission of context-dependent rules would be tantamount to a denial of the strict universality and necessity of the logical laws – the strict universality and necessity of which Fregean anti-psychologism was designed to protect. That Levi can even consider context-dependent rules simply indicates that he is not working in the context of EP_1.

But perhaps this last paragraph needs revision. The context-dependent rules of which Levi speaks are not the logical laws. So perhaps Levi's introduction of context-dependent rules poses no threat to Fregean anti-psychologism. But what is, perhaps, more interesting is that despite his distinction between fallibilism and corrigiblism, Levi maintains, at least for the context of *The Enterprise of Knowledge*, that the laws of classical logic and mathematics are not only epistemologically infallible, but incorrigible as well. And if this is not anti-psychologism in the Fregean sense, then Frege was not an anti-psychologist.

Nevertheless, Levi also directs his criticism against Popper, who, according to Levi, suffers miserably from the curse of Frege. But this seems strange. Popper, despite his anti-psychologism, is everywhere adamant that scientific inquiry begins with problem situations. Moreover, Popper's schema for understanding and scientific growth – $P_1 \rightarrow TT \rightarrow EE \rightarrow P_2$ – is not intended to provide an escape from problem situations, but to underscore the point that one problem situation properly engenders another. As far as I can see, what Popper regards as psychologistic is not the denial of method, but the method of justifying statements by sense experience. But if this is correct, then for Popper the choice between psychologism and anti-psychologism is also mutually exclusive. For either one allows that statements can be justified by sense experience, or one does not. Perhaps what Levi really wants to suggest is that psychologism, as traditionally understood, is unavoidable, but no cause for alarm. A prioricity or not, we can still claim epistemological infallibility for our beliefs. And with this I fully agree. We can always *claim* it.

Where do we stand with regard to these issues?

As far as I can see, the crux of the psychologism/anti-psychologism debate is the issue of cognitive authority — whether and to what extent our theories can claim cognitive authority, and on what basis can such authority legitimately be claimed. This issue of cognitive authority underlies our notions of objectivity and rationality as well. For the characterization of a theory as objective or subjective, rational or irrational, is ultimately an evaluation of the legitimacy of that theory's claim to authority. Moreover, the issue of cognitive authority is what motivates all justificationist programmes and, ironically, the rejection of justificationism as well. Frege maintained that logic and mathematics have absolute cognitive authority, but argued that such authority must ultimately be based on the Reason or Intellect (*a priori* valid statements), for sense experience can never insure apodeictic certainty for strictly universal statements. Mill acknowledged the cognitive authority of logic and mathematics, but cautioned that such claims to authority must be tempered by a recognition of the fallible nature of sensation. Finally, Popper's anti-psychologistic anti-justificationism seems to result primarily from the fear that claims to cognitive authority based upon psychologistic justification might tend to outstrip their legitimate grounds.

On my view, claims to apodeictic certainty, in the twentieth century, betray a sort of ignorance, if not, less charitably, a sort of arrogance. Regardless of whether we construe thoughts as third realm entities or merely descendents of sense perceptions, the fundamental human situation is one in which men disagree even with regard to the most basic of beliefs. The development of technology has simply served to place these disagreements in sharper relief. Not to be aware of such disagreements betrays a sort of ignorance; to be aware of the disagreements, but infallibly certain of our own beliefs, a sort of arrogance. The difficulty with this situation is not that we are devoid of good theories, but that we are endowed with too many good alternatives. The problem with these alternatives is not that they are unintuitive, but that they assault our most basic intuitions, leaving us without non-question begging grounds for adjudication. We find ourselves, as Peirce put it, aboard a ship in the open sea, with no one aboard who understands the rules of navigation.[26]

This situation may seem to pave the way for a thoroughgoing psychologism in the sciences and in logic and mathematics as well. For if we cannot appeal to the evidence of our senses, then the enterprise of knowledge is lost. Nevertheless, it would be too simple to think that cognitive authority should be based upon psychologistic justification alone. It is often said of history that each generation rewrites it in its own image. On my view, the same is true of philosophy. The philosophical developments of the twentieth century have not taught that knowledge is impossible. They have simply made us aware of the extent to which human knowledge is dependent upon human conventions and decisions. And this, I think, is no cause for despair. But if we persist in claiming cognitive authority at all, then we should desist in pawning off the responsibility for such claims on the Reason or the Senses. Rather, we should own up to the responsibility for our decisions.

Popper wrote that Kant was right to think that our theories are psychologically *a priori*, but wrong to think them *a priori* valid. With this, I fully agree. And so long as claims to cognitive authority are tempered with the recognition of the fallible character of psychologistic justification and the importance of human conventions, psychologism threatens no harm. But I am also sensitive to Popper's fear that the tendency of justificationism is to dismiss new ideas and stifle cognitive growth. As Peirce put it:

> ... one may be sure that whatever scientific investigation shall have put out of doubt will presently receive *a priori* demonstration on the part of the metaphysicians.[27]

So long as justificationism seeks to put issues beyond doubt and establish truths that can be held "come what may", claims to cognitive authority need to be tempered. If this is psychologism, then it is, on my view, psychologism without tears. But once we reject claims to *a priori* certainty, the question that remains is "Whither philosophy?"

Throughout our discussion we have considered psychologism and anti-psychologism as quasi-epistemological/quasi-metaphysical *theses*. But one cannot exaggerate the influence that anti-psychologism has had on the methodology of philosophical inquiry. Here I want to be explicit. Once philosophers abandon the hope for *a priori* validity, they can no longer appeal to logical necessity as a ground for justification and logical possibility as a standard for criticism. If nothing else, the rejection of the analytic/synthetic distinction, taken seriously, snaps all intuitions as to what is or is not logically possible and logically necessary. But if this is the case, then philosophy must abandon the hope of compelling belief, at least with regard to transcendental questions, through the force of rational argument. To the extent to which philosophy remains a game played out through the moves of justification and criticism, the game is intramural. But so long as philosophers maintain that the distinction between philosophy and the natural sciences turns on the distinction between the *a priori* and the *a posteriori*, this poses a very real problem for the self-image of philosophy. If philosophy is investigation into the *a priori*, then there is nothing left to investigate!

No so very long ago, philosophy regarded herself as the queen of the sciences, the ultimate arbitrator in all disputes concerning cognitive authority. But the rejection of her best held candidates for the status of *a priori* synthetic truth exposed her as a pretender to the throne. And with the emergence of Logical Positivism, she soon became accustomed to her role as handmaiden. According to positivist reforms, philosophers can clarify what the scientists say and they can check for consistency. But insofar as cognitive authority is concerned, science must fend for herself. Nevertheless, analytic philosophy could still claim authority in dispute concerning logical or conceptual (i.e., *analytical*) matters. But the denial of the analytic/synthetic distinction, for all intents and purposes, renders logic a natural science like all others. And this, to put it bluntly, leaves

220

no place for *a priori* philosophy at all. Rationalists, of course, will dissent from this view. For them, it is business as usual. But Wittgenstein seemed to think it put an end to philosophy as traditionally conceived. And the pragmatist attitude, where pragmatists are self-conscious about such matters, seems to be: Forget philosophy; do science!

Let me suggest an alternative. If the denial of *a priori* validity poses a threat to the self-image of philosophy, it is only because philosophers have for too long assumed that cognitive growth can be achieved only through judgment — what's true and what's false, who's right and who's wrong, what's good and what's bad. This conception of cognitive growth fostered the role of the philosopher as a sort of intellectual judge. And taking this role seriously gave rise to epistemology as the fundamental philosophical discipline, with objectivity, rationality, and rigorous justification as the fundamental epistemological norms. But this always presupposed that the questions, "Is it true or false?", "Is it right or wrong?", "Is it good or bad?" have "Yes" or "No" answers. What I wish to suggest as an alternative to the conception of the philosopher qua judge is simply that of the philosopher as a sort of intellectual interpreter. Simply put, when confronted with philosophical disagreement, the task of the philosopher is not to determine who's right and who's wrong, but simply to understand, and to help others to understand, the theories which give rise to the dispute. I do not think that the task of understanding is a simple one. Nor do I think it insignificant. In science, and the world at large, we find judgment enough. What is sorely lacking is understanding.

Perhaps I can better express this through a bit of counterfactual fancy. We are all familiar with the fabulous story of Plato's Cave — the saga of the philosopher's long and arduous journey by which he escapes from the imprisonment of the cavern of shadows and emerges on top of the mountain to bask in the sunlight of absolute truth. Some of us even recall the suggested sequel — the philosospher's equally long and arduous descent back into the cavern of shadows and his attempt to free his fellows. I think it is impossible to exaggerate the impression that this tale has made on centuries of philosophers. Nevertheless, it must be remembered that Plato was an idealistic type, and it is only natural that his story should have an idealist twist. Consider, for a moment, a slightly different scenario...

Socrates: Picture children imprisoned in rooms for a twelve year period of five to six hours a day. Conceive them as sitting at desks, so that they remain in the same spot, able to look forward only, and prevented by their guards from turning their heads. Picture also a blackboard running from one end of the room to the other upon which their guards write mathematical equations which they proclaim as true and which they compel their prisoners to copy in notebooks and memorize by rote.

Glaucon: All that I see.

Socrates: See also, then, these guards threatening these children with ominous looking exams upon which they must reproduce their notes with the warning that it is only accurate reproduction that will free them from prison and enable them to get high-paying jobs and large houses in the suburbs.

Glaucon: A strange image you speak of, and strange prisoners.

Socrates: Like unto us, weren't you told of the value of a high school diploma? Now tell me Glaucon, do you think that these prisoners could have any idea of mathematics other than what their guards told them?

Glaucon: How could they, if they wanted to get into medical school?

Socrates: And again, would not the same be true of whatever else the guards wrote on the blackboards?

Glaucon: Surely.

Socrates: If then they were allowed to talk with one another, do you think that each would be delighted to find that all the others agreed that two plus two is four, and that nobody bothered to ask, "What's a two?"

Glaucon: Necessarily.

Socrates: And if in this prison there were some lowly recalcitrant types who persisted in asking, "What's a two?" and "How do you know it's *always* four?", and who were subsequently forced to stand in the corner, or retained in the prison, or released but compelled to become janitors, do you think they would pay them much attention?

Glaucon: By Zeus, I do not.

Socrates: Then in every way, such prisoners would deem as true nothing else than what their guards told them.

Glaucon: Quite inevitably.

Socrates: Consider then what would be the manner of the release and the healing from these bonds and this folly if in the course of nature something of this sort should happen to them. Suppose that toward the end of their imprisonment the guards told them that the most intelligent among them could enter another prison, in which they would be kept in fetters for four years, but which, in the end, would enable them to learn more truth, and get even higher paying jobs, and even larger houses in the suburbs. And suppose that when they entered the new prison new guards told them that a lot of what the other guards had told them wasn't true at all, or true only to a degree, and that something else is really the truth. Don't you think they would regard what these guards told them as far more true?

Glaucon: Far more true, Socrates.

Socrates: But suppose that's not what happened.

Glaucon: What else Socrates?

Socrates: Suppose they just found a lot of smart-looking guys running around saying all sorts of different things. How do you think they'd react?

Glaucon: Well, I don't know. They'd probably think they were idiots.

Socrates: Quite right, my dear Glaucon. But which they?

Suppose that when Plato's philosopher finally emerged from the cave he found not one sun, but many. More naturalistically, suppose he simply found a lot of smart-looking guys running around saying all sorts of different things. Just as in Plato's version, his initial reaction might be to crawl back into the cave. True, the lighting there was poor, but there was a lot less confusion. But the impulse to epistemology, i.e., the impulse to judgment, is ingrained in us long before our philosophical curiousity is awakened. From birth, we are taught the fundamental dichotomies — good and bad, right and wrong, true and false. So if our philosopher were a serious sort, as he must have been just to make it this far, then he might take it upon himself to determine who's right and who's wrong, and to instruct them in what's true and what's false. And here, he most probably would measure right and wrong, true and false, on the best standards available, i.e., whatever he had been taught since childhood. But were our philosopher to have had an unhappy childhood, were he, for example, to have experienced philosophical disagreement at an early age, and if that experience had made an impression, if it had been traumatic, then perhaps he would not feel so confident. Perhaps he would realize that such matters cannot be decided by rule of thumb. And if he were serious, then perhaps he would set out to construct an epistemology. And were our philosopher *very* serious, then perhaps, by the middle of the twentieth century, he would have become a scientist.

Frege, certain of the strict universality of the laws of logic, felt confident to dismiss any and all deviant logics as heretofore unknown types of madness. Popper, a little more wary of authority, would prefer to see an argument. But there are some of us for whom the experience of philosophical disagreement has been especially traumatic. And the pitiful result of this is that we suffer from a pathetic insecurity which compels us to doubt, when we find ourselves in disagreement with others, whether we have fully understood their point of view — or anything else for that matter. Let me be the first to say that none among us particularly likes this state of affairs. It's especially difficult to make judgments. And were we able to be certain, we most certainly would. But it doesn't seem to be a voluntary thing. And even when we try to close our eyes and *claim* to be certain, there are always those restless nights. We've tried to construct epistemologies, to help us determine who's right and who's wrong. But it was impossible to decide which one to adopt. We've even thought of getting out of this business. But it seems that everyplace we look — everyplace *interesting* that is — we find the same sorts of disputes.

On my view, the business of philosophy is not with knowledge, i.e., truth, justification, and cognitive authority. Rather, it is with understanding, or, if you will, wisdom. On my view, the philosopher's task is not to adjudicate philosophical disagreement, but simply to figure out what's being said. It is not to prove that there are other minds, but to try to understand how other minds might try to prove things. To do this properly, the philosopher must think himself into a conceptual framework in which reasoning according to "deviant" laws — logical or otherwise — is *not* a heretofore unknown type of madness. He must see the world in such a way that these "deviant" laws no longer seem deviant. Most importantly, it is the philosopher's task not to stifle cognitive growth by clinging priggishly to cognitive authority, but to promote cognitive growth by encouraging creativity. That's right — cognitive growth! For on my view, cognitive growth occurs not through judgment, but through understanding. In following this path, the philosopher will not find objectivity, justification, and the third world. But he will find cognitive growth enough. For in the end, he will himself able to recognize the world from many different perspectives, instead of just one. And it is this, more than anything else, that *I* regard as cognitive growth.

I know that many philosophers have characterized epistemological relativism as a morally degenerate position — presumably because it does not pay proper respect to truth. But on my view, it is epistemological infallibilism that risks moral degeneration. So long as the epistemological infallibilist maintains that there is no serious possibility that his beliefs are mistaken, he has no reason to consider the conflicting beliefs of others seriously. On my view, the epistemological infallibilist risks moral degeneration by not paying the proper respect to persons.

Finally, I know that many philosophers will dissent from my vision of philosophy — "It's not serious enough!" But then, what do you mean by "serious"? I would never claim that my philosopher is likely to end up with a high paying job and a house in the suburbs. But he might, if he's lucky, have some fun.

NOTES AND REFERENCES

1. See above, chapter 6.

2. See above, chapter 3.

3. Aristotle; *Analytica Posteriora*; in *The Basic Works of Aristotle*; ed. by Richard McKeon; Random House (New York, 1941) p. 110. (71^a, 1-8).

4. *Ibid.* (71^a, 11-15).

5. *Op. cit.*; Frege; *The Foundations of Arithmetic*; p. 4^e.

6. *Ibid.*

7. *Op. cit.*; Frege; *The Basic Laws of Arithmetic*; p. 23.

8. See chapter nine, above.

9.   Mill, John Stuart; "Coleridge"; in *Essays on Ethics, Religion and Society*; ed. by J.M. Robson; University of Toronto (Toronto, 1969) p. 125.

10.   Carnap, Rudolf; *The Philosophy of Science*; ed. by Martin Gardner; Basic Books (New York, 1966) p. 126.

11.   Reichenbach, Hans; *The Philosophy of Space & Time*; trans by Maria Reichenbach and John Freund; Dover (New York, 1957) p. 6.

12.   *Ibid.*

13.   See chapter 6, above.

14.   I call this denial of the analytic/synthetic distinction "pragmatist" because, aside from the fact that Quine is generally considered a pragmatist, it can be found in a footnote to William James' *The Principles of Psychology* (See: James, William; *The Principles of Psychology*; Dover (New York, 1950) Volume 2; pp. 661-662). This denial, of course, can be found in other places, and I cannot be sure that Quine was influenced by James. Nevertheless, I find it somehow comforting to think that Quine's reputation might be built on a footnote of James.

15.   Quine, Willard van Orman; "Two Dogmas of Empiricism"; in *From a Logical Point of View*; Harper & Row (New York, 1953) pp. 42-43.

16.   Putnam, Hilary; "The Logic of Quantum Mechanics"; in *Mathematics, Matter and Method*; by Hilary Putnam; Cambridge University Press (New York, 1975) p. 174.

17.   Putnam, Hilary; "It Ain't Necessarily So"; in *Op. cit.*; *Mathematics, Matter and Method*; p. 248.

18.   *Op. cit.*; Haack; *Philosophy of Logics*; p. 237.

19.   *Op. cit.*; Haack; *Deviant Logic*; p. 15.

20.   *Ibid.*; p. 32.

21.   *Op. cit.*; Putnam; "It Ain't Necessarily So"; p. 248.

22.   Parsons, Charles; "Ontology and Mathematics"; in *Philosophical Review*; (80), 1971; pp. 152-153.

23.   Harman, Gilbert; *Thought*; Princeton University Press (Princeton, 1973) p. 18.

24.   *Ibid.*; pp. 18-19.

25.   Levi, Isaac; *The Enterprise of Knowledge*; The MIT Press (Cambridge, Massachusetts, 1980) p. 428.

26.   Peirce, Charles Sanders; "The Fixation of Belief"; in *Philosophical Writings of Peirce*; ed. by Justus Buchler; Dover (New York, 1955) p. 8.

27.   *Ibid.*; p. 19.

WORKS CITED

Books:

1. Anscombe, G.E.M., and Geach, P.T. *Three Philosophers*. Oxford: Basil Blackwell, 1961.
2. Aristotle. *Analytica Posteriora*. In *The Basic Works of Aristotle*. Edited by Richard McKeon. New York: Random House, 1941.
3. Benacerraf, Paul, and Putnam, Hilary, eds. *Philosophy of Mathematics*. Englewood Cliffs, New Jersey: Prentice-Hall, 1964.
4. Beth, Evert. *Mathematical Thought*. Dordrecht: Reidel, 1965.
5. Brentano, Franz. *Psychologie vom empirischen Standpunkt*. Leipzig: Duncker & Humblot, 1874.
6. Brentano, Franz. *Psychology from an Empirical Standpoint*. Edited by Linda L. McAlister. Translated by Antos C. Rancurello, D.B. Terrel, and Linda L. McAlister. New York: Humanities Press, 1973.
7. Carnap, Rudolf. *Logical Foundations of Probability*. Chicago: University of Chicago Press, 1950.
8. Carnap, Rudolf. *The Philosophy of Science*. Edited by Martin Gardner. New York: Basic Books, 1966.
9. Chazan, Barry I., and Soltis, Jonas F., eds. *Moral Education*. New York: Teachers College Press, 1973.
10. Dewey, John. *The Quest for Certainty*. London: George Allen & Unwin, 1930.
11. Dummett, Michael. *Frege: Philosophy of Language*. New York: Harper & Row, 1973.
12. Dummett, Michael. *Truth and Other Enigmas*. Cambridge, Massachusetts: Harvard University Press, 1978.
13. Farber, Marvin, ed. *Philosophical Essays in Memory of Edmund Husserl*. New York: Greenwood Press, 1968.
14. Feigl, Herbert, and Brodbeck, May, eds. *Readings in the Philosophy of Science*. New York: Appleton-Century-Crofts, 1953.
15. Feyerabend, Paul; *Against Method*. London: Verso, 1975.
16. Frege, Gottlob. *Begriffsschrift, eine der arithmetischen nachgebildete Formelsprache des reinen Denkens*. Halle, 1879.
17. Frege, Gottlob. *Begriffsschrift*. In *Source Book in Mathematical Logic, 1879-1931*.
18. Frege, Gottlob. *Die Grundlagen der Arithmetik, eine Logisch-mathematische Untersuchung über den Begriff der Zahl*. Breslau: Wilhelm Koebner, 1884.

19. Frege, Gottlob. *Grundgesetze der Arithmetik, begriffsschriftlich abgeleitet.* Band I. Jena: Hermann Pohle, 1893.

20. Frege, Gottlob. *Nachgelassene Schriften.* Edited by H. Hermes, F. Kambartel, and F. Kaulbach. Hamburg: Felix Meiner, 1969.

21. Frege, Gottlob. *Posthumous Writings.* Translated by Peter Long and Roger White. Chicago: The University of Chicago Press, 1979.

22. Frege, Gottlob. *The Basic Laws of Arithmetic.* Translated by Montgomery Furth. Los Angeles: University of California Press, 1967.

23. Frege, Gottlob. *The Foundations of Arithmetic.* 2d ed. Translated by J.L. Austin. Evanston: Northwestern University Press, 1968.

24. Frege, Gottlob. *Translations from the Philosophical Writings of Gottlob Frege.* Edited and translated by Peter Geach and Max Black. Oxford: Basil Blackwell, 1970.

25. Haack, Susan. *Deviant Logic.* New York: Cambridge University Press, 1974.

26. Haack, Susan. *Philosophy of Logics.* New York: Cambridge University Press, 1978.

27. Hall, A. Rupert, and Trilling, Laura, eds. *The Correspondence of Isaac Newton, Volume V.* Cambridge: At the University Press, 1975.

28. Harman, Gilbert. *Thought.* Princeton: Princeton University Press, 1973.

29. Heyting, A. *Intuitionism: An Introduction.* Amsterdam: North-Holland Publishing Co., 1956.

30. Hume, David. *An Enquiry Concerning Human Understanding.* 1748. Edited by Eric Steinberg. Indianapolis: Hackett, 1977.

31. Hume, David. *A Treatise of Human Nature.* 1739. Edited by L.A. Selby-Bigge. 2d ed., revised by P.H. Nidditch. New York: Oxford University Press, 1978.

32. Husserl, Edmund. *Logical Investigations.* 2 vols. Translated by J.N. Findlay. New York: Humanities Press, 1970.

33. Husserl, Edmund. *Logische Untersuchungen.* Halle: M. Niemeyer, 1900.

34. Husserl, Edmund. *Phenomenology and the Crisis of Philosophy.* Translated by Quentin Lauer. New York: Harper & Row, 1965.

35. James, William. *The Principles of Psychology.* 2 vols. 1890. Reprint. New York: Dover, 1950.

36. Kant, Immanuel. *Critique of Pure Reason.* Translated by Norman Kemp Smith. New York: St. Martin's Press, 1965.

37. Kant, Immanuel. *Kritik der reinen Vernunft.* Riga: Johann Friedrich Hartknoch, 1787.

38. Kant, Immanuel. *Logic.* Translated by Robert Hartman and Wolfgang Schwarz. New York: Bobbs-Merrill, 1974.

39. Kant, Immanuel. *Logik.* Edited by Benjamin Jasche. Konigsberg: Friedrich Nicolovius, 1800.

40. Kant, Immanuel. *Prolegomena to Any Future Metaphysics.* Translated by Paul Carus. Revised by James W. Ellington. Indianapolis: Hackett, 1977.

41. Kant, Immanuel. *Prolegomena zu einer jeden kunftigen Metaphysik die als Wissenschaft auftreten Können.* Riga, 1783.

42. Kolakowski, Leszek. *Husserl and the Search for Certitude*. New Haven: Yale University Press, 1975.
43. Kuhn, Thomas S. *The Structure of Scientific Revolutions*. Chicago: The University of Chicago Press, 1970.
44. Lakatos, Imre, and Musgrave, Alan, eds. *Criticism and the Growth of Knowledge*. Cambridge: Cambridge University Press, 1970.
45. Levi, Isaac. *The Enterprise of Knowledge*. Cambridge, Massachusetts: The MIT Press, 1980.
46. Locke, John. *An Essay Concerning Human Understanding*. 1690. Edited by P.H. Nidditch. New York: Oxford University Press, 1975.
47. Mill, John Stuart. *An Examination of Sir William Hamilton's Philosophy*. 1865. Edited by J.M. Robson. Toronto: University of Toronto Press, 1979.
48. Mill, John Stuart. *A System of Logic*. 2 vols. 1843. Edited by J.M. Robson. Toronto: University of Toronto Press, 1973.
49. Mill, John Stuart. *Autobiography*. 1873. Edited by Jack Stillinger. Boston: Houghton Mifflin, 1953.
50. Mill, John Stuart. *Essays on Ethics, Religion, and Society*. Edited by J.M. Robson. Toronto: University of Toronto Press, 1969.
51. Mohanty, J.N., ed. *Readings on Edmund Husserl's Logical Investigations*. The Hague: Martinus Nijhoff, 1977.
52. Morrell, J., and Thackray, A. *Gentlemen of Science*. London: Oxford University Press, 1981.
53. Nagel, Ernest. *Teleology Revisited*. New York: Columbia University Press, 1979.
54. O'Hear, Anthony. *Karl Popper*. Boston: Routledge & Kegan Paul, 1980.
55. Peirce, Charles Sanders. *Philosophical Writings of Peirce*. Edited by Justus Buchler. New York: Dover, 1955.
56. Popper, Karl R., and Eccles, John C. *The Self and Its Brain*. New York: Springer, 1977.
57. Popper, Karl R. *Conjectures and Refutations: The Growth of Scientific Knowledge*. New York: Harper & Row, 1963.
58. Popper, Karl R. *Objective Knowledge: An Evolutionary Approach*. New York: Oxford University Press, 1972.
59. Popper, Karl R. *Realism and the Aim of Science*. Totowa: Rowman and Littlefield, 1983.
60. Popper, Karl R. *The Logic of Scientific Discovery*. London: Hutchinson & Co., 1959.
61. Popper, Karl R. *The Open Society and Its Enemies*. 2 vols. 5th ed., rev. Princeton: Princeton University Press, 1966.
62. Putnam, Hilary. *Mathematics, Matter and Method*. New York: Cambridge University Press, 1975.
63. Quine, Willard van Orman. *From a Logical Point of View*. New York: Harper & Row, 1953.
64. Quine, Willard van Orman. *Philosophy of Logic*. Englewood Cliffs: Prentice-Hall, 1970.

228

65. Quine, Willard van Orman. *Word and Object*. Cambridge, Massachusetts: The MIT Press, 1960.
66. Reichenbach, Hans. *The Philosophy of Space & Time*. Translated by Maria Reichenbach and John Freund. New York: Dover, 1957.
67. Reichenbach, Hans. *The Rise of Scientific Philosophy*. Berkeley: University of California Press, 1951.
68. Rorty, Richard. *Philosophy and the Mirror of Nature*. Princeton University Press, 1979.
69. Rorty, Richard, ed. *The Linguistic Turn*. Chicago: The University of Chicago Press, 1967.
70. Russell, Bertrand. *An Inquiry Into Meaning and Truth*. London: Allen and Unwin, 1940.
71. Ryle, Gilbert. *Collected Papers*. 2 vols. New York: Barnes & Noble, 1971.
72. Schlipp, Paul Arthur, ed. *The Philosophy of Karl Popper*. 2 vols. La Salle: Open Court, 1974.
73. Sluga, Hans. *Gottlob Frege*. Boston: Routledge & Kegan Paul, 1980.
74. Strawson, P.F., ed. *Philosophical Logic*. New York: Oxford University Press, 1967.
75. Toulmin, Stephen. *Human Understanding*. Princeton: Princeton University Press, 1972.
76. Turnbull, H.W., ed. *The Correspondence of Isaac Newton, Volume I*. Cambridge: At the University Press, 1959.
77. van Heijenoort, J., ed. *Source Book in Mathematical Logic, 1879-1931*. Cambridge, Massachusetts: Harvard University Press, 1966.
78. Wittgenstein, Ludwig. *On Certainty*. Edited by G.E.M. Anscombe and G.H. von Wright. New York: Harper & Row, 1972.
79. Wittgenstein, Ludwig. *Philosophical Investigations*. Translated by G.E.M. Anscombe. New York: Macmillan, 1953.

Encyclopedias:

1. *Encyclopedia Britannica*. London: William Benton, 1964.
2. Edwards, Paul, ed. *The Encyclopedia of Philosophy*. New York: Macmillan, 1967.

Articles:

1. Abbagnano, Nicola. "Psychologism". Translated by Nino Langiulli. In *The Encyclopedia of Philosophy*.
2. Benacerraf, Paul. "Mathematical Truth". *The Journal of Philosophy* LXX (November 8, 1973).
3. Brouwer, L.E.J. "Consciousness, Philosophy, and Mathematics". In *10th*

International Congress of Philosophy. Amsterdam: North-Holland Publishing Co., 1940. Reprinted in excerpt in *Philosophy of Mathematics*.

4. Brouwer, L.E.J. "Intuititionism and Formalism". Translated by Arnold Dresden. *Bulletin of the American Mathematical Society* 20 (November, 1913). Reprinted in *Philosophy of Mathematics*.

5. Buchner, Edward Franklin. "A Study of Kant's Psychology". *The Philosophical Review* (January, 1897).

6. Caponigri, H. Robert. "Vincenzo Gioberti". In *The Encyclopedia of Philosophy*.

7. Carnap, Rudolf. "Empiricism, Semantics, and Ontology". *Revue Internationale de Philosophie* IV (1950). Reprinted in *The Linguistic Turn*.

8. Currie, Gregory. "Frege on Thoughts". *Mind* LXXXIX.

9. Dummett, Michael. "Frege's Philosophy". In *Truth and Other Enigmas*.

10. Einstein, Albert. "Geometry and Experience". In *Sidelights of Relativity*. New York: E.P. Dutton, 1923. Reprinted in *Readings in the Philosophy of Science*.

11. Feyerabend, Paul. "Consolations for the Specialist". In *Criticism and the Growth of Knowledge*.

12. Frege, Gottlob. "Der Gedanke". *Beitrage zur Philosophie des deutschen Idealismus* 1 (1919).

13. Frege, Gottlob. "On Sense and Reference". Translated by Max Black. In *Translations from the Philosophical Writings of Gottlob Frege*.

14. Frege, Gottlob. "Review of Dr. E. Husserl's *Philosophy of Arithmetic*". Translated by E. Kluge. In *Mind* LXXXI (July, 1972).

15. Frege, Gottlob. Review of E. Husserl. *Philosophie der Arithmetik. Zeitschrift für Philosophie und philosophische Kritik* 103 (1894).

16. Frege, Gottlob. "The Thought: A Logical Inquiry". Translated by A.M. and Marcelle Quinton. In *Mind* 65 (1956). Reprinted in *Philosophical Logic*.

17. Frege, Gottlob. "Über Sinn und Bedeutung." *Zeitschrift für Philosophie und philosophische Kritik* 100 (1892).

18. Gödel, Kurt. "Über Formal Unentscheidbare Satze der *Principia Mathematica* und Verwandter Systeme, I". In *Monatshefte für Mathematik und Physik* 38 (1931).

19. Husserl, Edmund. "A Reply to a Critic of my Refutation of Logical Psychologism". Translated by Dallas Willard. In *Readings on Edmund Husserl's Logical Investigations*.

20. Husserl, Edmund. "Phanomenologische Psychologie". In *Husserliana* 9.

21. Husserl, Edmund. "Philosophie als strenge Wissenschaft". *Logos* 1 (1910).

22. Husserl, Edmund. "Philosophy as Rigorous Science". Translated by Quentin Lauer. In *Phenomenology and the Crisis of Philosophy*.

23. Husserl, Edmund. Review of M. Palagyi. *Der Streit der Psychologisten und Formalisten in der modernen Logik. Zeitschrift für Psychologie und Physiologie der Sinnesorganie* 31 (1903).

24. Husserl, Edmund. "The Task and the Significance of the *Logical Investiga-*

tions". Translated by J.N. Mohanty. In *Readings on Edmund Husserl's Logical Investigations*.

* 25. Kitcher, Philip. "Frege's Epistemology". *The Philosophical Review* LXXXVIII (April, 1979).
26. Kneale, William Calvert. "Scientific Method". In *Encyclopedia Britannica*.
27. Kraus, Oskar. Introduction to the 1924 Edition of *Psychologie vom empirischen Standpunkt*, by Franz Brentano. Reprinted in *Psychology from an Empirical Standpoint*.
28. Kuhn, Thomas S. "Logic of Discovery or Psychology of Research?" In *Criticism and the Growth of Knowledge*.
29. Kuhn, Thomas S. "Postscript-1969". In the 1969 edition of *The Structure of Scientific Revolutions*.
30. Kuhn, Thomas S. "Reflections on my Critics". In *Criticism and the Growth of Knowledge*.
31. Lakatos, Imre. "Falsification and the Methodology of Scientific Research Programmes". In *Criticism and the Growth of Knowledge*.
32. Lieberson, Jonathan. "Critical Control and Objectivity in Popper's Theory of Scientific Methods". Ph.D. dissertation, Columbia University, 1978.
33. Mill, John Stuart. "Coleridge". In *Essays on Ethics, Religion, and Society*.
34. Morgenbesser, Sidney. "Approaches to Ethical Objectivity". In *Moral Education*.
35. Musgrave, Alan E. "The Objectivism of Popper's Epistemology". In *The Philosophy of Karl Popper*.
36. Nagel, Ernest. "Carnap's Theory of Induction". In *Teleology Revisited*.
37. Nagel, Ernest. "Modern Science in Philosophical Perspective". In *Teleology Revisited*.
38. Nagel, Ernest. "Philosophical Depreciations of Scientific Method". In *Teleology Revisited*.
39. Nagel, Ernest. "The Quest for Uncertainty". In *Teleology Revisited*.
40. Parsons, Charles D. "Foundations of Mathematics". In *The Encyclopedia of Philosophy*.
41. Parsons, Charles. "Ontology and Mathematics". *Philosophical Review* 80 (1971).
42. Peirce, Charles Sanders. "The Fixation of Belief". In *Philosophical Writings of Peirce*.
43. Popper, Karl. "A Realist View of Logic, Physics, and History". In *Objective Knowledge*.
44. Popper, Karl. "Back to the Presocratics". In *Conjectures and Refutations*.
45. Popper, Karl. "Conjectural Knowledge: My Solution of the Problem of Induction". In *Objective Knowledge*.
46. Popper, Karl. "Epistemology Without a Knowing Subject". In *Objective Knowledge*.
47. Popper, Karl. "Facts, Standards, and Truth: A Further Criticism of Relativism". In *The Open Society and Its Enemies*.

48. Popper, Karl. "Normal Science and Its Dangers". In *Criticism and the Growth of Knowledge*.

49. Popper, Karl. "On the Sources of Knowledge and of Ignorance". In *Conjectures and Refutations*.

50. Popper, Karl. "On the Theory of the Objective Mind". In *Objective Knowledge*.

51. Popper, Karl. "The Demarcation Between Science and Metaphysics". In *Conjectures and Refutations*.

52. Popper, Karl. "Two Faces of Common Sense". In *Objective Knowledge*.

53. Putnam, Hilary. "The Logic of Quantum Mechanics". In *Mathematics, Matter and Method*.

54. Putnam, Hilary. "It Ain't Necessarily So". In *Mathematics, Matter and Method*.

55. Putnam, Hilary. "The 'Corroboration' of Theories". In *The Philosophy of Karl Popper*.

56. Quine, Willard van Orman. "Two Dogmas of Empiricism". In *From a Logical Point of View*.

57. Ryle, Gilbert. "Knowing How and Knowing That". In *Collected Papers* Volume 2.

58. Schneewind, J.B. "John Stuart Mill". In *The Encyclopedia of Philosophy*.

59. Sluga, Hans. "Frege and the Rise of Analytic Philosophy". *Inquiry* 18.

60. Sluga, Hans. "Frege's Alleged Realism". *Inquiry* 20.

61. Sober, Elliot. "Psychologism". *Journal for the Theory of Social Behaviour* 8 (July, 1978).

62. Tarski, Alfred. "The Semantic Conception of Truth and the Foundations of Semantics". *Philosophy and Phenomenological Research* 4.

63. Wild, John. "Husserl's Critique of Psychologism: Its Historic Roots and Contemporary Relevance". In *Philosophical Essays in Memory of Edmund Husserl*.

64. Willard, Dallas. "The Paradox of Logical Psychologism: Husserl's Way Out". In *Readings on Edmund Husserl's Logical Investigations*.

INDEX OF NAMES

INDEX OF SUBJECTS

240

242

250

inessential properties of   58, 68
laws of   87
ontological character of   33, 40, 66, 73
processes   144
toleration   132
translation   183, 184, 212, 213
radical   184, 213
true, being as opposed to being
thought to be   24, 29, 31, 32, 47, 49, 100, 106, 111, 148, 206
truth(s)   2, 13, 24, 29-32, 35, 36, 41, 56, 57, 67, 72, 87, 88, 89, 93, 100, 112, 136, 137, 149, 156, 162, 179, 181, 222
absolute   3, 39, 40, 94, 100-107, 128, 136, 137, 190, 206-210, 220, 223
arithmetical   45, 79, 100
as a criterion of knowledge *see* justificationism
as a regulative ideal for belief   105, 112
as a regulative ideal for scientific inquiry   137, 139, 171, 188-191, 193-195
as a semantic notion   34
as a third realm entity   19, 101
as consistency   191
as manifest   118, 207
as opposed to the construction of a model   86
as relative   89, 190
conflation of concept with criterion 191-193
correspondence theory of   100, 101
criterion of   190-195
eternal   3, 4, 27, 69, 89, 101, 146, 155, 175
Frege's theory of   60, 100
ideal   18
immutable   3, 4, 101, 175
inductive   41, 42
laws of   87
logical   73, 216
mathematical   51, 72, 208
not a relation   100, 101
objective   18, 19, 24, 39, 40, 54, 68, 69, 136, 190
primitive   51
pure   18
scientific   132

subject-independent   67, 89, 101
subjective   67
timeless *see* truth, eternal
values as objects   100

underdetermination (of theories by evidence)   86, 211
understanding   11, 12, 21, 84, 86, 96, 150-152, 156, 157, 159, 161, 180, 197, 217, 222, 223
as the business of philosophy 222, 223
contingent laws of   84
final   151, 152, 184
necessary laws of   84, 90
unification (of science)   179, 196, 197
universality (universal statements)   28, 80, 88, 89
absolute   90
comparative   104
conflated with objectivity   88
strict   13, 26, 30, 31, 73, 85, 103-107, 126, 127, 163-165, 169, 171, 182, 205-208, 210, 217, 222
not empirically verifiable   116, 123, 127, 206, 218

validity   13, 14, 27, 51, 216
and circularity   204
of arguments   128, 164, 165, 204
of knowledge   13
of logical laws   30
of thought   29, 53
variability argument *see* argument(s), Frege's variability
verifiable (verifiability)   198
as a criterion of demarcation 116, 127
as a criterion of meaning   114, 116, 119, 209
of singular statements   119, 205
of universal statements   119, 127, 206
verification(s) (verificationism)   77, 119, 127, 133, 137, 138, 160, 179, 180, 181, 211
verisimilitude   136, 137, 139
Vienna Circle   114, 115, 135, 209

wisdom   222
words   35, 70, 71, 81, 96, 183
world(s)   40

NIJHOFF INTERNATIONAL PHILOSOPHY SERIES

1. Rotenstreich N: Philosophy, History and Politics – Studies in Contemporary English Philosophy of History. 1976. ISBN 90-247-1743-4.
2. Srzednicki JTJ: Elements of Social and Political Philosophy. 1976. ISBN 90-247-1744-2.
3. Tatarkiewicz W: Analysis of Happiness. 1976. ISBN 90-247-1807-4.
4. Twardowski K: On the Content and Object of Presentations – A Psychological Investigation. Translated and with an Introduction by R. Grossman. 1977. ISBN 90-247-1726-7.
5. Tatarkiewicz W: A History of Six Ideas – An Essay in Aesthetics. 1980. ISBN 90-247-2233-0.
6. Noonan HW: Objects and Identity – An Examination of the Relative Identity Thesis and Its Consequences. 1980. ISBN 90-247-2292-6.
7. Crocker L: Positive Liberty – An Essay in Normative Political Philosophy. 1980. ISBN 90-247-2291-8.
8. Brentano F: The Theory of Categories. Translated by R.M. Chisholm and N. Guterman. 1981. ISBN 90-247-2302-7.
9. Marciszewski W (ed): Dictionary of Logic as Applied in the Study of Language – Concepts / Methods / Theories. 1981. ISBN 90-247-2123-7.
10. Ruzsa I: Modal Logic with Descriptions. 1981. ISBN 90-247-2473-2.
11. Hoffman P: The Anatomy of Idealism – Passivity and Activity in Kant, Hegel and Marx. 1982. ISBN 90-247-2708-1.
12. Gram MS: Direct Realism – A Study of Perception. 1983. ISBN 90-247-2870-3.
13. Srzednicki JTJ and Rickey VF (eds): Leśniewski's Systems – Ontology and Mereology. ISBN 90-247-2879-7.
14. Smith Joseph Wayne: Reductionism and Cultural Being – A Philosophical Critique of Sociobiological Reductionism and Physicalist Scientific Unificationism. 1984. ISBN 90-247-2884-3.
15. Zumbach C: The Transcendent Science – Kant's Conception of Biological Methodology. 1984. ISBN 90-247-2904-1.
16. Notturno MA: Objectivity, Rationality and the Third Realm: Justification and the Grounds of Psychologism – A Study of Frege and Popper. 1985. ISBN 90-247-2956-4.
17. Dilman I (ed): Philosophy and Life. Essays on John Wisdom. 1984. ISBN 90-247-2996-3.
18. Russell Joseph J: Analysis and Dialectic. Studies in the Logic of Foundation Problems. 1984. ISBN 90-247-2990-4.
19. Currie G and Musgrave A (eds): Popper and the Human Sciences. 1985. ISBN 90-247-2998-X.